1 MONTH OF FREE READING

at

www.ForgottenBooks.com

By purchasing this book you are eligible for one month membership to ForgottenBooks.com, giving you unlimited access to our entire collection of over 1,000,000 titles via our web site and mobile apps.

To claim your free month visit:

www.forgottenbooks.com/free811000

* Offer is valid for 45 days from date of purchase. Terms and conditions apply.

ISBN 978-0-365-47867-6
PIBN 10811000

This book is a reproduction of an important historical work. Forgotten Books uses state-of-the-art technology to digitally reconstruct the work, preserving the original format whilst repairing imperfections present in the aged copy. In rare cases, an imperfection in the original, such as a blemish or missing page, may be replicated in our edition. We do, however, repair the vast majority of imperfections successfully; any imperfections that remain are intentionally left to preserve the state of such historical works.

Forgotten Books is a registered trademark of FB &c Ltd.
Copyright © 2018 FB &c Ltd.
FB &c Ltd, Dalton House, 60 Windsor Avenue, London, SW19 2RR.
Company number 08720141. Registered in England and Wales.

For support please visit www.forgottenbooks.com

Commission of Conservation
Canada

HONOURABLE CLIFFORD SIFTON, Chairman
JAMES WHITE, Secretary

REPORT

OF THE

FIRST ANNUAL MEETING

HELD AT OTTAWA, JANUARY 18th TO 21st, 1910

To His Excellency the Right Honourable Sir Albert Henry George, Earl Grey, G.C.M.G., &c., &c., Governor General of Canada.

May it Please Your Excellency:

The undersigned has the honour to lay before your Excellency the Report of the First Annual Meeting of the Commission of Conservation for the fiscal year ending March 31, 1910.

      Respectfully submitted

          CLIFFORD SIFTON
             Chairman

OTTAWA, April 18, 1910

SIR,—

I have the honour to transmit herewith the Report of the First Annual Meeting of the Commission of Conservation which was held at Ottawa, January 18th to 21st, 1910. Included therein are the reports of the meeting, the addresses of the Chairman and of the specialists who addressed the Commissioners, also copies of the Act establishing the Commission, the names of the members of the Commission and of the various committees of the Commission.

I have the honour to be,

Sir,

Your obedient Servant

JAMES WHITE
Secretary

HON. CLIFFORD SIFTON, Chairman
  Commission of Conservation

TABLE OF CONTENTS

	PAGE
Act Establishing the Commission of Conservation.	vii
Amending Act respecting the Commission of Conservation.	ix
Order in Council appointing Commissioners	xi
Committees of the Commission.	xv
Inaugural Address.	1
Hon. Clifford Sifton	
Address by His Excellency, Earl Grey.	27
Scientific Forestry in Europe: its Value and Applicability in Canada.	29
Dr. B. E. Fernow	
The Conservation of Agricultural Resources.	42
Dr. James W. Robertson	
Possible Economies in Production of Minerals of Canada.	60
Dr. Eugene Haanel	
The Conservation of the Natural Resources of Ontario.	75
Hon. Frank Cochrane	
The Conservation of the Water-powers of Ontario.	82
Hon. Adam Beck	
Fish and Game in Ontario.	100
Kelly Evans	
Fur-bearing Animals in Canada, and How to Prevent their Extinction.	107
F. T. Congdon, M.P.	
Measures for the Maintenance and Improvement of the Public Health.	114
P. H. Bryce, M.D.	
Diseases of Forest Trees.	135
H. T. Gussow	
Insects Destructive to Canadian Forests.	142
Dr. C. Gordon Hewitt	

The Water Wealth of Canada, with Special Reference to the
  Ottawa River Basin................................. 152
        Charles R. Coutlee, C.E.
Discussion on Organization................................ 170
Committees... 175
Reports of Committees:—
  (a) Forests... 176
  (b) Fisheries, Game and Fur-bearing Animals.......... 188
  (c) Minerals.. 189
  (d) Waters and Water-powers......................... 191
  (e) Lands... 191
  (f) Press and Co-operating Organizations............. 193
  (g) Public Health................................... 195
General Discussion....................................... 196

ACT ESTABLISHING THE COMMISSION OF CONSERVATION

8-9 EDWARD VII

CHAP. 27

AN ACT TO ESTABLISH A COMMISSION FOR THE CONSERVATION OF NATURAL RESOURCES

[Assented to 19th May, 1909]

HIS Majesty, by and with the advice and consent of the Senate and House of Commons of Canada, enacts as follows:—

1. There shall be a body to be known as "The Commission of Conservation," hereinafter called "the Commission."

2. In addition to ex-officio members, the Commission shall consist of twenty members appointed by the Governor in Council, and who shall hold office during pleasure.

3. The Minister of Agriculture, the Minister of the Interior, the Minister of Mines and the member of each provincial government in Canada who is charged with the administration of the natural resources of such province shall be ex officio members of the Commission.

4. Of the members appointed by the Governor in Council, at least one member appointed from each province shall be a member of the faculty of a university within such province, if there be such university.

5. The Governor in Council may appoint one of the members of the Commission to be its chairman.

6. The chairman shall preside at all meetings of the Commission, take the necessary steps for carrying into effect the decisions and recommendations of the Commission, direct the work of the permanent officers hereof, and generally act as the administrative head of the Commission.

7. The Commission shall meet annually on the third Tuesday in January, in the city of Ottawa, or in such other place in Canada as is

decided by the Commission or by any committee thereof appointed to decide upon the place of meeting.

8. The chairman may, with the concurrence of five members of the Board, summon a special meeting of the Commission at any time or place.

9. No fees or emoluments of any kind whatever shall be received by the chairman or other members of the Commission, but they shall be repaid their actual reasonable disbursements incurred in travelling to, returning from, and remaining at meetings of the Commission. The chairman shall be paid any similar disbursements incurred in travelling or otherwise attending to the work of the Commission. Before any such payment is made a statement shall be rendered by the member of the Commission to whom payment is to be made, which statement shall be certified by the secretary and countersigned by the chairman, and thereafter payment may be made out of any moneys appropriated by Parliament for the purpose of the Commission.

10. It shall be the duty of the Commission to take into consideration all questions which may be brought to its notice relating to the conservation and better utilization of the natural resources of Canada, to make such inventories, collect and disseminate such information, conduct such investigations inside and outside of Canada, and frame such recommendations as seem conducive to the accomplishment of that end.

11. The Governor in Council may appoint a secretary to the Commission and such officers and clerks under him as are deemed necessary for carrying on the work of the Commission. Such officers and clerks shall be appointed under *The Civil Service Amendment Act*, 1908.

12. The Commission may, notwithstanding the provisions of *The Civil Service Act*, employ such assistants as are necessary for the purpose of any special work or investigation, and the remuneration and expenses of such assistants in carrying on the work committed to them may be paid out of the said Parliamentary appropriation on the certificate of the chairman and the secretary; but no permanent officer or employee shall be appointed by the Commission, and the employment of such assistants shall terminate immediately upon the completion of the special work for which they were employed.

13. The Commission shall make its report to the Governor in Council at the end of each fiscal year, and the said report shall be printed, and laid before both Houses of Parliament.

AN ACT RESPECTING THE COMMISSION FOR THE CONSERVATION OF NATURAL RESOURCES.

(Passed the House of Commons, April 8, 1910).

HIS Majesty, by and with the advice and consent of the Senate and House of Commons of Canada, enacts as follows:—

1. Chapter 27 of the statutes of 1909, intituled "An Act to establish a Commission for the Conservation of Natural Resources," may be cited as *The Conservation Act*.

2. Section 7 of the said Act is repealed and the following is substituted therefor:—

"7. The Commission shall meet annually in the city of Ottawa, or in such other place in Canada as is decided by the Commission or by any committee thereof appointed to decide upon the place of meeting.

"2. The annual meeting shall be held on the third Tuesday in January, unless the Commission, by resolution, shall fix another date."

3. Section 8 of the said Act is amended by adding thereto the following subsection:—

"2. The chairman and the chairman of a committee may summon a meeting of such committee at any time or place."

4. Section 9 of the said Act is amended by adding after the word "Commission" in the seventh line thereof the words, "The members of the Commission, when attending meetings of the committees of the Commission, shall be repaid their actual reasonable disbursements incurred in travelling to, returning from, and remaining at the meetings, or attending to the business thereof."

5. Section 12 of the said Act is amended by adding thereto the following subsection:—

"2. Any committee of the Commission may, with the approval of the chairman of the Commission, exercise all the powers conferred upon the Commission by this section."

6. Section 13 of the said Act is amended by adding thereto the following subsection:—

"2. In addition to the annual report the Commission shall report from time to time to the Senate or to the House of Commons, through the Speaker thereof, whenever directed to do so by resolution of the Senate or of the House of Commons, as may be."

7. The said Act is amended by adding thereto the following sections:—

"14. All mailable matter addressed to the Commission or to the secretary, at Ottawa, shall be free of Canada postage under such regulations as are from time to time made in that regard by the Governor in Council.

"15. No person appointed as secretary or as officer or clerk under him, or person employed as an employee for the purpose of any special work or investigation, shall, while appointed or employed as aforesaid,—

"(a) purchase, lease, acquire or obtain, on royalty or otherwise, any Dominion or provincial franchises, fishery rights, water powers, water privileges, lands, mines, mineral lands or timber limits, or in any way contract therefor or acquire any interest therein, either for himself or as agent for any other person or corporation;

"(b) locate military or bounty land warrants or land scrip, or act as agent of any other person in such behalf;

"(c) disclose to any person, except to members of the Commission, any discovery made by him or by any of them, or any other information in his possession relating to matters under the control of the Commission, or in relation to their investigations, until such discovery or information has been reported to Parliament.

"16. Every person guilty of any violation of any provision in section 15 of this Act shall forfeit to His Majesty all property or interest so acquired or obtained, and shall also incur a penalty of one thousand dollars for each such violation.

"2. The acquisition of each item of property or interest therein or contract therefor, as aforesaid, shall be deemed a separate violation of the said section.

"3. Such penalties shall be recoverable on information filed in the name of the Attorney General of Canada, and a moiety thereof shall belong to His Majesty, and the other moiety thereof shall belong to the informer."

ORDER IN COUNCIL APPOINTING THE MEMBERS OF THE COMMISSION OF CONSERVATION

Certified copy of a Report of the Committee of the Privy Council, approved by His Excellency, the Deputy Governor General, on the 3rd September, 1909

The Committee of the Privy Council, on the recommendation of the Right Honourable Sir Wilfrid Laurier, advise, under the provisions of Chapter 27 of 8-9 Edward VII, "An Act to establish a Commission for the Conservation of Natural Resources," that a Commission be appointed to be known as "The Commission of Conservation," and that the same be composed of the following gentlemen, to be members ex-officio:—

> The Honourable Sydney Fisher, of Ottawa, Minister of Agriculture;
> The Honourable Frank Oliver, of Ottawa, Minister of the Interior;
> The Honourable William Templeman, of Ottawa, Minister of Mines;
> The Honourable Francis L. Haszard, of Charlottetown, Premier of the Province of Prince Edward Island;
> *The Honourable William Thomas Pipes, of Halifax, Attorney General of the Province of Nova Scotia;
> The Honourable Ward Chipman Hazen Grimmer, of Fredericton, Surveyor General of the Province of New Brunswick;
> The Honourable Jules Allard, of Quebec, Minister of Lands and Forests of the Province of Quebec;
> The Honourable Frank Cochrane, of Toronto, Minister of Lands and Mines of the Province of Ontario;
> The Honourable Hugh Armstrong, of Winnipeg, Provincial Treasurer of the Province of Manitoba;
> The Honourable James Alexander Calder, of Regina, Commissioner of Education and Provincial Treasurer of the Province of Saskatchewan;

---

* On the decease of Hon. Mr. Pipes, he was succeeded by Hon. A. K. Maclean as Attorney General of Nova Scotia and also, therefore, as a member of the Commission of Conservation.

The Honourable Alexander Cameron Rutherford, of Edmonton, Premier and President of the Executive Council of the Province of Alberta;

*The Honourable Frederick John Fulton, of Victoria, Chief Commissioner of Lands of the Province of British Columbia;

and of the following members:—

The Honourable Benjamin Rogers, of Alberton, Prince Edward Island;

Professor Howard Murray, B.A., of Dalhousie University, Halifax, Nova Scotia;

Mr. Frank Davison, of Bridgewater, Nova Scotia;

Mr. Cecil C. Jones, M.A., Ph.D., LL.D., Chancellor of University of New Brunswick, of Fredericton, New Brunswick;

Mr. William B. Snowball, lumber merchant, of Chatham, New Brunswick;

Mr. Henri S. Béland, M.D., M.P., of St. Joseph de Beauce, Quebec;

Mr. Frederick Debartzch Monk, K.C., D.C.L., M.P., of Montreal, Quebec;

Doctor J. W. Robertson, C.M.G., Director of Macdonald Agricultural College, of Ste. Anne de Bellevue, Quebec;

Monseigneur J. C. K. Laflamme, Superior and Rector of University of Laval, of Quebec, Province of Quebec;

Sir Sandford Fleming, K.C.M.G., LL.D., M.I.C.E., Chancellor of Queen's University, of Ottawa, Ont.;

The Honourable Senator William Cameron Edwards, of Ottawa, Ontario;

Mr. Edmund Boyd Osler, M.P., of Toronto, Ontario;

Mr. Charles Arthur McCool, lumber merchant, of Ottawa, Ontario;

Mr. J. F. Mackay, journalist, of Toronto, Ontario;

Professor Bernard Fernow, of Toronto, Ontario;

The Honourable Clifford Sifton, K.C., M.P., of Ottawa, Ontario;

The Reverend George Bryce, M.A., D.D., LL.D., F.R.S.C., of the University of Manitoba, Winnipeg, Man.;

Doctor W. J. Rutherford, Deputy Minister of Agriculture and member of Faculty of the University of Saskatchewan, of Regina, Saskatchewan;

Professor H. M. Tory, M.A., D.Sc., LL.D., President of University of Alberta, of Edmonton, Alberta;

---

* Since the passing of this Order in Council, Hon. Price Ellison has succeeded Hon. Mr. Fulton as Chief Commissioner of Lands and Works for British Columbia, and also, therefore, as a member of the Commission of Conservation.

Mr. John Hendry, lumber merchant, of Vancouver, British Columbia.

The Committee, on the same recommendation, further advise that the Honourable Clifford Sifton, of Ottawa, Ontario, be chairman of the said Commission of Conservation.

       (Sgd.) RODOLPHE BOUDREAU
             Clerk of the Privy Council

COMMITTEES OF THE COMMISSION OF CONSERVATION

Committee on Fisheries, Game and Fur-Bearing Animals:—Hon. F. L. Haszard, Chairman; Hon. Hugh Armstrong, Hon. Frank Cochrane, Hon. Price Ellison, Hon. W. C. H. Grimmer, Hon. A. K. Maclean, Dr. Howard Murray.

Committee on Forests:—Senator W. C. Edwards, Chairman; Mr. Frank Davison, Dr. B. E. Fernow, Mr. John Hendry, Mgr. J. C. K. Laflamme, Hon. Frank Oliver, Mr. W. B. Snowball; and the ex-officio members of the Commission who represent the various provinces.

Committee on Lands:—Dr. J. W. Robertson, Chairman; Dr. Geo. Bryce, Hon. Sydney Fisher, Hon. Benj. Rogers, Dr. W. J. Rutherford; and the ex-officio members of the Commission who represent the various provinces.

Committee on Minerals:—Dr. H. S. Béland, Chairman; Mr. John Hendry, Dr. Howard Murray, Hon. W. Templeman; and the ex-officio members of the Commission who represent the various provinces.

Committee on Press and Co-Operating Organizations:—Mr. J. F. Mackay, Chairman; Hon. Jules Allard, Dr. Geo. Bryce, Dr. Howard Murray, Dr. H. M. Tory.

Committee on Public Health:—Mr. E. B. Osler, Chairman; Dr. H. S. Béland, Hon. J. A. Calder, Hon. Sydney Fisher, Sir Sandford Fleming, Dr. Cecil C. Jones.

Committee on Waters and Water-Powers:—Mr. F. D. Monk, Chairman; Hon. Jules Allard, Hon. Frank Cochrane, Hon. Price Ellison, Hon. W. C. H. Grimmer, Mr. C. A. McCool.

PROCEEDINGS

OF

THE COMMISSION OF CONSERVATION

AT

The First Annual Meeting

Ottawa, Canada

The inaugural address of the Chairman, Honourable Clifford Sifton, at the first annual meeting of the Commission of Conservation held in the Carnegie Library, was delivered at 11 o'clock on the morning of January 18, 1910.

INAUGURAL ADDRESS

In opening the meeting, Mr. Sifton said:—

Your Excellency and Gentlemen:

The occasion upon which we meet is one of very great importance. I need not say I am glad to welcome such a gathering as we have here this morning. I should, perhaps, say a word or two in regard to the preliminary arrangements for our meeting. The Commission was constituted by the Act which was passed at the last session of Parliament. There was necessarily a considerable amount of delay in the making of appointments to the Commission because communications had to be made with the gentlemen whose names were mentioned and the appointments were not completed, therefore, until late in the summer. When we returned for work in the fall, the first duty was to select a Secretary, who is the chief officer of the Commission, and whose appointment is, therefore, a most important one. After a good deal of deliberation and consideration we decided upon Mr. James White, who is now the Secretary of the Commission. I do not need to say to any of you who have had any experience of Mr. White's work that his appointment is one of the best we could possibly have made. Those of you who are not familiar with his work will become familiar with it in the future, and I have no doubt you will confirm the judgment of those of us who have been acquainted with his work in the past.

Then it was necessary to proceed with the organization of a staff. That, I may say, has been somewhat slow. The Secretary of the Commission, together with the Civil Service Commissioners, is giving his attention to the matter but the getting of the right kind of technically qualified men has not yet been successfully performed, except in the case of one member of the staff. The appointments, however, will be made in due course as soon as the proper men can be found. I may say that the Secretary of the Commission and the Civil Service Commissioners are giving their attention to the matter with the sole object of getting the men who are the best qualified for the work which we have for them to do.

Then there was the question of making the arrangements for this meeting. I had thought of calling a preliminary meeting of the Commission to arrange details of the meeting, but that, on consideration, appeared impracticable, and so I undertook the responsibility of making the arrangements myself with the co-operation of Mr. White.

It appeared to me that it would be well at this meeting to make some remarks indicating my own ideas as to the way in which the work of the Commission should be carried on, but I need not say that, in doing so, I have no idea of trying to impose my own views upon the Commission. On the contrary, what I desire is that the members of the Commission should make use of me in the fullest possible way for the purpose of carrying out their views in regard to the great and important subject which we have to consider.

We have met to-day under the mandate of the Parliament of Canada for the purpose of inaugurating a work which is fraught with most important consequences to the people, not only of our own generation, but of the future. Parliament has deemed it wise to constitute this Commission for the purpose of promoting the conservation of our natural resources. The Bill was introduced by the Government; it passed both Houses of Parliament without a division, and may therefore be taken to represent the unanimous view of all parties in the House of Commons and the Senate.

The Commission, it is to be noted, is exceptional in its character.

First, it is not a portion of the ordinary governmental administration for which the Government is politically responsible. It is a Commission created by Parliament and entrusted with certain duties, upon the performance of which it is to report from time to time. The funds necessary for carrying on the work must, it is true, be procured by application to the Government of the day, which will introduce the necessary estimates; but, otherwise, the work is totally independent of the ordinary administration of affairs.

Second, the Commission is constituted in such a way as to secure upon its membership three members of the Federal Government and one member of the Government of each Province, insuring, therefore, the presence of a sufficient proportion of members actually engaged upon and experienced in the details of administration in the various parts of the country.

Other provisions requiring the appointment of members from the Universities, provide for the presence of a considerable proportion of men who have attained distinction in connection with our scholastic institutions. It is therefore evident that Parliament has legislated with the object of securing upon the Commission a high degree of scholarship, of scientific knowledge and of administrative experience in order to ensure the work being successfully undertaken.

Having accepted this important public trust, it becomes our duty to unite in discharging our responsibilities with whole-hearted enthusiasm and with single-minded determination to advance the public interest in every way possible within the legitimate scope of the powers conferred upon us.

The Commission is not an executive nor an administrative body. It has no executive or administrative powers. Its constitution gives it power to take into consideration every subject which may be regarded by its members as related to the conservation of natural resources, but the results of that consideration are advisory only. In a sentence, the Commission is a body constituted for the purpose of collecting exact information, deliberating upon, digesting and assimilating this information so as to render it of practical benefit to the country, and for the purpose of advising upon all questions of policy that may arise in reference to the actual administration of natural resources where the question of their effective conservation and economical use is concerned.

The effectiveness of our work will depend upon its own merits. We can only study, investigate and advise. The Governments concerned must take the responsibility of accepting or rejecting what we recommend. So far as the work consists in collecting and digesting information, it will, in any event, be of great value. When it comes to the acceptance by Governments of specific recommendations for action, or the adoption of policies, then the strength of the advice, its effectiveness and influence, must depend upon its own inherent and obvious wisdom and the soundness of the reasons advanced in its support. Obviously, therefore, there will be no room for haphazard conclusions or careless or unscientific work. Each question dealt with must be approached with an absolutely open mind and an unyielding determination to make the investigation thorough and complete and to reach the best possible conclusions. If the work be undertaken in such a spirit, it may reasonably be hoped that it will bear important fruit. The men who are in charge of the administration of our natural resources are, we may assume, desirous of giving the best administration possible. But it is most difficult for them always to know what is best. The subjects are complicated and the information necessary to a really intelligent conclusion often widely scattered, difficult to procure, and of such a character as to require much time and long study to digest. This is peculiarly true in Canada—a country of sparse population and of immense resources yet comparatively little known. One man, in Canada, is often charged with the administration of resources so vast in extent that it is difficult for him to gain even the most cursory knowledge of the details of his own department. The life of the political head of a Department under our system, is a strenuous and busy one. He may often recognize that there is need for progress and improvement, but it takes time to work out the lines of such progress. Further, he is often deterred by the fear of hostile criticism, to which he could only oppose his own individual opinion. His motives are criticized and the wisdom of his measures impugned. Thus the boldest administrator, sooner or later, becomes disposed to adopt the policy of *laissez faire*. Under such circumstances, competent and disinterested support in carrying out the needed measures of reform ought to be welcome, and if, by the publication of the results of the work of this Commission, a strong and intelligent public opinion has been created in support of such measures, the way is made easy for their adoption.

One further word in regard to the methods and principles of action to be adopted in carrying out our work. It is absolutely essential to make it clear that it is not the province of the Commission, and it will not be its practice, to interfere with, to hinder, or to belittle the work of any other bodies, persons, associations or institutions. Our province should be to help, not to hinder. Where any person, organization, association or institution is engaged in doing work looking to the same result as that which we are aiming at, viz., the conservation of natural resources, it is our duty to support that work by every means in our power. There is no room for jealousy, there is abundant scope for all. There should be a community of interest and a harmonious co-operation all along the line, resulting in a great and strong movement for the adoption of the most effective policies.

The history of the movement which has resulted in our meeting is comparatively brief. The President of the United States having appointed the Inland Waterways Commission of the United States, that Commission on October 3rd, 1907, addressed to the President a memorandum suggesting that the time had arrived for the adoption of a national policy of conservation and suggesting that a conference of the Governors of the States of the Union should be held at the White House to consider the question. The President acted upon the suggestion, and the Conference, duly summoned by the President, met at the White House in May, 1908. Leading publicists in the United States declared that no more important gathering had ever taken place on the continent. It comprised not only the Governors of the States, but members of the United States Cabinet, Members of Congress, Justices of the Supreme Court and many distinguished scientific men. A declaration of principles was adopted and steps taken to promote joint action between the Federal and State Governments. Later, a National Commission was appointed, which proceeded to make perhaps the first and only attempt to formulate an inventory of the natural resources of a nation.

Following this action, President Roosevelt, recognizing that the principles of the conservation of resources have no international limitations, invited the representatives of Mexico and Canada to meet at Washington in a joint North American conference. This conference adopted a declaration of principles, copies of which have been furnished to you. Upon the receipt of the report of the Canadian delegation, our Government determined to adopt the recommendations contained in that declaration of principles, and to constitute a permanent Commission of Conservation.

In determining the lines upon which action should be taken, it was recognized that there was grave danger that the authorities of the Provinces might look with jealousy upon any Commission created by Federal legislation, and the provisions of the Act were expressly framed in such a way as to preclude the possibility of any ground for such a feeling, the representation being, in fact, such as to secure, as far as possible, the most effective representation of the views of each Province. The Commission is, in fact, probably the most truly national in its composition of any body that has ever been constituted in Canada.

If I may be permitted to make a personal reference, I desire to say that, so much impressed have I been with the importance of this consideration that I determined, when accepting the position of Chairman, to dissociate myself altogether from active participation in party political affairs, believing that the work of the Commission will occupy a great share of my time and attention, and that, by such a course, I can reasonably hope to secure the complete and hearty cooperation of all the members of the Commission.

I must admit that, although I have, during the greater portion of my life, made it my business to become acquainted, as far as possible, with the natural resources of our country, the most pronounced feeling that I have experienced in attempting to realize the scope of our work has been one of utter inability to do so. The least consideration of any class of resources impresses one painfully with the inadequacy of his intellectual equipment to grasp the significance of a subject where each minute branch is properly the work of a lifetime of expert and highly specialized research. Nevertheless, it is our duty to address ourselves to the work courageously, trusting that painstaking and systematic labour will bring satisfactory results.

Some general considerations are at once apparent from an examination of existing conditions. It is evident, for instance, that our circumstances differ materially from those of the United States in important particulars. There they have a large population, and the development of their resources has proceeded very far. In our case the facts are different. Our population is sparse, our resources only in an initial state of development. So much so is this the case, that I have heard the view expressed that what Canada wants is development and exploitation, not conservation.

This view, however, is founded upon an erroneous conception, which it must be our work to remove. If we attempt to stand in the way of development, our efforts will assuredly be of no avail either to stop development or to promote conservation. It will not, however, be hard to show that the best and most highly economic development and exploitation in the interests of the people can only take place by having regard to the principles of conservation.

It is further evident, from an examination of the publications relating to the work in the United States, that many of the lines of policy which have resulted disastrously there, have not been followed at all in Canada. As a fact, the policy followed in Canada in some cases is that which the United States are now trying to reach. A notable case of this kind is the disposition of the timber lands. In the United States the policy has been to sell the timber lands outright, which removes the land and timber from Government regulations. Forest experts deplore the fact that the great bulk of the timber in the United States is now privately owned, and that the local taxation, based upon totally uneconomic principles, is made so heavy that it becomes an incentive to the timber owner to clear off the forest and to realize on it as quickly as possible by the most destructive methods.

In Canada, on the contrary, the amount of timber land privately owned is comparatively trifling. Only, I think, in the province of

Quebec is it a factor. Our Governments—Federal and Provincial—have followed the policy of leasing the right to cut timber under regulations which permit the most absolute control by the Governments concerned and preserve the right to alter the regulations from time to time. There is therefore in the state-owned timber lands of Canada —Provincial and Dominion—a free field available for the adoption of improved regulations.

Another respect in which our position differs, to our great advantage, from that of the United States is that the lands surrounding the head-waters of some of our greatest and most important water courses are still in the ownership of our Governments, so that extensive reserves can be made with little expense to the public treasury.

As an illustration of the importance of this fact, it may be mentioned that, for the last twenty-five years, it has been recognized in the United States that forest reservations were necessary to protect the head-waters of the streams that arise in the Appalachian mountains. Thousands of newspaper and magazine articles have been written on the subject. Bills have been introduced into Congress; influential associations and deputations have implored Congress to take action; presidents have recommended it; but no action has yet been taken. So difficult is it to secure intelligent attention to a subject which involves the welfare of whole states, once the land has passed from Government control.

Where the scope is almost infinite the effort should be to choose that which is immediately practical and useful. And first of all it appears clear to me that provision should be made for making a comprehensive and accurate inventory of our natural resources, so far as our available information extends. The beginning of all proper investigations is the ascertainment of facts, and there is no country that I know of where it is more urgently necessary in the public interest that the natural resources should be tabulated and inventoried than it is in Canada. When the Commission was appointed by the Canadian Government to go to Washington last winter, we set on foot a preliminary movement to tabulate information. The results of that work are now among our records. It is, I may say, of the most fragmentary description. It was surprising to find how difficult it was to get anything like accurate information. Statistical information of the class which our census officers prepare is abundant and accurate, but it does not assume to deal with the question of natural resources. At the present moment there are but few publications of any Government in Canada which give accurate and comprehensive information upon these subjects.

The utility of such an inventory hardly needs discussion. Both for the purposes of development and of conservation it is the first essential to have an accurate and complete statement of the facts, readily available, accessible to all, and couched in language that the average reader can understand.

You have no doubt made yourselves familiar with the declaration of principles adopted by the North American Conservation Conference at Washington. Let me quote from it one paragraph which, I think, should be regarded as embodying the guiding principle of our work.

> "We recognize as natural resources all materials available for the use of man as means of life and welfare, including those on the surface of the earth, like the soil and the waters; those below the surface, like the minerals; and those above the surface, like the forests. We agree that these resources should be developed, used and conserved for the future, in the interests of mankind, whose rights and duties to guard and control the natural sources of life and welfare are inherent, perpetual and indefeasible. We agree that those resources which are necessaries of life should be regarded as public utilities, that their ownership entails specific duties to the public and that, as far as possible, effective measures should be adopted to guard against monopoly."

Let it be understood, that in this declaration, there was no intention of reflecting upon any government or upon any person. There is probably no government in North America and no man for any considerable time connected with administration of public affairs, as a representative or as an administrator, who has not frequently been a party to measures inconsistent with this declaration of principles. But it is only by recognizing the neglect and omissions of the past and by endeavouring to avoid them in the future, that progress can be made. The object in framing this declaration was to embody the results of experience and the highest wisdom attainable. The laws and the practice, as they exist to-day, are far from conforming to these ideal principles, but the ideal is our guiding star, and, towards its attainment, we should devote our most strenuous efforts.

The natural resources may be grouped generally under a number of headings:—The Minerals, The Fisheries, The Public Health, Inland Waters, The Land and The Forests.

Minerals—Up to the present moment, in the history of Canada, the sole effort has been to secure the exploitation of our mineral wealth. There is no reason why such exploitation should be discouraged; but there is every reason why intelligent consideration should be given to the more economic use and production of minerals. Improvement in methods of production may mean scores of millions added to the available mineral wealth and long continued enjoyment of the results of mineral production. Improved methods of saving and separating minerals will result in great quantities of mineral being profitably used which are now consigned to the refuse heap. The various Provinces have departments which have the care of their mining industries. The Dominion also has established a Department of Mines. The Dominion Department of Mines has lately been devoting attention to the issuing of useful reports containing exact information upon a variety of subjects. Investigations of an important character have been undertaken. Questions relating to processes for more satisfactory and economical extraction of ore are constantly arising. There is always the difficulty, however, that the Minister or official, whether in the Province or in the Dominion, who strives to advance, is faced with the difficulty, not only of doing his ordinary and usual work, but of overcoming the natural inertia which opposes itself to progress and the adoption of new and advanced ideas. A careful survey of the work done by the various Departments of Mines will undoubtedly result in making clear the lines of practicable progress, stimulating co-operation between the different departments, strengthening the hands of those who desire to follow a progressive policy, and also, which is hardly less important, eliminating classes of work, the utility of which is not apparent.

It would be quite outside of my scope to undertake to speak at large upon the mineral resources of Canada. Let me mention a few salient facts.

1. In 1905, the mineral production of Canada was $20\frac{1}{2}$ millions.
In 1908, the mineral production of Canada was 87 millions.

2. If you look at the geological map of Canada, you will see that the development has taken place, practically, (leaving out the Yukon) only in territory lying fairly near to the southern boundary, that is, to the inhabited and settled territory.

3. Wherever prospecting has been done farther north, indications of valuable minerals have been found, and, by accident, great wealth has been uncovered in some cases.

4. Our whole country north, from Ungava to Yukon, is of a geological formation which renders it almost certain that it is rich in valuable minerals.

5. There are in the province of Ontario, large bodies of certain classes of iron ore which are, at present, useless. They can be utilized,

so far as our present knowledge goes, only by the introduction of electric smelting. The water-power is abundantly available. Our Government has taken the lead of all the governments of the world in the investigation of the subject. Economic plants for electric smelting of iron ore are now being established in Norway and Sweden. We have led the way in investigations, but we are behindhand in the application of the knowledge acquired. A great industrial development lies ahead of Canada in connection with this subject. Our Government should be urged to spare no effort in its encouragement.

Waste prevails to a very large extent. Let me illustrate,—

1. In the Cobalt camp the mine owners are largely at the mercy of foreign smelters and refiners.* Much valuable mineral is taken and not paid for or accounted for. It is lost to the owners and to this country because there is no effective method of treating these ores in Canada. Thorough investigation by experts is highly necessary. Probably the valuable mineral lost in the Cobalt camp in one year would pay for the whole investigation, and build the plant necessary to treat the ores under proper guarantees.

2. In the utilization of coal deposits, most wasteful methods are employed.† Coal difficult to mine, is not taken out and the shafts are blocked up and the deposits lost forever; so of iron. In making coke it is alleged that uneconomic methods largely prevail.

3. In British Columbia, until lately, no account was taken at all of zinc contents in the ores, and a large amount of this very valuable metal was lost. The Federal Department of Mines has investigated the subject, but further action is necessary.

4. In the Yukon, large deposits of gold-bearing gravels have been covered by tailings and rendered extremely expensive or impossible to work.

5. Upon the subject of mine accidents I speak subject to correction; but my information is that Canada makes almost the worst showing in the world. The fatality rate in coal mining in the United States and Canada appears to be steadily increasing. Increased knowledge, scientific development and modern methods are apparently not being devoted to protecting the lives of helpless employees.

In the Transvaal, with Kaffir labour, the death rate in 1906 was 5 per 1,000 employees employed underground. This was considered so great that a Royal Commission was appointed to enquire into it. In

---

*The present position is that, owing to recent improvements, the provision for treatment of high-grade ores in Canada is now fairly good. The low-grade ores are still sent to foreign smelters.

† This remark does not apply to coal mining in Nova Scotia.

the Cobalt district in 1908, I am told the death rate was 24.8 per 1,000*
employees employed underground, or nearly five times as great as among
the Kaffir labourers of the Transvaal.

Much of this is, no doubt, due to the fact that Canadians have not,
until the last few years, been a mining people. New mining districts
have been opened up in great haste. Work has often, almost of necessity, been placed in incompetent and inexperienced hands. This has
been, perhaps, to some extent, inevitable in the early stages of mining
development. But we do not desire that, in Canada, the rush for the
wealth of the mines should be characterized by the same coarse disregard of human life that has been evident in some other countries.
We have got far enough now to take stock of the position and adopt
a forward policy. If a man is employed to take charge of a boiler and
engine on a small steamboat, he requires to show that he has passed a
rigid examination as to his qualifications. Is it not equally necessary
that there should be a standard of qualification for the man who takes
charge of the development of a mine, where the lives of employees are
constantly at stake? While it is most undesirable that the mining industry should be too much hampered by governmental interference,
public opinion would surely, in view of the above figures, support the
Government in going much farther in the way of regulation and
inspection.

Fisheries—This is one of the greatest of our national resources, the
means of livelihood of a large and important branch of our population. No effort should be spared to promote its perpetuation and
continuation. Ever since Confederation there has been a department
especially charged with the duty of conserving the fisheries, and extensive expert investigations have repeatedly been made. A Committee
on Fisheries has lately been added to the list of select standing committees of the House of Commons, and I believe that efforts are made
in the selection of the members of that Committee to appoint gentlemen who are familiar with the subject. Some of the Provinces also

---

* The figures respecting Mining Accidents in the Cobalt district were based
upon the Eighteenth Annual Report of the Bureau of Mines of Ontario, 1909, Volume
XVIII, Part I. On page thirteen appears the following statement,—

"The number of men employed in the silver mines of Cobalt, including also
those engaged in the works for the reduction of ores at Copper Cliff, Deloro and
Thorold, was 2414. The amount paid out in wages, $2,159,055.00. Of these
1089 were under ground workers and 1325 above ground."

Another portion of the Report shows that there were 27 fatalities underground
in the silver mines of Cobalt.

It has since transpired that the above quoted statement is not strictly accurate,
and was intended to apply to "producing" mines only. The Deputy Minister of
Mines of Ontario states that the correct figures would be a little less than 12
per 1000 of those employed underground.

have Departments who are charged with the care of the fisheries and pursue an active policy. It will be a matter for you to decide as to what course can best be adopted to strengthen the hands of those who are charged with the important duty of dealing with this subject.

Public Health—The physical strength of the people is the resource from which all others derive value. Extreme and scrupulous regard for the lives and health of the population may be taken as the best criterion of the degree of real civilization and refinement to which a country has attained. It cannot be said that it has received too much attention, though the Provinces, the Dominion, and the municipalities have health laws and health administrations all doing effective and useful work. There are, however, many branches of the subject, general in their character, which merit attention.

The Dominion spends hundreds of thousands of dollars in eradicating the diseases of animals, and the work, it is pleasing to know, is being done with thoroughness. But no similar effort is made by Province or Dominion to meet the ravages of diseases among human beings, such, e.g., as tuberculosis. Lately this subject was brought before the House of Commons by Mr. George H. Perley, M.P., and an illuminating debate followed. It is probable that Parliament would readily consent to the necessary appropriation for undertaking to deal with the evil. This, however, is one of the subjects upon which Federal and Provincial jurisdictions overlap, and in which any effective action will require to be carefully worked out and agreed to between all the Governments concerned. A sub-committee from this Commission, representing as it does, all the Governments, might well be able to work out an acceptable and useful plan which would receive general assent.

Other questions, such as the pollution of waters and streams, demand attention. There is a Bill at present before the Senate, dealing with this question, to which, it is understood, some of the municipalities affected to object. A study of the question will, no doubt, reveal the best method of dealing with it so as to obviate disputes and accomplish the desired results.

Waters—Rainfall and snowfall are the sole sources of our supply of fresh water. It is the universally essential natural resource. It is as essential to life as the heat of the sun.

Canada is exceptionally favoured in that there is no part of its great area which, under natural conditions, is entirely arid. It will be our own fault if it becomes so, as it will, in some portions, unless preventive measures are taken in time.

Of the total supply of fresh water which descends in the form of rain and snow, perhaps one-half is evaporated, about one-third finds its way to the sea, and the remainder, about one-sixth, is used. Waters are useful for:—

1. Human and animal use to sustain life.

2. For vegetable use to sustain vegetation and render agriculture possible.

3. For navigation.

4. For power.

5. Under modern systems of sanitation, we make use of water for flushing sewers, carrying away and destroying the most valuable of fertilizers, and at the same time polluting the water into which it is carried. This may be characterized rather as a monumental misuse than as a use of water.

The practical utility of water for domestic purposes is measured by its purity. When polluted, it becomes the worst of all sources of disease. In our present state of civilization it would be thought that, at least, we would be careful to provide pure water. Such is not the case. In this city at the present time, families who are especially careful are buying water for drinking purposes, while Montreal is struggling with a serious outbreak of fever, probably the result of the use of impure water.

The utility of the streams for the purposes of power and navigation is measured by the volume at the low-water stage. At the high-water stage, the excessive flow is wasted, and, not only so, but it always does serious damage. The damage is not, as popularly supposed, measured by the destruction of houses, buildings, fences and other visible property. The more serious damage is by the erosion of soil and consequent loss of fertility.

Most of the rainfall and snowfall which does not evaporate or run to the sea remains in the soil. This water is essential to the production of vegetation. Without it, crops become an impossibility. When the supply is lowered beyond the necessities of the crops the fertility and productive power are lowered. It is popularly supposed that nature regulates this. So it does, but under the influence of conditions created by man, and, where evil conditions are allowed to arise, the necessary supply of ground-water diminishes. It is, for instance, a known fact that, in certain upland parts of the eastern United States the average level of the ground-water, that is, the water held in the soil, has fallen by from 10 to 40 feet, while springs and wells have permanently failed. In these districts thousands of abandoned farms are to be found.

While the stock of water from rain and snow cannot be increased, the quantity available for use can be greatly augmented:

1. By methods of agricultural treatment which diminish the run-off and hold the proper quantity for absorption by the soil.

2. By catchment areas which prevent the spring freshets, obviating the destructive force which results in erosion, and making use of the water stored to supplement the flow in seasons of low water. Works of this character are now being constructed on the upper reaches of the Ottawa, and similar works will undoubtedly be required in many sections of the country. These works are essential to securing the full and proper use of our natural advantages in water supply. It is not an academic question, nor one to be relegated to the distant future. A little investigation will show that a surprisingly large and increasing number of our streams do great damage by spring freshets, and are rendered of little service for power purposes by the meagreness of the flow in low water.

3. By preserving forest growth which furnishes the best possible reservoir.

Recognition of the above facts, and action upon them, to be useful, should be brought about without undue delay. Enormous development will take place in Canada during the next few years. It should proceed on lines that will conserve, improve and increase the water supply, rather than diminish it.

One of the greatest industrial developments of our time consists in the utilization of water by means of electrically transmitted power. The flowing waters of Canada are, at the moment, apart from the soil, our greatest and most valuable undeveloped natural resource. They are more valuable than all our minerals, because, properly conserved, they will never be exhausted; on the contrary, they can be increased. In great areas of our country they are capable, when fully developed, of supplying our entire urban population with light, heat and power, operating our tramways and railways, and abolishing the present methods with their extravagance, waste and discomfort. The time when this dream will be realized need not be, and probably is not, far distant.

What are to be the conditions under which this development will take place? Is this great national boon to be handled in such a way that the people shall forever continue to pay tribute and interest upon the continually growing unearned increment of value, or is the development to take place under conditions that will ensure due economy, full utilization, reasonable rates and a participation by the people in the profits?

The subject is comparatively new in Canada. Few vested rights exist. The field is, therefore, comparatively an open one for intelligent legislative effort. The old common law of England, the principles of which, in the main, regulate the rights to waters, is largely inapplicable to modern conditions under which water and its uses have become of prime importance. The subject requires to be dealt with by legislation in a fundamental fashion.

In California, where the use of water is a necessity of agriculture, a great body of water-right law has been built up. The people found it necessary to deal with the subject in the public interest, and they have done so. In Canada, the time has arrived when the subject should be considered, and when the rights of the public to water and the use of it should be defined.

I know of only two instances in Canada where this subject has been approached and dealt with in a progressive spirit. The first is the case of the provinces of Alberta and Saskatchewan, in which, by the Federal North West Irrigation Act, passed before the provinces were formed, the waters are vested in the Crown and can only be taken and used for irrigation under license.

The second illustration is found in the province of Ontario, the Government of which Province has the credit of being the first to inaugurate a really progressive policy in regard to water-powers. I understand that conditions are inserted in the leases of water by that Province, protecting the interests of the public. Further, a policy has been adopted, under the operation of the Hydro-Electric Power Commission, of giving the people the greatest possible benefit from the possession of water resources. I am glad to say that, during the session of this Commission, we shall have an authoritative statement from a member of the Ontario Government as to the exact scope of the policy.

For myself, I am free to say that I think the necessities of the case demand further and more radical action. It is open to serious question if the time has not arrived when all water-power development should be under the control of the Governments concerned, requiring a license for development, and subject to general laws making regulations in the public interest, and taking a share of the profits for the public treasury with power, in the future, to readjust tolls.

Let me give you a striking illustration of what is ahead of us if this is not done. It is not in the densely settled east, but in the West where one would think that such a state of affairs had hardly, as yet, sufficient time to develop.

"The Central Colorado Power Company now claims as its "market an area from Grand Junction on the west, to fifty miles "east of Denver and 100 miles north and south of this line—an "area of 50,000 square miles, a commonwealth in itself.

"In this area this Company, holding the best powers, with "sufficient power already in process of development to supply the "demand for years, and, with its command of the market referred "to, controls the territory for the present, but also for the future "development as well, since there will be no possibility of equality "of competition for future competitors, either in meeting the cost "of producing power or in obtaining equal marketing facilities."

Boston (Mass.) Traveller

A present necessity in this connection is an agreement between Federal and Provincial Governments as to the limits of their respective jurisdictions. Such an agreement should be easily arrived at, and it would be more seemly and more in the public interest that it should come about by an amicable agreement than be reached through prolonged and expensive litigation, which may result in a determination founded upon technical principles of law remote from any consideration of public convenience and interest.

The water-powers of Canada are extensive and widely distributed. The reports of the Hydro-Electric Power Commission, so far as they have gone, deal satisfactorily with Ontario; but anything like an accurate estimate for the whole country has never been made. The best information at present available, points to the following figures as approximately correct:—

	POSSIBLE H. P.	DEVELOPED H. P.
Yukon	470,000	3,000
British Columbia	2,065,500	73,100
*Alberta	1,144,000	1,333
*Saskatchewan	500,000	..
Manitoba	504,000	18,000
North West Territories	600,000	none
Ontario	4,308,479	331,157
Quebec (exclusive of Ungava)	6,900,000	about 75,000
New Brunswick	150,000	no records available
Nova Scotia	54,300	13,300
Total	16,696,279	514,890

* Unfortunately, in Saskatchewan and Alberta, most of these powers are somewhat far removed from the settled portions of the Provinces.

At 22 tons of coal per horse-power per annum (24 hours) the total possible horse-power is equivalent to 367,318,118 tons of coal per annum. The horse-power actually developed—514,890—used to the full extent, will displace 11,327,580 tons of coal per annum. The development in Ontario alone, utilized to the full extent, will displace no less than 7,285,454 tons of coal annually.

Let me call your most particular attention to the fact that water-power at the present time, in the infancy of its development, furnishes the equivalent of nearly the entire quantity of coal consumed in Ontario.

Ontario, it is to be noted, imports its coal from the United States. Last year the quantity imported was:

Bituminous	6,635,388 tons
Anthracite	2,035,117 tons
Total	8,670,505 tons

This includes the quantity brought in through Port Arthur and Fort William for western use. The supply of coal in the United States is being used up with tremendous rapidity, and though, in our generation, there is no possibility of exhaustion, there is not only the possibility, but the certainty, that increasing scarcity and expense in production will greatly enhance the cost to our consumers within a very few years.

Upon the subject of water-power development, we, in Canada, are distinctly behind the times. It may be surprising to some, as it was to me, to find that little Switzerland to-day leads the world in the development of water-powers, both in regard to advanced legislation on the subject, and also, though, perhaps not so decidedly, in regard to the economical and successful development and use of power. In an interesting and able publication by Mr. Charles Mitchell, C.E., of Toronto, containing an account of his study of European installations, I find the following:—

> "In that branch of engineering science devoted to the development of hydraulic works and equipment for the generation of power, European engineers undoubtedly lead."

And again, he says that:—

> "Viewed from the hydro-electric standpoint of engineering, Switzerland undoubtedly has led all other countries, and it is there the engineer must go, even to-day, to obtain ideas as far ahead of American as are the European fashions."

If this is the verdict of the engineer, the verdict of the lawyer must be equally decisive in favor of the pre-eminence of Switzerland. Her people found themselves, like Ontario, paying enormous tribute to foreign countries for coal; they found that their water-powers were hampered in their development and in danger of being monopolized by defective laws. They went to the root of the matter; had it fully and carefully investigated by a commission of jurists and experts, and submitted a constitutional amendment which was ratified by referendum, and thus placed the law upon a workable and satisfactory basis.

This constitutional amendment gave the Federal Congress greater powers, but I do not suggest that here it is necessary that greater powers be given to our Federal Government—that is not what, in our case, is required. What we require is that we should proceed in the same businesslike and systematic way as Switzerland has done, and secure a clear and definite agreement, settling doubtful points and leaving the way open for systematic and progressive legislation, under which all development will be properly regulated in the interests of the people. If anyone doubts the necessity of such an arrangement, let him consider the position which we find existing to-day, under which the holders of a Dominion charter are claiming the right to exploit a stream in defiance of the Government of the Province, and municipalities have already been involved in litigation on the subject.

Forests—When the Federal Government established a small Forestry Branch a few years ago, it is said that there was not employed, at that time, in the Dominion of Canada a single educated forester. Since that time there has been progress. A number of skilled foresters are in the employ of the various Governments, and much careful and conscientious work is being done. Chairs of Forestry have been established, and many young men are qualifying themselves for scientific forestry. The Canadian Forestry Association, formed a few years ago, is constantly labouring to arouse public interest in the subject. Yet it must be said that, in regard to this, the greatest and most available field for the conservation of an important natural resource, the work is only beginning.

The outstanding and important fact is that, in the last ten years, enlightened public opinion has clearly grasped the necessity for the conservation of the forests, and we can rely upon such public opinion being unanimous in support of all well-considered measures having that end in view. Frequent public discussions during the last few years have rendered the main facts to be considered fairly familiar. I shall not burden my remarks with statistics upon the subject of our supply of merchantable timber. The figures obtainable at the present time

One of the best homesteads in the Crowsnest Valley. Little of the land is fit for agriculture, being too rough and stony.

Land originally forested, but burned over and washed until the stony subsoil is exposed. This particular location has been homesteaded.

Pine reproduction on land burned over fourteen years ago.

Douglas Fir, which has defied fire, growing on the lower terraces.

Young Spruce seedlings coming up under Jack-pine.

are far from accurate or reliable. It is certain, however, that the quantity of merchantable timber in Canada, outside of British Columbia, is much less than was popularly supposed up to a short time ago. It will be one of our first duties to thoroughly sift and supplement the presently available statistics and prepare a full and reliable statement.

A few facts stand out very clearly:—

(1) Under the policy adopted by our Governments—Provincial and Dominion—the timber lands leased to operators are still subject to the fullest regulation by the Governments concerned. The field is open, therefore, for improvement in regulations.

The generally admitted evils in the present methods of lumbering are:—

(a) Destruction of young growths.
(b) Cutting of trees not sufficiently matured.
(c) Leaving of inflammable refuse and débris upon the ground.

(2) The great foe of the forest is fire. A good deal has been done in the way of fire protection, but much more requires to be done. Notwithstanding everything that has been said and written on the subject, and the measures of prevention taken, it remains a fact that the devastation of forests by fire is going on at a rate that is simply appalling when one considers the ultimate and not far distant result. It is doubtful if one person in ten thousand realizes the actual meaning of even the partial and fragmentary information which we have on this subject. I commend to the attention of the members of this Commission a careful perusal of a little book issued by Mr. J. F. Whitson, O.L.S., of the Ontario Department of Lands, Forests and Mines, 1908, in which the subject is ably dealt with.

Tree planting in the west is important; the renewing of the white pine forests is important; the pulp-wood question is important; many other phases of the question are important, but the all-essential thing in regard to the question of forests is to get the community wakened up to the idea that an absolutely new departure must be made and at any cost the destruction of forests by fire must be stopped.

On a certain night during the past summer, I was in a log mining camp in one of the northern mining districts. The men in charge of that camp were up all night watching and fighting fires to prevent the destruction of the camp. On three sides as far as could be seen the fire was raging in a country covered with forest. It destroyed not only the timber, but the young growth and the covering of moss and forest mould, which is the only thing that sustains vegetable life on those hills. In that district the soil covering is very thin, and, once the fire goes through, there is nothing left but the barren rocks interspersed with lakes. For such destruction there is absolutely no excuse, and the most drastic enforcement of the law should be had to prevent it. A few striking examples will quickly disseminate the knowledge that no mercy will be shown to those who violate the law in this respect, and the fires started by careless prospectors and miners will cease. A sure reward in public recognition and gratitude awaits the man who will initiate such action.

(3) While the conservation of our actual supply of merchantable timber is important, yet of equally great importance is the treatment of the land, properly described as forest land, upon which there is at present no merchantable timber standing. These lands are many times larger in extent than those occupied by merchantable timber. They are, at present, excepting a few districts like the Algonquin Park, very largely neglected. The presence of a forest growth upon these lands is an absolute essential to the continued prosperity of the country. They conserve and regulate the water supply of our rivers. Without them we shall have, as they now have in many parts of the United States, destructive floods in the spring, followed by low and contaminated water all summer.

Without the protection of the forest growth and vegetable covering upon the soil the regular and even flow of our rivers will be forever a thing of the past. This is not a problem of the far distant future; it is a problem of the present. We have already reached the beginning of the results of deforestation promiscuously carried on. Within a few years we have seen on the St. Lawrence, Niagara, and Ottawa, extremes of high and low water of which we should take notice. The Federal Government is even now constructing extensive conservation works at the head-waters of the Ottawa. Artificial works, however, can only supplement, never supply, the place of nature in the regulation of stream flow.

There are some practical steps which can be taken at once, and which are of the utmost immediate importance. At the last session of Parliament the select standing Committee on Forests and Waterways investigated the question of the flow of water from the east slope of the Rocky mountains through the plains of Alberta and Saskatchewan. It was shown in evidence before the Committee that, to preserve the water-supply of those Provinces, it was necessary to prevent the destruction of the timber upon the east slope of the mountains. It was shown that the destruction of the timber meant the disappearance of the regular water-supply of those Provinces, the agricultural production of

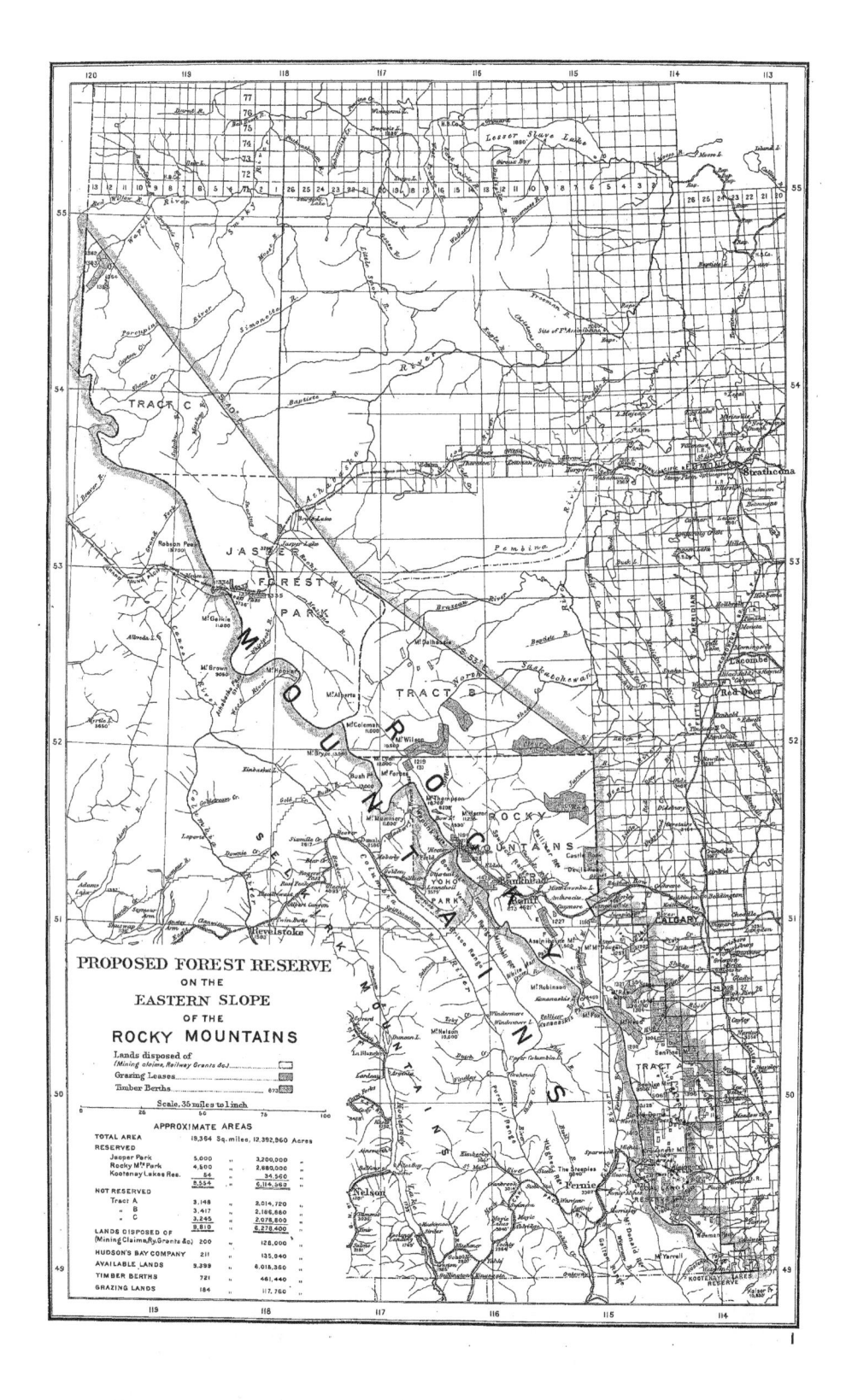

PROPOSED FOREST RESERVE
ON THE
EASTERN SLOPE
OF THE
ROCKY MOUNTAINS

Lands disposed of
(Mining claims, Railway Grants &c)
Grazing Leases
Timber Berths

Scale, 35 miles to 1 inch

APPROXIMATE AREAS

TOTAL AREA	19,364 Sq. miles,	12,392,960 Acres	
RESERVED			
Jasper Park	5,000	"	3,200,000 "
Rocky M'n Park	4,500	"	2,880,000 "
Kootenay Lakes Res.	54	"	34,560 "
	9,554	"	6,114,560 "
NOT RESERVED			
Tract A	3,148	"	2,014,720 "
" B	3,417	"	2,186,880 "
" C	3,245	"	2,076,800 "
	9,810	"	6,278,400 "
LANDS DISPOSED OF			
(Mining Claims, R'y Grants &c)	200	"	128,000 "
HUDSON'S BAY COMPANY	211	"	135,040 "
AVAILABLE LANDS	9,399	"	6,015,360 "
TIMBER BERTHS	721	"	461,440 "
GRAZING LANDS	184	"	117,760 "

which is the pride and the hope of Canada. It was further shown that by proper steps, not only can the present available supply of water be conserved, but that it can be greatly increased. Accordingly, the Committee recommended that practically the whole of the forest lands of the east slope of the mountains, which are still under the control of the Government, be formed into a permanent forest reserve, be placed in charge of a competent warden with a sufficient staff of assistants, and that it be governed by careful and stringent regulations.

Within the last few days I have been informed that the Government has decided to act upon the report of the Committee, and that a Bill for the purpose is now in course of preparation by the Minister of the Interior.

In the northern district of Ontario there is need of action. Of late years, the Governments of Ontario and Quebec have set apart large forest reserves. I am not fully conversant with the policy pursued by Quebec, but I understand that the Government of that Province has lately initiated an advanced policy on the subject, and has been conducting expert investigations into the question of preserving the source of supply of head-waters. We shall have a discussion of that subject from one of our members who is thoroughly competent to speak upon it. The Government of Ontario is pursuing a progressive and praiseworthy policy, having for its object the conservation of its valuable merchantable timber. The principal obstacle in the way of carrying out this policy is destruction wrought by fire. The enactment of more stringent laws on this subject should be considered.

But there is a field for work in the northern districts of Ontario in relation to the territory which does not bear high grade merchantable timber. Consider the position of the vast region stretching from Sudbury to Port Arthur and lying to the south of the height-of-land. A comparatively small part of this great tract bears merchantable timber. A further very small fraction is fit for cultivation. As to all the rest, apart from minerals, the only use to which it can be put is the growth of timber. So far as can be ascertained, prior to 1850, this tract was probably covered with timber, most of it of merchantable value. Fires, sometimes running for hundreds of miles, have travelled over it.

I quote from the above-mentioned pamphlet of Mr. Whitson.

> "To-day you will scarcely find a township in the white and
> "red pine country that has not been burned, or partly burnt over,
> "and, in many instances the fire has swept over them several times.

"The fire of 1871 started almost at every point of the compass
"along the north shore from French River to Kaministikwia on
"Lake Superior.

"This fire swept with fierce energy over an area of more than
"2,000 square miles, leaving blackened and giant pines to be a
"reminder for more than half a century of the immense destruc-
"tion there and then caused, converting a virgin forest into a barren
"and desolate wilderness."

He refers you to a fire of 1855,

"which burnt easterly to the shores of Lake Timiskaming, up the
"Montreal River to its source, and westerly along the height-of-
"land for over 200 miles, to near Michipicoten." Two thousand square miles were devastated. I give these brief quotations as a slight indication of what has taken place.

Particularly since railway construction began, the greater portion of this tract has been, and is being, repeatedly burned over. If you look through the car windows as you travel through it, you will see stretches of bare and rocky hillside followed by brulés, followed again by tracts upon which extensive young forests of jack-pine rise to the height of ten, fifteen and twenty feet. But over this country fires are repeatedly passing, and the territory is quickly and surely getting to the point when every vestige of forest will be gone. Following this comes the stage in which, robbed of the protection of the trees, the vegetable mould and moss, which is the only covering of the rocks, dries out and becomes inflammable. Then it burns. It is happening every year. I could show you places which, within thirty years, were covered with forest, where the successive steps have taken place, and nothing remains but the bare rocks. There is nothing more absolutely certain in nature than that, unless steps are taken to protect it, the whole territory mentioned, with the exception of the few and small tracts fit for agriculture, and occupied as such, and small settlements along the railway, will be completely denuded, not only of trees, but of the soil, within the lifetime of men now living. No one can tell the physical effect on climate of such a catastrophe, but, apart from that, the mind shrinks from the very idea of such a rocky waste in the heart of the country.

My information is to the effect that the fires are almost wholly caused by railway locomotives. Fires occurring from any other causes can be pretty effectually prevented by stringent laws and effective enforcement by the Province, but Dominion railways must be dealt with by Federal legislation. The laws of Canada relating to fires caused by railway engines certainly require amendment. Upon what prin-

Crowsnest Valley from Coleman to McLaren's Mill. The meadow land is fit for agriculture, if drained; the terraces on the left are fit only for growing timber.

Burned valley of Oldman river, showing forest replaced by an unproductive sod.

ciple do we permit railways to spread abroad destruction of public and private property? The time may have been when the necessities of transportation and the comparative poverty of the railway companies made it impracticable to enforce stringent laws, but that time has surely passed, and I have no doubt the great companies will themselves readily realize their duty in this respect.

This question of prevention of fires arising from railways is a very large and difficult subject, but we must be prepared to face large and difficult subjects if we desire to accomplish important results. Throughout the whole of the district which I have mentioned the land immediately adjoining the railway track is covered with inflammable material, which, in dry weather, will generate fire from the smallest spark. As conditions exist, frequent fires are inevitable. The condition is one for which a remedy ought to be insisted upon.

With proper protection from railway fires, the Government of Ontario could make a reserve of the whole district, and place it in charge of a warden and staff who would protect it from fire at a comparatively slight cost, and arrest the course of destruction which is going on. Given the slightest chance, the land will reforest itself. Even now there are extensive growths of young trees along the railway line, but unfortunately, under existing conditions, they are doomed to destruction. Planting might be easily and economically carried on to a considerable extent, but, without that, throughout the greater extent of the territory, reforestation will be effected by nature.

Here is the greatest opportunity that any Government ever had to conduct an extensive operation in forestry—at trifling expense and with certainty of valuable returns. The territory would be a mine of wealth.

Railway ties are every year becoming more scarce and difficult to obtain. I am told they are now worth from fifty to sixty cents per tie. Great quantities of ties are required now and the demand is steadily growing. In the United States, an important railway company has actually bought land and commenced to plant trees in order to supply ties for the future. The cut-over and burned-over Crown lands of Ontario and Quebec would, in time to come, if properly protected and fostered, supply ties for the whole of Canada from the New Brunswick line to Regina, and the Governments of these provinces would draw revenues from them which would be counted in millions.

The trouble with us in Canada is that our country is so great we are apt to overlook its possibilities. Especially are we prone to neglect what does not produce present results. It is no doubt true that present and pressing problems demand incessant attention. Nevertheless, we must look also to the future. The man who takes up this subject, grapples with it and fights it to a successful conclusion will write his name very clearly and distinctly in the history of the country.

Then there is the great northern region of Quebec and Ontario, and that portion of New Brunswick through which the National Transcontinental railway is being constructed. The House of Commons' Committee on Forests and Waterways made a partial investigation into the question of prevention of fires in these districts at the last session of Parliament, the record of which will be available as a basis for further work. It appears that the Transcontinental Commissioners have been giving attention to the subject in conjunction with the Provincial Governments, with, so far as is known, fairly satisfactory results. I understand also that the Government of Quebec has recently had the matter under serious consideration. The investigation to which I referred was necessarily somewhat cursory, and the matter should be systematically and thoroughly gone into in order to make it absolutely certain that the same unfortunate results which have followed railway building in other forest districts will not follow there also.

In referring to this matter I speak with perfect frankness. As between Governments and political parties and public men, if there has been neglect we have all been to blame. What is required now is direct and cordial co-operation between Dominion and Provincial authorities.

Lands—Agriculture is the foundation of all real and enduring progress on the part of Canada. It is one of the striking facts of the present social condition in the United States and in Canada that, with a few exceptions, those men who, by reason of strength of character and intellectual pre-eminence, take the lead in public affairs, in professional life and in scholarship are, as a rule, removed not more than one or, at most, two generations from ancestors who tilled the soil.

The possession of a preponderating rural population having the virtues and strength of character bred only among those who follow agricultural life, is the only sure guarantee of our national future. The possession of such a population depends upon the maintenance of the fertility of the soil.

The idea that such fertility will endure without the most anxious and strenuous care is contradicted by the well-known facts of history. The countries from which Xerxes led his hosts to the attack of Greece were highly populous. Persia, Babylonia, Palestine and surrounding countries were the homes of dense populations of many millions, and all our information about them leads to the conclusion that the inhabitants lived in a high degree of comfort. To-day these countries are comparative deserts. Egypt, the ancient store-house of the world, became largely barren, and remained so for centuries, with its rural population sunk in wretchedness and poverty, until British engineering skill and administrative ability gave it a new lease of life. Spain, under the Saracens, is declared by high authority to have been more highly developed agriculturally than any country of modern Europe up to twenty-five years ago. Peru and Mexico were agriculturally in a better condition, with more enlightened laws relating to agriculture before the days of Pizarro and Cortez, than they are now, though Mexico, under the present administration, is making wonderful progress. Coming closer home, there are thousands of farms in the New England states which are practically abandoned through depleted fertility of soil.

We have no great reason to be proud of our treatment of the soil in modern countries. We have never approached the economic wisdom of the biblical law which governed the Jews in their treatment of the land. Not long since I read that, in the time of the Incas, the breeding of the birds which produced guano, off the coast of South America, was strictly protected by law, while modern civilization has permitted the supply of this most valuable fertilizer to be seriously diminished by ruthless exploitation.

On the whole, the most successful efforts to preserve the fertility of their soils under the pressure of a great population have been made by China and Japan, countries which we are disposed to think can teach us nothing, but have everything to learn from us. As a matter of fact, China and Japan alone go the whole possible length in avoiding the waste of fertilizers and restoring to the soil everything that is taken from it. Speaking generally, and leaving Japan out of consideration, in the words of a recent authority, "wherever in this world there is "a large population dependent for its livelihood upon soil which has "been cultivated for upwards of two centuries, there is extreme and "depressing poverty."

We are, in the practice of our best agriculturists, more fully abreast of the most advanced nations in agriculture than we are in the treatment of any other branch of natural resources, but our advanced agriculturists are far too few in number. The development of scientific agriculture is now being promoted among us by a large number of institutions supported by public and private funds. Experimental farms and agricultural colleges are rendering services of the highest value. The application of agricultural chemistry affords a vast field for constructive effort. In connection with these institutions such men as Dr. J. W. Robertson and Dr. W. Saunders, Director of Experimental Farms, have done a work the importance of which it is impossible to over-estimate.

Is there, therefore, nothing for us to do in this department? On the contrary, speak for a few minutes with any minister administering such institutions, and, if his heart is in his work, he will tell you that there are whole fields of labour, of valuable research and investigation, which he is unable to attack for lack of men and means.

We are fortunate in having among our membership men eminently qualified to direct our deliberations upon this subject, and under their advice it will, no doubt, be possible to do much valuable work.

Let me conclude by calling your attention to the unique position occupied by Canada at the present period of its history. For many years, the progress of the country was comparatively slow. A combination of circumstances was responsible for that fact. Sparse population, great natural obstacles to transportation, peculiarities of geography, our proximity to the more wealthy and attractive United States—all combined to retard progress. It has taken the toil of generations to attain the present position. Now our time has come. Population is flowing in; development of resources is proceeding rapidly; trade is growing. In all human probability a period of great expansion and prolonged prosperity lies before us.

It is as certain as that day follows night, that this condition will bring a large influx of capital, particularly from the country to the south. This capital will come with the object of acquiring whatever revenue-producing assets Canada possesses. It will not come for philanthropic purposes. It will come to acquire and to monopolize. It will come with a volume and a power that no single individual or corporation can resist. I could, if I chose, give you some very striking illustrations of how this movement has already begun, but that is not necessary. It does not take a very profound observer to see that, within ten years, United States capital will be on the spot to acquire nearly every one of our great natural sources of wealth, except our farm lands and fisheries, which, in the nature of things, cannot be monopolized, though they may be heavily tolled by monopolists.

If, then, we are desirous that Canada shall remain Canadian, a good place for Canadians to live in, and a good place for our children to make their homes, it is in the highest degree important that we should endeavour to promote such improvements in the organic laws of the country as will prevent the monopolization of the sources of wealth, and, at least, ensure to the people their full share of the wealth which is produced therefrom. We have the experience of other countries to draw from, and it will be our own fault if we do not profit by it.

This Commission can exert a powerful influence in the right direction. It can strengthen the hands of all who are desirous of following progressive policies. It can help to render the labour of investigations in the various branches of scientific thought available for the service of the country. It can be the vehicle by which enlightened and educated men can bring an influence directly to bear on the administration of affairs. In a word, it can, if it will, be the embodiment of public spirit and advanced thought.

After concluding his inaugural address, Mr. Sifton said:—

We are fortunate in having with us to-day, as an indication of his interest in the important subject which is before us, the representative of His Gracious Majesty, His Excellency, the Governor General. I may say it is a source of great satisfaction to us to know that a gentleman in his exalted position takes a deep and intelligent interest in work of the kind which is coming before this Commission. I am sure you will be delighted to have a few words from His Excellency, if it will please him to address you.

EARL GREY'S ADDRESS

Mr. Sifton and Gentlemen:—

It is hardly necessary for me to assure you that I am not going to inflict on you anything like a dissertation on the natural resources of Canada or how to develop and conserve them. I have come here in a spirit of sympathy with this movement, and with the desire to learn something of your plans. Perhaps the most illuminating remark in the patriotic and able address, so replete with important and interesting facts, to which we have just listened from Mr. Sifton, was his confession that he was determined to divest himself of his party coat in order that he might put up a shirt-sleeve and effective fight in the interests of conservation. The constitutional limitations of my office prevent me from divesting myself of my gubernatorial robes; but, so far as I may be permitted, I will give you and the Conservation Commission every assistance in my power to enable you to fulfil the objects of your work.

I do not think anyone who has listened to this illuminating address, or anyone who may read it—and I hope it may be reported verbatim in the public journals—will fail to realize that the future well-being of Canada depends on the loyal acceptance by its people of the principles which aim at the profitable and scientific development and conservation of your natural resources. I recognize that the future prosperity of Canada depends on scientific research and upon the efficient application of the results of that research to the industrial and physical life of the people. The character of this assembly, recruited from every part of Canada, shows that this Conservation Commission will help in consolidating the Dominion; and it appears to me that another important advantage which will result from this movement is that the teaching of conservation undoubtedly carries with it a lesson, viz., that the interests of the individual must be subordinated to the greater interests of the State, and that any practice, however advantageous it may be to the individual concerned, which militates in any way against the greater interest of the State, is a practice which cannot possibly be indulged in by any but an absolutely selfish man.

    I have come here, Mr. Sifton, to listen to your address, to show the sympathy which I feel with the Conservation movement which you are leading and to show that I think the object of this movement is one which aims at the promotion of the national welfare and the development of individual duty.

    The Commission then adjourned.

WEDNESDAY MORNING

The Commission met on the morning of Wednesday, January 19, at 10 o'clock, in the Carnegie Library. At the opening of the proceedings the Chairman of the Commission called to the chair Hon. Frank Cochrane, Minister of Lands, Forests and Mines in the Ontario Government, who presided during the morning sitting.

Hon. Mr. Cochrane: I appreciate the honour done me in asking me to take the chair. The gentlemen forming this Commission have met here not only in the interests of the Provinces—one of which I represent—but in the interests of this great Dominion. There is, in my opinion, no question before Canadians to-day of greater importance than that of the conservation of our natural resources. I congratulate the Honourable Mr. Sifton on the able address he delivered yesterday and the foundation which he laid in it for matters for our consideration. When the Commission gets down to business I trust that one of the first things done will be to order the printing of that very able address of the Honourable Mr. Sifton, so that it may be circulated broadcast throughout the Dominion. I believe that a perusal of that address will set the people of Canada thinking about the magnificent natural resources which Providence has bestowed on their country, and the all-important necessity of conserving them for us of to-day and for our descendants. As the business of to-day is somewhat technical, I shall not prolong my remarks.

Hon. Mr. Cochrane then called upon Dr. B. E. Fernow, Dean of the Faculty of Forestry, University of Toronto, who read a paper on

SCIENTIFIC FORESTRY IN EUROPE: ITS VALUE AND APPLICABILITY IN CANADA

Dr. Fernow said:—

At the invitation of your Chairman, I am to bring before you information as to what has been accomplished by scientific forestry in other countries and to indicate how far similar methods may be applicable in Canada.

The first part of my task, being a matter of description, is simple enough. I need only condense what I have enlarged upon in two volumes which I have compiled. The second part, however, being a matter of judgment, would require a rather more comprehensive analysis of Canadian conditions than the brief time at my disposal would permit. It would, moreover, in part, anticipate the work of this Commission, and it can, therefore, be treated by me only suggestively.

Perhaps your Chairman, in formulating the first query, did not, when using the term "scientific," realize that this, to a technical man, suggests the application of technical knowledge to secure practical results; that, at first sight, it limits the enquiry to the result of methods of silviculture and technical forest management. It differs from the application of scientific politics—the statesman's inauguration of policies—to the treatment of forest resources. Nevertheless, to the discussion of this I shall also, in a later part of my address, devote a few minutes.

The first, and more limited, question of technical results from scientific treatment is quickly answered. The result of scientific treatment, i.e., as compared with letting unsystematic exploitation and nature take their course, must lie in the production of larger and more valuable forest products per acre in a shorter time. That this result has been achieved wherever scientific procedure has been followed, can be proved by figures. It must, however, be realized that the results always come only in the long run, for forests grow slowly, much more slowly than is usually realized. Prussian state forests—not by any means the best or even best managed in Germany—in 1830, when systematic management had been applied for only a short time, produced only 29 cubic feet per acre per year, of which less than 20%, or under 6 cubic feet, was of log size fit for the arts. By 1907, thanks to the forester's art, the product had increased to 61 cubic feet per acre per year, 52 cubic feet of which was over 3 inches diameter, and the percentage of saw timber had increased to 63 per cent., or 33 cubic feet per acre per year. The forester, then, had succeeded in making, not two, but three to five blades grow where one grew before. Or, if you translate this material result into financial form, you will find that the gross revenue per acre of 72 cents and the net revenue of 44 cents in 1830, had grown, in 1907, to $4.55 for gross and $2.52 for net revenue. That is to say, there was an improvement in the net result, annually, of $2\frac{1}{4}$ per cent. compounded, while the principal—the forest—was continuously improving and becoming more efficient.

It is to be understood that these results came from annual growth, the wood capital on which they accumulated remaining untouched, so that this, or a better cut, can go on forever.

In this financial result, the increases in price of stumpage play, of course, a part, but, since wood prices during the period have hardly

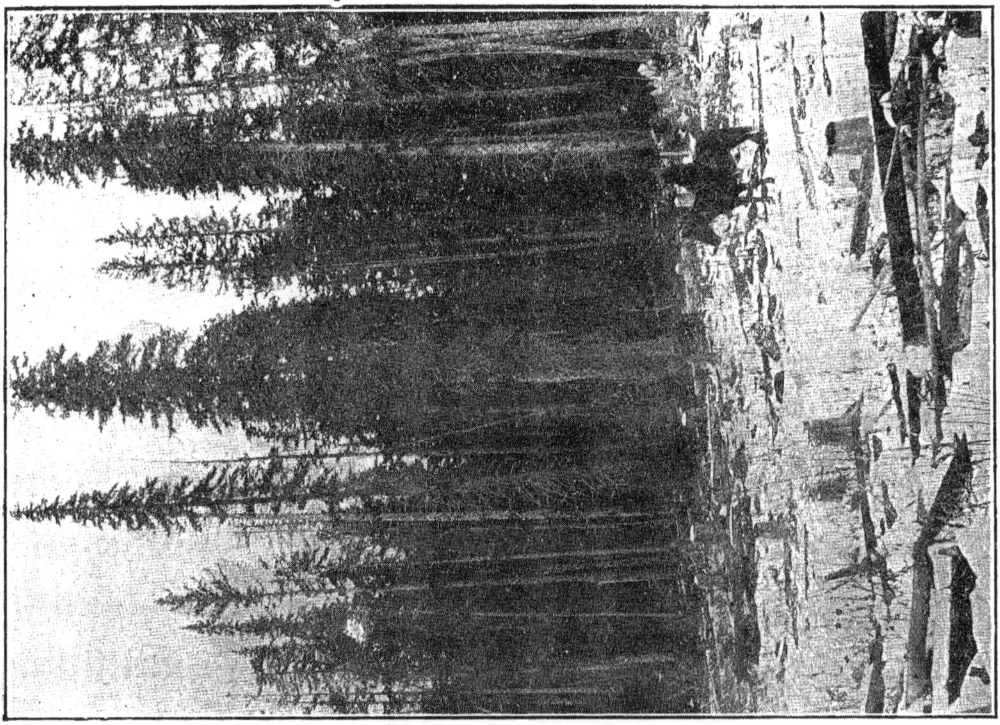

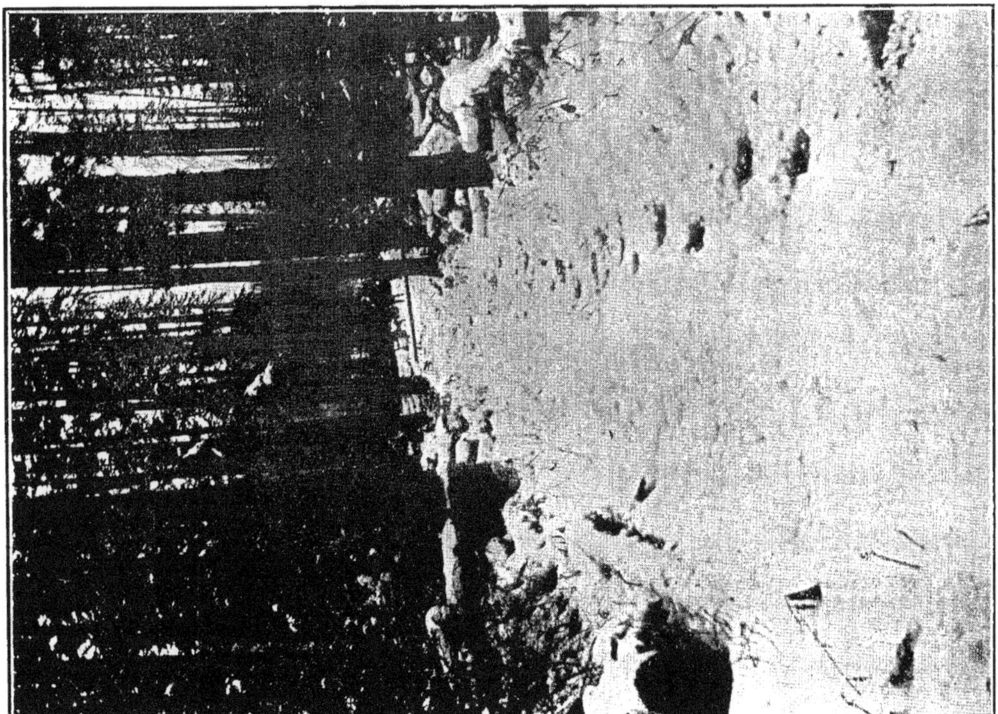

trebled while the income, as we have seen, has more than quintupled, the forester's art claims almost as much credit for the result as the economic changes which influenced the price.

While this is the outcome of a large and somewhat extensively managed property of 7 million acres, which still entails much dead work for improvement, and hence promises a still better revenue for the future, the smaller State properties of Saxony and Württemberg show still more striking rewards—rewards which are, indeed, two or three times as high. In Saxony, with somewhat less than half a million acres of state forest, mostly spruce, but most intensively managed, the cut increased from 60 cubic feet per acre in 1817–26, to 94 cubic feet in 1905. The timber-wood increased from 17% to 66%, or 62 cubic feet per acre; the gross revenue from $1.57 to $8.00, and the expenditures from 95 cents to over $5.00.

That still further improvement is possible, is shown in the last four years, for, in 1909, the cut of timber-wood had still further increased to over 78 cubic feet, which comes near the maximum attainable. The gross income was over $9.00, and the net revenue $6.00. Saxony, in 50 years, had taken some $200,000,000 from her small forest property without impairing its producing value.

In the same year, Württemberg, with 90 cubic feet per acre, and a net yield of $740, probably reached the top notch, at least of material production, for a large and varied forest property. Altogether, the forests of Germany, 35 million acres, produce around 1,700 million cubic feet of wood in annual growth, of which about 41% is saw material, or 20 cubic feet per acre (about 150 feet B.M.).

Comparing this with the 33 cubic feet stated for Prussia, we are at once confronted with the important fact that State forests, which represent only one-third of the forest area, produce not only a larger amount of growth per acre than do private forests, viz., over 50 per cent. more, but they also produce the better class of wood in larger proportion, that is to say, nearly 20 per cent. more. The State-controlled forests take an intermediary position. In other words, Prussia from an acreage which is about one-half the area now under license in Ontario, derives annually at least seven times the net income of Ontario, and that not, as does Ontario, by depleting its capital, but by merely taking the interest the annual growth. Moreover, the interest is increasing now at a rapid rate, while the capital also is continually enhancing in value.

It might be suggested that the difference lies in the difference of stumpage values. While this is true in part, it is not the whole difference, for the average stumpage value in Prussia is now less than $10, and the highest price for pine is in the neighborhood of $18, which is hardly more than double the stumpage rate in Ontario.

There is, then, no doubt that the difference lies largely in the manner of management. I should add that the results in Prussia by no means represent the final possibilities. There are still many areas in her State forests which are not yet in full productive condition; there are waste areas still awaiting planting; there are other areas still inaccessible to markets; and there is no reason why the saw timber percentage should not reach that of Saxony, namely 80%.

To cite one more case of financial result of forest management, I may refer to waste land planting in France, which was carried on with State aid, by municipalities and private enterprise. Here, in the last 60 years, 2,300,000 acres of absolute waste land of various descriptions were reclaimed by forest planting at a total cost of $15,000,000. These areas are now estimated to be worth $135,000,000 and furnish annual crops valued at $10,000,000, or, in other words, yield 67% on the initial outlay. These examples of the profitableness of practical or, if you will, scientific forestry can be multiplied indefinitely wherever it has been carried on long enough.

What does this scientific treatment that leads to such results consist in? First of all, in a difference of attitude, namely, in considering timber as a crop capable of reproduction, and not looking on the forest as a mine which is bound to be exhausted. Instead of allowing a lumberman to cut down and carry off all that is good and marketable, and leave the poorer materials and the slash to burn, or permitting a reproduction of the good, bad and indifferent species which nature unaided might chance to establish, the forester first of all ascertains in detail the character and composition of the forest property. He then makes a plan—a working plan—in which it is determined how much of a felling budget may be taken properly and yet assure continuous crops. He then proceeds to cut with a view to securing the new crop, first improving the composition by removing or killing the weed trees to give a better chance for the valuable species, and then cutting the old crop gradually, as the young crop needs more light. Or else, he may clear the entire stand and replant the area, a method under which 65% of the Prussian forests is managed. There are a number of other methods, each adapted to given conditions. The one difference between forester and lumberman—and the only one—is the obligation on the part of the former to provide for the future, to leave a forest crop in place of the harvested one.

Unfortunately, this crop takes a long time to mature. Only he who can afford to work and wait for the distant reward can engage

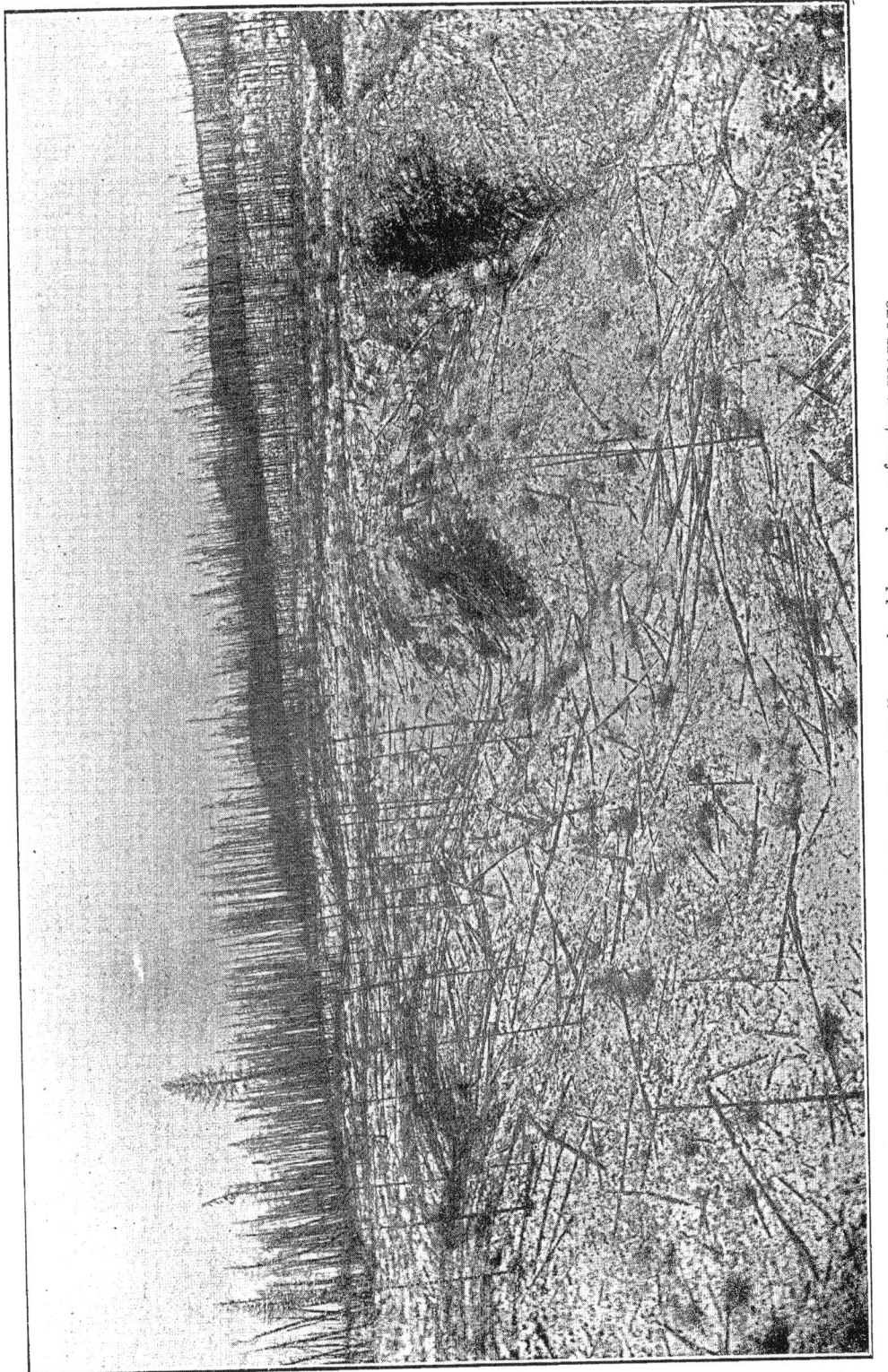

Good reproduction in Lyon Creek Valley on land burned over fourteen years ago.

in and find profitable, the management of timber lands for continuous revenue, at least from saw timber. Only the State or other persistent corporations can do this. If history teaches anything, this is the lesson taught by European experience.

How did the countries which apply such treatment to their forest resources come at it? How did forestry originate? Precisely as any other industrial art comes into man's life—by the necessity or desirability of it appearing. There are three reasons for the practice of the art of perpetuating forests. The most obvious is to secure continuous wood supplies; another, mainly of local import, comes from the fact that the forest cover influences soil and water conditions, and the third, a reason of sound political economy, is that areas unfit for farm uses may still be made productive by forest cropping.

Although, in Germany, sporadic attempts at forest cropping date back to the 14th and 15th centuries, systematic forest management did not become general until the end of the 18th century when a timber famine was actually threatening certain portions of Germany. The fact that, at that time, wood was the only fuel, that rivers were practically the only means of transportation, and that the dense population in the river valleys had used up near-by forest supplies and turned the lands into farms, while the extensive forests of mountain and hinterland were largely inaccessible, will explain the existence of this timber famine. At that time, German forests were largely in the condition in which we now find much of our Canadian forests—largely culled, slashed, burned or inaccessible. For instance, in 1778, it was reported from eastern Prussia that "not a single acre could be found in the province that had not been burnt in earlier or later times," and that "the people are still so much accustomed to the ruthless use of fires that no punishment could stop them."

All the nostrums which are now advocated in Canada, and more particularly in the United States, to relieve the situation, were recommended then, and, in part, practised. These included the planting of rapidly growing trees, the fixing of diameter limits below which trees might not be cut, marking the trees which might be felled, even on private property, and other interferences with private rights. Restrictions in the use of wood for buildings, coffins and other manufactures; in the use of Christmas trees and in the use of fences, were instituted. Even the number of buildings for any community was under regulation. The wood trade generally was regulated by laws. Finally, however, the forester, by using common sense and scientific knowledge, and especially by properly using the commonplace natural conditions at hand, showed the way out.

It is not my purpose to trace the history of development of modern forest policy in Europe, but I wish merely to point out that we may learn from that history as well what to avoid, as what to do, to meet similar conditions.

During the 19th century, one European nation after another came to recognize the necessity of substituting management of its forest resources for ruthless exploitation. The governments conceived it as their duty, in the exercise of their providential functions, to provide for the future. The last to fall in line—and they are still uncertain and undeveloped in their forest policies—were naturally the countries exporting forest products, Russia and Sweden; and, now, the United States and Canada—the countries which erroneously suppose themselves to have a surplus of forest resources to dispose of—are joining the ranks.

While local considerations, such as the prevention of soil erosion, of torrents and floods, of sand drifting and the necessity of using waste lands, have led to measures of reforesting, the main and universal incentive to the practice of scientific forestry is the necessity of obtaining wood supplies.

To discuss this question at length would lead us too far. Indeed, it should be understood that accurate statistics, and, in many cases, even reasonable approximations to conditions, are lacking. Hence only very general statements are possible. All data available, however, show that, at the present time, all countries, except the southern ones, cut more than the actual annual growth of their forest area, that they are cutting into capital, and are within measurable time of the exhaustion of their supplies of timber of serviceable size.

The value of the forest areas of the southern hemisphere, largely located in the tropics, is in doubt, since they produce woods which, under present methods of use, have but limited application. While the wooded area of the world may be figured at over four billion acres, the really productive forest area capable of furnishing the kind of timber which plays a rôle in the markets of the world is probably not over half that figure. The annual consumption of wood is tolerably closely known to be in the neighbourhood of forty billion cubic feet; and this, besides supplying home consumption, gives rise to an export trade of $300,000,000. If we were to take 40 cubic feet as a fair average production per acre—in Sweden it is figured at 25, in Germany at nearly 50 cubic feet—it would appear that a large enough area is on hand to furnish all supplies, provided it were managed for such production. And it is such management that we, in this Commission, are called upon to bring about.

All the varied methods which have been applied to secure an economic and scientific handling of forest properties for reproduction can be briefly classified under four heads:

1. Government ownership and management, based on the *paternal* function of government.

2. Municipal ownership and government supervision of its management by exercise of the *fiscal* function of the State.

3. Regulation of private forest management by exercise of the *police* function of the State.

4. Encouragement of private forest management by exercise of the *educational* function.

State ownership and management, which, at the end of the 18th century, under Adam Smith's teaching, had been discredited, is now considered the most efficient means of securing results. Nowhere else are public ownership and administration for the public interest so essential and indispensable as in the case of forests.

The conclusive arguments for State ownership are, that the long time element involved in forest cropping—60 to 120 years—is discouraging to private enterprise, and that the protective function of a forest cover on mountains and in other locations, which requires ultra-conservative use, imposes the duty on the State of maintaining proper forest conditions.

Practically every European state, therefore, owns forest property, and, during the last thirty to forty years, the tendency is, at least in some countries, notably Germany, to enlarge it by taking over mismanaged private forests, buying and reforesting waste areas, and exchanging farm lands for forest. Prussia, for instance, in 1902, not only provided for a naval programme which now has suddenly aroused attention, but set aside some $30,000,000 for purchase of waste lands; and in addition, she annually spends nearly half a million dollars in reforesting these. During the last forty years she has increased her forest property by nearly 13 per cent. Yet the actual ownership of forest by the governments of the different German States does not exceed 33 per cent. of the total forest areas, as against 62 per cent. in European Russia, and over 35 per cent. in Sweden.

These State properties are managed under well organized forest departments, the administration performing all the forest work down to the cutting of the wood, selling logs and cordwood, etc., in the forest, or else, as is frequently done in France and Russia, selling the year's cut on the stump and carefully supervising the cutting.

Municipal ownership is especially well developed in France, where 23 per cent. of the total forest area is under municipal authority. In Germany only 15 per cent. is municipally owned. The management of these municipal forests, which are, in many cases, most valuable sources of income for city or town, is closely controlled by the governments in various ways, e.g., by requiring professional foresters to be placed in charge, by having working plans submitted for sanction, by giving expert advice, and, in some cases, as in Baden, by the Government managing them directly for an annual charge per acre. Altogether, this supervision is of a fiscal character to prevent the dissipation of municipal property, and is based on the same principle as that by which we limit the debt which a municipal corporation may incur.

Private property, which, in Germany, represents one-half of the forest area, is much less controlled by Government than is usually supposed. Yet about one-half is in some manner or degree controlled, so that only 25 per cent. of the entire forest area is without any control whatever, and this portion is easily distinguished by its poor condition.

The State supervision over private property is of two kinds. Entailed properties are looked after, like municipal properties, under a family compact with the Government, by which the Government is obliged to prevent dissipation of the property. In the southern and southwestern states, which are mountainous, the control is of a police character, for the purpose of preventing improvident clearing, which might lead to soil washing, torrential action, etc. Otherwise, there is not much control, and, in Prussia and some other parts, it is entirely absent. Restrictive measures on private properties have always been found difficult to enforce, and, therefore, undesirable. Such paternalistic propositions as are now agitated for in the United States, e.g., restricting private owners generally from cutting below a certain diameter limit, would be considered childish and intolerable.

In France, the supervision of private forest management is much more developed than in Germany, and is much more strict. On the other hand, ameliorative or persuasive measures have been, especially lately, highly developed in Germany. The formation of forest planting associations to reclaim waste lands, or to manage small forest properties to better advantage by merging them and then employing professional foresters, is encouraged. Plant material is given to would-be planters, with advice, which is furnished, rarely free of charge, but yet at a low cost. Bureaus of information, with experts who act at a low charge, are established in each province in Prussia, and are developing remarkable activity in assisting forest owners to secure better results in forest and market. The large number of well-trained foresters of

A rollway of logs on Hon. P. McLaren's Limit.

West slope of McGillivray ridge. It has been burned over, but the forest will re-establish itself.

higher degree makes it possible to extend better technical procedure in all directions, the governments merely facilitating the way to its employment.

There are no fakes and nostrums of paternalism employed, but everything is conducted on business principles, such as should commend themselves to any democratic community. The Government simply uses its better facilities and greater credit to help the citizens to help themselves and the community.

Of course there are forest schools, mostly supported by governments, some eight higher schools to educate the eventual forest managers, and some eight or ten to educate the lower forest officers. The experiment stations are instituted to put practical forest management, which is relying still, to a large extent, on mere experience and empiricism, upon a more scientific basis. Such, then, are the scientific results of good forest politics.

I have confined myself largely to conditions in Germany, partly because I am personally more conversant with them, partly because here are exemplified all the different methods and policies that have been and are being used elsewhere, or have been tried and found wanting. For direct application to Canadian conditions this German development is, to be sure, too ideal, too far advanced, too intensive, and we should, perhaps, look at some country which is more nearly comparable to ours in its present condition of development, for points which we might utilize immediately. It is, however, my belief that all progress would be more rational if it were directed by the ideals that have shown practical value.

The country which most nearly resembles our own, both in physical character, forest conditions and methods of forest administration, is Sweden.

Sweden, with fifty million acres of forest on 50 per cent. of its land area, has been, and is still, one of the largest, if not the largest, exporters of forest products, mostly spruce and pine. For the last 20 years forest products contributed between thirty and forty and, including wood manufactures, over fifty-million dollars' worth annually to the export trade. Every year the cut per acre has increased, until now it may be a thousand million cubic feet. The realization that this important resource is being rapidly diminished has come, as with us, only within the last decade.

Hardly 10 per cent. of the country is cultivated, the rest is barren or wooded, at least 40 per cent. of which is State owned or partially controlled by the Government. Forest fires and the axe, as with us, have devastated and deteriorated large areas, especially in the northern zone, where the growth is as slow as with us (one inch of diameter in 12 to 15 years). Similar policies as with us have prevailed. To attract settlers, crown lands were given away freely, the settler selling the wood to lumbermen, while a loosely conducted license system handed the forest property over to the lumbermen. Licenses to cut timber limits were given on long terms (50 years; later, only for 20 years) for prices which were often realized from the forest in the first winter. A diameter limit of 12 inches, measured at 18 to 20 feet above ground, was usually the basis of the lease; but the licensee could somehow lease away smaller sizes, so that several persons secured rights in the same forest. In the absence of a sufficient force of forest guards, supervision was slack and wasteful practices abounded. Owners of iron works had the right to secure their wood supplies, charcoal, etc., from the State forests, but if, for any reason, the iron works were abandoned, the forest privileges were continued; the iron men turned lumbermen, or even sold the properties as if they were their own. This went on until, in 1896, the Government began to challenge titles and institute legal proceedings to recover its own. As a result, many were forced to secure the fee simple, and some thirty million acres of forest, or, including unreclaimable waste lands, over fifty million acres, became private property. Meanwhile the State, by purchase and reclamation of waste lands, still further increased its holdings.

Although sporadic attempts to control the exploitation to some extent date back centuries, and a commission of German forest experts was called in as long ago as 1760, while during the 19th century repeated attempts were made to create a saner forest administration, private interests were strong enough to render them nugatory. But, in 1903, as a result of a painstaking extended canvass by a legislative committee, a law was enacted which was to go into effect in 1905, placing the control of all private forest in the hands of Forest Conservation Boards. These Boards, one for each province, have surveillance of all private forests, the owners being obliged to submit felling plans to the committee for approval. The Board may also enforce reforestation of cut-over areas, may forbid clearing, and may order the adoption of specific measures of conservation; for the law itself refrains from formulating any rules.

These Boards consist of three persons appointed for three years, one by the Government, one by the County Council, and one by the managing committee of the County Agricultural Society. In addition, where the communities desire, elected forest commissioners may be added to the Board. The Board can enforce its rulings by court proceedings in which injunctions to prevent further lumbering, confiscation of logs or of lumber, or money fines, etc., may be adjudged.

An export duty of 4 to 8 cents per cubic foot on timber, and 8 to 14 cents per ton on dry wood-pulp is imposed to furnish funds for carrying out the law. A more systematic administration of the State forests, under the Domain Bureau of the Department of Agriculture, was also provided, and the time limit for timber licenses reduced to five years. The management of municipal forest properties is placed under the State administration, the corporation paying for such service.

To be sure, the forest management of the State, as well as of private owners, can still be only extensive, and the methods of lumbering —usually the stumpage being sold—resembles ours, while forest fires are still not infrequent. But there is supervision by professionally educated foresters, and, to judge from the publications of the Association of Foresters and of the forest experiment stations, remarkable progress has lately been made. I would advise that the character and actual practical working of these attempts in Sweden be submitted to a closer inspection by this Commission.

I shall now add a few suggestions respecting the applicability in Canada of policies which elsewhere have proved advantageous.

The first objection which so-called practical men urge against adopting policies or methods practised elsewhere is that our economic and political conditions are so different as to preclude such adoption. This is, of course, true, and only a visionary would think of transplanting bodily a system which has no natural affinity to its new surroundings. Nevertheless, the principles underlying that system may be recognized as desirable, and a knowledge of the experience had in applying these principles to a given system may assist the judgment in altering it to suit new conditions. Any practicable plan must take into account the conditions as they exist, and, before any change in the present methods of waste and destruction can take place, the causes of such waste must be analyzed to see how, and to what extent, they can be removed.

The first and greatest need is, however, a change, a radical change, in the attitude of our people and Governments from that of exploiters to that of managers. We should realize that existing methods of treating timber lands are bad, and that a change is imperatively needed. Only when there is doubt implanted as to the propriety of our present methods of forest management, and only when people realize the urgent need of change, will the radical reform be inaugurated that we believe necessary. When that attitude is established which demands that our forests shall be managed, not merely exploited, all the rest will be comparatively easy, and it will then astonish the practical men to find how much European methods and systems are really applicable, just as it lately surprised the Americans across the line.

To secure the change of attitude, more knowledge is needed. Just as the Swedes based their recent legislation upon a more or less careful ascertainment of their forest conditions, so should we endeavour to ascertain more precisely where we stand. Our knowledge as regards our forest resources is, at present, to a great extent, guesswork. While it would be too expensive to make actual forest surveys of the whole country, yet a more authoritative collation of known facts, presented in such a way as to suggest the needs of future methods of treatment, is possible and desirable. Such a forest survey as I conducted for the province of Nova Scotia last summer at a cost of less than 25 cents a square mile would be more than sufficiently accurate for the purpose. Here are the results of that survey:—

Mapped 7,400 square miles = 4,700,000 acres; twenty per cent. in farms or capable of farm use; some 21,000 acres of natural meadow; 24,000 acres open bogs, capable of utilization; some $2\frac{1}{2}$ million acres, or 53%, of forest land, of which (1) only 75,000 remains virgin, or nearly so, (2) 445,000 lightly culled, (3) 1,115,000 severely culled, (4) 130,000 young thrifty growth, besides 34,000 second growth pine ready for cutting, and **280,000** acres, or a little over 1%, recently burned; 25%, or 480,000 acres of old burns, and 690,000 acres of barren land, which could be made partially useful; 2%, or 90,000 acres unknown.

State ownership of the bulk of the forest property being the actual condition in most parts of the Dominion, it should be comparatively easy to change from the present methods of administering it to better ones. The experience of other nations, that State ownership has invariably furnished better results than private management, either without or with State control, should make us adhere to State ownership as a principle. If this is agreed to, then the installation of properly manned and properly endowed forestry bureaus in each province to manage this property on forestry principles, following the example of the Dominion Government, should be the next step. Perhaps, however, before such bureaus are established, it might be advisable to appoint Royal Commissions for each Province, or possibly, Committees of this Commission, as the Chairman has suggested, similar to the Swedish Forest Conservation Boards, to formulate plans of procedure. This would very acceptably remove the reform from the political arena. For one thing, it can be proved beyond doubt that the existing license systems are the greatest hindrance to reform, and the most difficult task would be to adjust equitably the rights of licensees and yet secure this change, without which no hope for the future can be entertained.

Timber left on a tract logged to the 10-inch diameter limit. Many of the standing Spruces have died.

Each province and sections in each province vary to such an extent, when it comes to application of technical methods, that each bureau must be left to work out by itself the proper way of handling its problems. That is to say, legislation, even provincial legislation, should be as little specific as possible, leaving to the administration the formulation of rules, just as is done in European countries. Such a thing, for instance, as a general diameter limit to which cutting may be allowed, is a mistake.

Every method to cope with forest fires which is used elsewhere is applicable somewhere in Canada, and none should be left untried. Every silvicultural practice used in Germany or Sweden is practicable in Canada somewhere, with proper judgment. The only reason that should keep it out is expense. But even this reason is only apparent, and very temporary. We know, for instance, that white pine stumpage in this country has now reached the figure which will cover the cost at which it can certainly be reproduced by artificial planting and return at least 4% compound interest; and soon other species will have reached the stumpage price which represents cost of production. To be sure, the results are realized only in the long run, and, hence, only the Government or municipalities are fit to engage in such ventures, which must, however, in time, turn out as profitable as the undertakings of Germany or France. Every method employed in the old countries to encourage private forestry, especially by education, expert advice and other assistance, is applicable now in Canada, except, perhaps, for the lack of experienced personnel. Only the restrictive measures on the exercise of private property rights need to be carefully scrutinized. And these, we have seen, are largely of historical development and not favoured in their own country when other methods are possible. While we may have to vary the precise method by which we attain results, it is my belief that every principle which has been found to work elsewhere can be put in practice in Canada, and can be practically applied now, if we so desire.

It may be useful to summarize the six essential points made in this statement:—

1. Wherever forestry, i.e., managing timber lands as a crop, has been practised for long enough time, its results have shown themselves in increased production per acre and in greatly increased revenues.

2. Every principle involved in the successful systems inaugurated in other countries can, with proper judgment, be applied somewhere in Canada, even now.

3. To secure such application of improved methods in handling timber-lands, first of all a change of attitude towards the forest on

the part of Governments and people is necessary, namely, from considering it as a mine to be exploited, to conserving it as a crop which can be perpetuated by management.

4. Such change of attitude may be secured by more definite and reliable information regarding our timber supplies, and the need or desirability of their conservative use—information which it should be the first business of this Commission to collate.

5. The timber license systems are inimical to the radical reform which is believed necessary in order to secure such conservative use. Hence, comprehensive plans for an equitable adjustment of the rights of licensees, which will, however, restore the full control of the properties to the provincial Governments, need to be formulated.

6. This can best be done by royal commissions or special forestry committees for each province, unhampered by political considerations, and leading eventually to the creation of special bureaus for the organization of a forest service.

HON. MR. COCHRANE: The information given in this paper by Dr. Fernow is most interesting, and although his suggestions are pretty radical, yet I think a great many of them might be put into effect without doing injury to the individual.

I regret to say that Hon. Mr. Allard had to return to Quebec last night on account of illness in his family, and so will be unable to address us. I call upon Dr. James W. Robertson, who will address us upon

THE CONSERVATION OF AGRICULTURAL RESOURCES

Dr. Robertson said:

May I offer one word of explanation before I speak on this large subject? I have been separated from my office—from my books and papers—since I was asked to prepare this address; consequently, it will not be so compact nor so full as I would like it to be for an occasion like this. I am sure your indulgence will be generous under these circumstances.

On Friday of last week, just five days ago, the President of the United States sent a special message to Congress, on "Conservation of the Natural Resources of the Nation," and, since the movement for conservation in the two countries has been not only concurrent, but cordial, and has been going forward with harmonious co-operation, I may be permitted to begin by quoting one passage from the message of President Taft.

"In considering the conservation of the natural resources of the country, the feature that transcends all others, including woods, waters, minerals, is the soil of the country. It is incumbent upon the government to foster by all available means the resources of the country that produce the food of the people. To this end the conservation of the soils of the country should be cared for with all means at the government's disposal. Their productive powers should have the attention of our scientists that we may conserve the new soils, improve the old soils, drain wet soils, ditch swamp soils, levee river overflow soils, grow trees on thin soils, pasture hillside soils, rotate crops on all soils, discover methods for cropping dry-land soils, find grasses and legumes for all soils, feed grains and mill feeds on the farms where they originate that the soils from which they come may be enriched.

"A work of the utmost importance to inform and instruct the public on this chief branch of the conservation of our resources is being carried on successfully in the Department of Agriculture."

That presentation of the question may be taken as appropriate to Canada also. The recognition by President Taft of the valuable work of the Department of Agriculture in his country may be applied with equal aptness and pride to Canada by anyone who knows what the Dominion and the Provincial Departments of Agriculture have done and are doing.

The agricultural resources of Canada may be regarded as the chief asset in the landed estate of the people of the Dominion. A vast heritage has come to us from our ancestors, who won it by labour, courage, and privations, careless of personal ease that their children might have a good start, a good chance and good homes. Their main thought was for us and for their country, and all that that stands for in its broadest interpretation and its widest application. We have entered upon the unearned ownership of what they acquired and what they achieved. Why did they come to Canada? (I speak with some knowledge, at least regarding one family, because I was present at the family councils and discussions). They came because this was a land of liberty for individuals; and I think none of us need fear that this Commission will encroach upon that. They came because it was a land of respected law; and, if we help to secure better laws adapted to our new conditions, then so much more insistent and powerful will the call be to all of us to preserve our right to that reputation. They came, above all, because it was a land of opportunities for children; and I happen to be one of the many who have found it to be a good land in that sense. Why did those born in this country toil for its development? For similar reasons, and chiefly that it might be a good place for homes when the children came to their inheritance.

While this Commission is not charged with the conservation of all these priceless possessions, it may be expected not to contravene these birth-rights, but to help in extending their enjoyment through the wise use of what we have in the several departments of the nation's property. Our landed estate is not fully known to any one mind, but we have many minds capable of grasping something of its real significance and possibilities. There is nothing on record yet with anything like fullness as to what we have, what we are doing with it, or what we may do with it. Our youth accounts for that, but our intelligence and growing sense of responsibility require us to correct that condition. We have not owned the place long enough to have made a full survey or investigation of what it contains.

We certainly have a fine property. We own half a continent extending one-sixth of the way around the globe. From the Atlantic westward we have 1,000 miles of land, with possibilities which no man can adequately describe, as a place for homes for a dominant people, a people dominating others not by suppressing them, but by lifting them up to our level. That area, 1,000 miles wide, is characterized in its natural resources by two important qualities that indicate great things for our future,—soil and climate conducive to the growth of apple trees in vigour and abundance, and the summer air fragrant with clover blossoms. These mean possible homes for happy families and plenty of children, with the fertility of the land perennially renewed by clovers. Farther west come 1,000 miles of rock and lake and forest; a wilderness so far as agriculture is concerned, but such a wilderness is not a useless part of the earth's surface. I look upon that as Canada's great regulator of climate for ensuring regular and dependable rainfalls in summer, and, if that vast area be burned over and left bare, the winds sweeping over it will go where they list, licking up the moisture instead of dropping down refreshing showers. Ontario, Quebec and the Maritime Provinces, equally with Manitoba, Saskatchewan and Alberta, are concerned in conserving that regulator of our greatest material need— a reliable dependable climate with frequent rainfalls in summer.

Then we have 1,000 miles of prairie soil enriched by thousands of years of nature's far sighted economy, when she stored it with plant food immediately available for crops. There is a tremendous temptation for first settlers to become surface miners instead of real farmers who use and husband the treasures of the soil. The lure of the prairies is like unto the lure of the Yukon or the lure of the Cobalt: "Come and take something, ship it out and make yourselves rich." Surface mining is not agriculture; agriculture is something different; it is conserving the substance and fertility of the soil while taking a liberal toll of crops for our own sustenance and improvement. Over these western plains there is a great deal of good agriculture, notwithstanding the temptation to take from the soil its immediately available wealth. I think this Commission can strengthen the hands of these people by showing them that immediate profits to the largest extent can be obtained from good agriculture while conserving the crop-producing power of the land for the benefit of our descendants.

Between the prairies and the Pacific ocean we have 500 miles of mountains, where not devastated by fire, carrying timber of untold value and rich with minerals, precious and common; while the valleys produce crops from wheat to peaches and all those fine fruits that give us not only nourishment, but delight. A great asset is that stretch, 500 miles in breadth, of mountains and fertile valleys.

That is a hurried and brief survey of our estate, not in acres, but in areas of the half-continent. It is worth while taking care that it shall pass on, not merely undiminished and unimpaired, but improved and enriched by intelligent labour and good management.

May I say a word in a general way regarding agriculture? The object of agriculture, of course, is crops; crops the best in quality and the largest in quantity that can be obtained. I would not think it at all prudent to enter here upon a discussion in detail of the processes and operations of agriculture, but would ask you to join me in considering what we obtain and may continue to obtain in even greater plenty from our agriculture, while I drive a few stakes of statement here and there on which to present suggestions and evidence regarding the conservation of these resources.

Crops—crops for food; and all our foods, with the exception of fish, come from some farm; tea and coffee, as well as bread and butter. One does not want to magnify the place and function of food in human affairs. It is worth saying, however, that a nation's greatness and its success rest upon its food and its ideals, and the poorly nourished people will be at the will of the well-fed race. The race that can utilize its resources for food for the wholesome nourishment of its children and its adults and for the development of energy in the highest realms, becomes a great people. It is worth while remembering that human life and human ideals at their best rest upon the basis of a healthy body nourished by plain, wholesome food. The raw materials for our clothing, with the exception of furs, come from the farm; and furs may be included in the survey of this Commission. Our animal servants that are bred and reared for our pleasure and for our comfort, come from the farm. What man lives who, having learned to ride in youth and having often been the partner in trot and canter with a spirited horse, has not got some kind of education that makes him more capable among men? In learning to dominate the lower animals by intelligence and kindness does there not come some ability to lead the higher by similar means? I like to think of a rural people that know how to ride. It is worth while as part of education. We get many other things from farms: flowers, which we do not eat, but which furnish real pleasure and inspire us with sentiment—lovely and sometimes lofty. "Consider the lilies how they grow." How much poorer we would be in much that conduces to beauty and strength and goodness, but for the richness of thought that flowers bring to us. Tobacco: I do not know that I have ever advocated the growing or use of tobacco, but I believe, as the founder of Macdonald College once said to me, that all from tobacco has not gone up in smoke. Drugs: We get even drugs from the farm. That is a brief survey of crops. Agriculture is for the gaining of crops, and the gaining of the best crops from a constantly improving soil depends upon the capacity and quality of the men.

Agriculture is not breaking clods or moving soil by hand or by machinery; it is the care of the surface of old mother earth. It is a task for men of the large vision, men of stout heart, men of kindly good-will towards their fellows. Out of their labours also abideth these three: faith, hope and love. The task of the race for many thousands of years has been to take care of old mother earth and make her a better home for children. Why the railway, why the art gallery, why the library, why the steamship, why the Dreadnoughts, why anything, but that the face of old mother earth may be a better place for homes for children? And the best result of all the effort is found in the culture of the farmer and of his family by intelligent labour. From the best agriculture comes the culture of the rural population, not only for this year's crop and next year's crop, but for the conservation and transmission of all they have acquired and achieved and become.

Crops in themselves represent labour and management, sun energy and materials. When a man sells a bushel of wheat he sells a small portion of the earth's surface, plus air and sunshine, plus labour and management. The processes which led up to that transaction are called cultivation. The best cultivation means the suppression of weeds, the control of injurious insects, the restraint of damaging disease; it implies the preservation of fertility and the increase of beauty. That is the essence of good cultivation, of good culture, wherever you find it whether on the fields or in human affairs. You will agree with me that agriculture includes the maintenance of an intelligent, capable, prosperous and contented rural population. I cordially agree with the thought of our chairman yesterday in which he indicated the great value to the nation of an intelligent rural population carrying forward their work and maintaining homes. Agriculture is a great mother and a prolific mothering occupation from which great leaders and patient workers have come in all ages. If Christ had not been born in a stable and cradled in a manger, I believe some great seer with power of interpretation would have invented the story to make it fit the facts of human experience.

Agriculture plays a great part in changing the forms and altering the values of materials and energies for human service. The primary sources of all crops that come through labour are the sun, air, water and soil. The contributing factors for crops are: soil, air and climate (which, after all, is not so elusive as to escape wholly the intelligent domination of the good farmer) seeds, labour and intelligence. These four—soil, air and climate, seeds, and intelligent labour are the constituent or contributory elements or factors for crops. The soils are merely broken down or broken up portions of the earth's rocky surface. The crust of the earth is not very thick. If some strange power, natural or supernatural, should come along with a jolt and upset the island of Montreal—well, the eastern end would be down in the molten, while the upper end would be with Macdonald College and the snow. That is about the thickness of the crust according to the statements of latest scientific imaginations; and the soil on it is still in the making in different regions at the rate of from one-tenth of an inch up to one inch per century. Soil fairly represents the rocky crust of the earth in its mineral or inorganic elements. The organic parts of the soil are the decaying remains of bodies which were once alive—roots and leaves and stalks and flesh and bones. All flesh is grass and all grass was sun, air, water and soil; and thus the rotation goes on. The decaying remains of things that once lived and the atmosphere are the source of nitrogen for crops. Nitrogen is one of the most important constituents of the flesh-forming parts of foods as distinguished from the starchy parts that give us heat and energy.

The soil contains living organisms at work. Soil is not a wholly dead thing, not the soil for crops. It is alive to the extent that it is the home of myriads of living things. Earth worms were the necessary forerunners of human life. Their function was the digestion of the crude elements of plant food, thus preparing the constituents necessary for the life of plants, which, in their turn, sustain the higher forms of life. Millions of bacteria also live in the soil, and, but for their labours, crops would soon cease to grow. All the available nutrients would very quickly be exhausted but for the continuous labour of these lower forms of life. By cultivation and good management the farmer can increase the population of his soils by many myriads of bacteria per cubic inch in the course of a few years. The farmer has a new interest in cultivating land when he knows he is managing life. The main purpose of cultivation is to give the life in the soil a chance to do the best for itself; and in proportion as this is done will the crops prosper. We are all interdependent. No man liveth unto himself. The man who gives the bacteria in the soil and all the other serviceable forms of life a good chance, will thereby provide a rich and profitable opportunity for himself. I think that law runs through the whole realm of nature's economy.

Water also is a constituent of the soil for farm purposes; it is not something extraneous and foreign. The rocky portion of the earth's surface broken down, the decaying remains of organisms, bacteria and other forms of life and water—these make soil. The series of changes, chemical and physical, which go on are due to the life and activity of these organisms in the soil. They are the cooks, without which plants cannot find their nourishment, even though it may be there in the crude form not far from the roots.

Certain substances are essential to plant life and plant growth, and these are only ten in number. The two chief constituents of farm crops are oxygen and carbon. These come directly from the air where they exist in unlimited quantities. Hydrogen is a constituent of water, and so long as there is plenty of rainfall or water in the soil there is no scarcity of that element. Nitrogen, a valuable constituent of plant food and human food, comes directly into plants from the soil and also into plants from the air. It comes into soil from the air by previous processes of growth followed by decay. There is plenty of nitrogen close by; over every acre there rests enough for 1,500,000 average crops of cereals. Since it may be taken into crops of the clover family through the agency of bacteria which live in the roots, the supply may be reckoned as inexhaustible when the agencies are effectively used. Once captured and combined into a plant, it may be kept in rotation through plants, animals and manures indefinitely.

You may remember the statement by Sir William Crookes that there was a danger that the nitrogen of the soils might be too scant for producing sufficient wheat crops. We learn from recent investigations that by means of the life of bacteria on the roots of clover, alfalfa and other legumes, the nitrogen is taken in direct from the air and thus prepared for use by other crops. By that process we can call on the free nitrogen of the air to the extent of our intelligence and our ability. That element is available in abundance subject to the limitations of our intelligence and our labour.

The other elements required by plants are phosphorus, potassium, magnesium, sulphur, calcium and iron. If the first seven inches of the soil are of the average composition of the crust of the earth, then the amount of phosphorus present is enough for average crops of cereals for only 250 years; and that is not a long span in the life of a nation. We run some risk of being short of that element, and if a crop is short of any one of these elements it cannot make use of the others; the crop is held up for want of nourishment and cannot go on. On the average the phosphorus in seven inches of the earth's surface represents enough for about 250 crops such as wheat; the potassium represents about 5,000 crops, if it could be all taken out without renewals; the magnesium represents 14,000 crops; the sulphur represents 20,000 crops; the calcium represents 100,000; and the iron 400,000.

There are only three elements likely to be deficient in agricultural soils, namely, nitrogen, potassium and phosphorus. Analyses by Dr. Frank T. Shutt, of the Experimental Farm, which are very comprehensive and among the best on the continent, give us the information that in the top foot of the good lands in Canada there is enough nitrogen for 150 large crops of cereals without renewals, if it could be all taken up; enough potassium for 300 crops of cereals if it could all be taken out without renewals, and phosphorus for 250 crops. You see, we are within measurable distance of the exhaustion of nitrogen, of potassium and phosphorus unless we have constant renewals. Only a small proportion of the total quantity of these elements in the soil is in available form at one time; they are mainly in a form not soluble and therefore not get-at-able by the plants. In fact, a very small proportion of what is present is ready for the use of plants; otherwise the rains would wash them out and leave the soil poor. While I have no desire to compare to the disadvantage of the mother-land the conditions there and here, it is worth mentioning in this connection that when the frosts of Canada seize the soil at the end of the growing season, all the soluble plant food is held fast in its frozen grip until spring, whereas in England the wastage into the sea between November and March on cultivated land without a growing crop, is sufficient to feed one whole grain crop. The frost of winter is not altogether a handicap; it holds the available soluble constituents of plant food and leaves them in position and condition ready for the use of the crops in spring. England could not have gone on reaping such harvests but for bringing on to the land these constituents in abundance by importations from other countries. She makes all lands pay tribute to her soil by her imports of foods and fertilizers. She can spare much leaching to the sea and never miss it. We cannot afford to do that.

Nitrogen can be supplied by manure spread on the land and by the growing of legumes. The application of manure will liberate by fermentation the potash as nothing else does. The supply of potash in the soil can be renewed by putting back on the land the manure from all the crops removed, or its equivalent. The phosphorus is somewhat deficient, and there is great danger for the future of farming in Canada unless we conserve that and put it back on the land.

The rotations of crops so generally advocated furnish for the next crops the decaying portions of roots and stalks and leaves. These may be the home for bacterial life. We must not forget that soil, which we formerly thought was dead, is the habitation of bacterial servants who work for us and, in supporting themselves, do tasks which we could not otherwise have performed at all. The rotation of crops first of all furnishes suitable conditions for bacteria. The humus or decaying organic matter also makes the land retain water, and this enables plants to obtain their food. Rotation of crops cleans the land from weeds; a most important function. It also cleans the land from what seem to be poisonous substances, which, in some little measure, so far as our latest investigations show, a crop leaves as its by-product in the soil. Clover sickness is not a grotesque notion of the ancients. We know that the by-product of one form of life, unless disposed of somehow, would make it impossible for that form of life to keep on living there. You may have five people living in a small valley for all time and thriving on the fruits, drinking pure spring water and rejoicing in all the surroundings; but let 50,000 people camp in that valley for a fortnight, and the by-products in their sewage may make the continuation of healthy life for them impossible. Sensible rotation puts in another kind of crop after oats, wheat or barley to renovate and purify the soil for the next crop. That also is a part of the conservation of labour which is worth thinking about. Rotation of crops also cleans the land from forms of injurious insects. It is not generally known by farmers that the two-and three-year old wire worm is the fellow that cuts the oats, and he cannot get to be three years old unless the pasture or hay is down for that length of time. If you can kill all the two-year old wire worms and white grubs by rotation, their power to do damage will be greatly reduced. There is a great conservation of labour and skill in getting at your foe in the right time. The distribution of labour over the whole season is a valuable plan in national administration. It is important that our people on the land should be occupied the whole year round rather than be rushed in the spring and harvest, with a temptation to loaf and rust during the rest of the year. Once, in Manitoba, I met a farmer on the train going west and asked him: "What are you going to British Columbia for?" His answer in substance was: "I cannot stand this long winter doing nothing." There is no salvation for man but in labour; if he wants to feel satisfaction within himself, labour in some form spread over the year is necessary. I restate part of the case for the rotation of crops in the following paragraphs.

It is admitted that the rotation of crops has been the chief means of improving the agriculture of Great Britain and some other portions of Europe during the last century. The practice itself consists in growing roots (or some other cultivated green crop) and leguminous crops (such as clover, beans or peas), or grass (or hay crops), alternately with cereal crops ripened for grain. The famous four-course Norfolk rotation was roots, barley, clover or beans and wheat. The chief point seems to be to make each of these crops follow others which have different requirements with respect to the time of the season when they benefit most by plenty of available plant food in the soil, and different habits of growth in other ways, particularly in the ranges of their roots. The rotation for any farm must have regard to the soil, the climate, the markets for crops and other local conditions. Not only the increase in the yield of crops has to be taken into account, but also the value and uses to which the crops can be put when grown.

Clover is a most valuable crop for use in a short rotation. It increases the substances of plant food in the soil for cereals, and makes conditions suitable for the activity of such germs in the soil as prepare other substances for the use of subsequent crops. The use of a clover crop, or some other plant of the same family—one of the legumes—in a rotation, has been demonstrated to be the best farm practice. In an experiment extending over thirty-two years, at Rothamsted, the records show an increased yield of wheat amounting to 114 per cent. when one crop in the rotation included clover or beans, as compared with the yield from wheat when cereal crops followed cereal crops.

The results on the experimental farms of Canada show that the yield of grains (wheat, oats or barley) after clover is from two to ten bushels per acre more than the yield of grain in the same season after a previous grain crop. The great increase in crops grown in rotation over those grown continuously seems to be because more nitrogen is available to the former; and perhaps because it is available during the early period of their growth from the preparation of it by the preceding crop or by the cultivation of that crop.

Other benefits from systematic rotation of crops are:—

(1) The distribution of the mechanical operations of the farm over the season; (2) The opportunity for cleaning the land; (3) The comparative freedom from damage by insects; (4) The production of a variety of products for feeding to live stock and for sale.

Now let us consider climate. The end of the whole process and effort and plan of agriculture is not changing the condition of soil, as in the forest primeval or in the unbroken prairie, to a cultivated surface. It is not breaking clods or moving soil; it is gathering sunshine into humanized wealth. Agriculture organizes wealth in humanized and usable forms out of what otherwise would continue as wilderness. The soil is only one of the means whereby the intelligent labour of man finds expression in crops. Seed is one of the means. Water is another of the essential means. If any one of these is defective or deficient the success of the human effort towards expression in crops is hindered. For every ton of dry matter that comes into our granaries there went through the plants 300 tons of water. Does not that commend to us a careful consideration of the conservation of that big forest reservoir up in the wilderness? Every ton of dry matter from the corn fields and the oat fields of Ontario and Quebec and the wheat fields of the West means that the plants transpired at least 300 tons of water. Therefore, the immense advantage of frequent showers in summer and of retentive soil that water may be available when and where the plant needs it, is plainly evident. The farmer is the manager of these means to capture the sunshine. His main business is the catching and converting of sun-power into food and materials for clothing for the human race.

The temperature of the first three inches of the soil is, to some extent, determined by the method of cultivation; the land may be warmer from being drained and properly cultivated than if left uncared for. The sunshine can be gathered into the crops earlier in the season by means of early ripening varieties. As to wind-storms and hail-storms, the wind bloweth where it listeth; but wind-storms and damaging rain storms and hail-storms do not often come where intelligent forethought and labour have set out and cared for trees and maintained the forests as a useful ally of agriculture.

It has been considered by many that the wastefulness of pioneers is in keeping with the prodigality of nature, and that the pioneer had the right to dissipate natural resources if he thereby improved himself and the prospects for his family. Take an illustration in a large way from the use of coal. During millions of years it was prepared and then stored in the earth—we suppose for human use. And we have been using it with fine prodigality, boasting of the millions of tons we mine every year. Yet we learn from some authorities that the probabilities are, that in seventy-five years the coal deposits of the United States will be pretty well exhausted, except those at the lower levels, more difficult of access and more costly to obtain. It seems all right in the meantime to be using up the coal which has given man, to a large extent, control over metals and the knowledge of and control over electrical energy. Thereby he has acquired ability to apply to his own service the inexhaustible resources of water-powers; and perhaps, by and by, he may be able to use sun-power direct. By harnessing the water-powers of the country we now generate heat, light and power from them, which man could never have done, as far as we can see, except for the use he made of coal in a large and liberal way during all these years of experimenting. There is a justification, if you please, for the extravagant use of that great natural resource, because of what has resulted from it. But when man exhausts the soil, what does he do? He helps to make the people more careless and less competent; he leaves them less power and more poverty in every respect. On the other hand, when he preserves and increases the fertility of the soil, the people thereby become increasingly efficient and capable. These two go together. It is for us to see that the fertility of our soil shall be maintained, and that there shall be continuously improving conditions for the rural population.

Already in our brief term of occupation the soil fertility is somewhat depleted. Is there no warning in the fact that the average yield of wheat per acre in the United States is only about one-half of the average yield per acre in old England? Let us see that the man on the land is informed of the difference between the privilege of the pioneer miner to be extravagant and seemingly wasteful, and the duty of the pioneer farmer to conserve the fertility of the soil. The greatest want on the farm is want of useful knowledge. Ignorance is always the mother of vice. Vicious farming is not done with malice aforethought; it is an inevitable outcome of ignorance regarding nature and her ways.

Seeds are important. The crops of Canada, in 1909, of wheat and oats and barley called for about 33,000,000 bushels of seed grain. Some years ago a competition was carried on in 450 places in Canada to determine the results obtainable by sowing selected seed. If you reason from the results, you shall find that an increase of 190,000,000 bushels of oats, wheat and barley might have been obtained by this one means, alone, in 1909. I do not say that improvement is immediately practicable or possible; but I do say it is attainable when all the fields of Canada are sown always with clean, well-selected seed. I can hardly realize what quantity 190,000,000 bushels represent. The figures by themselves do not convey clear, definite meaning; but I know that the quantity they represent is more than four times as much as all the grain and flour that went through the port of Montreal in any season before 1909. What a possibility of extending and expanding commerce. That 190,000,000 bushels of grain would fill 1,500 miles of railway grain cars. We are gradually, very gradually and slowly, coming to see the importance of pure seed.

One word more about the seed. We require seeds that suit the soil and climate. No man can tell without trial that a seed will fit into any particular set of conditions; but, so far as we know, the plant that has proven its ability to do well, to do the best of any of its kind in a locality, will give the seed that will produce the plant there again which will thrive best in that locality. The work of the experimental farms, particularly the work done by Dr. William Saunders, Director of Dominion Experimental Farms, and by Professor C. A. Zavitz, at the Ontario Agricultural College, is highly valuable. The work of the Seed Branch of the Department of Agriculture and of the Canadian Seed Growers' Association has also been exceedingly useful. Even in the few years that Macdonald College has been in existence, Professor Klinck has perfected an Indian corn for fodder and for ensilage which thrives admirably in Quebec. The experiments on the Dominion Experimental Farms have given the farmers of the West control over the climate to the extent of escaping frosts in great measure by means of varieties of wheat which will ripen some days earlier than was formerly the case. The work of the Ontario Agricultural College has given a barley to Ontario which yields on the average some four bushels more to the acre than any other variety so far known. A strain of barley especially well suited to Quebec and the Maritime Provinces has been evolved by Professor Klinck at Macdonald College. These are already achievements in the right direction.

Labour must also be considered. It is essential that labour, to be excellent and economical, should be performed by healthy people. The water supply of the farm houses has much to do with the labour of the people. Less attention is paid to the water supply of farmhouses than to that of other dwellings. While this would not be the occasion to discuss the pollution of streams generally, a reference must be made to the waste and the danger from allowing the sewage from cities and towns to escape into streams. Common opinion says that the stream purifies itself. Well, the sewage of Ottawa goes down past Macdonald College, a hundred miles distant, about four and a half days old, and it is not impaired in the vitality or vigour of its bacteria. I don't like that kind of water for drinking purposes. Why should anyone? This subject affords a great field for thought and action. The fact that the old farm well was put near the house without any reference to the drainage and seepage from the barn, the stables and the house itself, is in evidence everywhere. Typhoid on the farm—that old graveyard in Scotland holds my oldest sister and my oldest brother because we did not know the danger. Now that we do know, should we not protect our people? The farm home should be a place where typhoid and scarlet fever are unknown. Why should there not be a bathroom in every farm house? I would not live on a farm if I could not get the wholesome comfort of a bath daily, and I am only one man in many. Numbers of men who might enrich the nation's life would not live in the country without a good water supply on tap in the house. It can be had on every farm at small cost. How many men think of the value to the housewife of having running water in the house, to save her steps and give her pride in her home? We know that the pride of women in their own homes and families is a means towards national greatness. Anyone who has looked into the quality and sources of life and power knows something of the influence which the hopefulness and joy of the mother exercises on the vigour and spirit of her sons and daughters. The placing of a good pure water supply in farm homes is a conservation of one of our greatest agricultural resources.

We have made some headway at Macdonald College in considering the application of wind-power to the heating of homes on the prairies where the wind blows 20 hours a day. Can it not be turned into mechanical or electrical energy to give heat units to warm and light the house? In Canada we are away behind other countries on some of these matters. That is why some of us look to Switzerland and Denmark and Sweden to gain from their experiments and experiences lessons of real value. In some respects we have been so self-satisfied in Canada from self-laudations that we have not made earnest efforts to learn. Why should we not light and warm our prairie houses from the wasted energy of the winds? Cannot we grow special crops that will provide fuel close by? Maybe we can improve the sunflower until the stalks give us fuel and the heads a greater percentage of seeds and oil than before. Maybe an intelligent application of research and labour will enable us to utilize and conserve these resources.

Is intelligence in or for labour inherited? I do not think so. Every man is as lazy as he dares to be; that is what he inherits; and he is just as selfish as his education lets him be; that is our civilization. We cannot get intelligent labour by intuition; it comes only by instruction and by illustration and by training. The grown man is almost as susceptible as the young man to a form of instruction adapted to his years; you can provide means of education and training for him in a form in which he will take pride. When a man is old he is not past being educated, but the means must be acceptable and adequate. He will respond to illustrations of a system of farming which will be profitable to the farmer and his family while not reducing the crop-producing power of the soil or spoiling the beauty and attractiveness of the place. One of the problems of humanity is to maintain fertility by the activity of plants and bacteria while gathering a generous living from labour.

There is a vast field for the application of intelligent methods in the suppression of weeds and insects and diseases, and in laying the hand of intelligent control upon all our foes inside and outside. Insects alone take toll of our crops to the extent, perhaps, of 10 per cent. of their value. The magnitude of this toll can be realized from the fact that the field crops in Canada last year had a value of $532,000,000. If we cannot save all of this toll, we can save part of it by trying to bring into farm labour more and more intelligence regarding our natural resources and their management.

What are we doing as a people commercially and industrially with these agricultural resources? Last year in Canada (I quote from the excellent report and data provided by the Department of Agriculture) last year in Canada we grew on 30,065,556 acres, field crops to the value of $532,992,100 at local market prices. What could be done with that? It will feed our own people in the main, and the surplus will furnish the basis for a vast national commerce, domestic and export. It will furnish freight for railways and steamships, and the revenues and savings from it will furnish capital for banks and for business, and pay the wages of thousands and thousands of employees in our manifold industries. In part, we pay our outside debts by our exports. To every hundred dollars' worth of exports the main industries contribute as follows:—fisheries, $5, manufactures, $12, mining $15, lumbering $16, and agriculture $51. That is the way we pay what we owe outside.

There is evidence that we are getting more crop from the same land, apart from the question of whether we are depleting the soil of its fertility. Take wheat as a typical farm crop. We are doing fairly well in Canada because we are bringing virgin land by the million acres into crop, and that keeps our average up. The average in the United States last year (one of their big years) was 15·77 bushels to the acre while the average in Canada was 21·51 bushels to the acre, or about 5¾ bushels to the acre more than the average yield of the United States. The average in Russia was 8 bushels to the acre; and in Germany in recent years the average has been 29 bushels to the acre. Even in these long cultivated lands in Germany, not new virgin lands, there is a yield of some 10 bushels to the acre more than there was 25 years ago as the result of the application of more intelligent methods and better management. But what has Germany been doing during those 25 years? She has been importing wheat and such grains and exporting sugar, which takes out sunshine with carbon and water gathered through plants from the air. Sugar does not carry away any valuable plant food.

Denmark has been doing the same—importing wheat and corn, oil-cake and bran (which, by the way, we exported to the value of $888,900 in 1909) and such like, and exporting chiefly butter, bacon and eggs. The butter imported into the United Kingdom from Denmark was reported as 197,571,024 lbs., worth some $49,802,400, in 1909; and that $50,000,000 worth of butter carried less out of Denmark of the elements of fertility than did 1,000 tons of hay shipped out of Quebec. There is a contrast in the national administration of agriculture—$50,000,000 worth of butter impoverishing the land less than the export of 1,000 tons of hay, worth at the outside $14,000. In Hungary, on one of the large estates of which correct records have been kept, the increase in the yield per acre has been remarkable. Between 1851 and 1860 the yield of wheat was 10·9 bushels to the acre, and between 1891 and 1900 the average yield of wheat was 30·3 bushels to the acre. During 1851–1860 the yield of barley was 14·7 bushels to the acre; during 1891–1900 it was 43·9 bushels to the acre. The yield of oats was 17·1 bushels to the acre as against 51·3 bushels to the acre. The yield of Indian corn was 21·3 bushels to the acre during the former period, as compared with 41·6 bushels to the acre during 1891–1900. This has been brought about by intelligent and intensive cultivation instead of by following primitive methods.

And in England, dear old England—in England, big enough to represent in its own name the Empire of which I am proud to be a citizen; in England, not merely the mother of parliaments, but the mother of liberties for mankind all round this good old earth; in that kind of England with its sturdy agricultural population, the yield of wheat has been 31·39 bushels to the acre on the average for ten years. Last year (1909) it was 33·68 bushels to the acre. And in Scotland—that little land which modestly admits the ability of her own people—in Scotland during ten years they got an average of 38·86 bushels to the acre, and last year 41·19 bushels to the acre. Not so bad for the old land. It is written that 200 years ago England was harvesting only 8 bushels of wheat to the acre. The records of those ancient days are somewhat conflicting, as 26 bushels per acre were reported in the sixteenth century. This much is certain, the yield per acre now and in recent years is higher than ever before.

What did England and Scotland do? They imported foods and feeds, guano and other fertilizers. They were importing guano for the land in my early days on a Scotch farm. I doubt if I could have had as good an education as was my privilege but for the guano on the farm, which enabled us to take good crops from a reluctant and difficult soil. Will it pay Canadian farmers to do the same thing or something else to maintain phosphates? I think we are nearly at the point where we must consider that carefully. Phosphates are becoming scarce.

Our agricultural resources must be considered not only from the standpoint of the farmer following a particular occupation for profit, but also bearing in mind that agriculture is a great public interest, a great productive business having an influence and bearing upon the fortunes of the nation, the Empire and the race. Agriculture is one of the great mothering occupations for the maintenance of civilization. Three fundamental activities mother and nurture all the others in our civilization: farming, whence arise many good things; making homes, the object and glory of nearly all human effort; and teaching the young that they may have a correct knowledge of nature and a sound knowledge of human nature.

While it is easy in the case of Mines and Fisheries and Forests and Waterways and Water-Powers to do something definite by means of regulations laid down by legislation, it is immensely more difficult to accomplish much by that means in the case of lands, because the ownership and control are in the hands of multitudes of individuals each acting singly and independently. But because it is difficult it is none the less needful, nor should it be the less a task to which we should apply ourselves.

Can anything more be done to attract our own people to stay on the land, particularly to keep the young men and young women satisfied on the land? What are other peoples doing, and with what success? Let us find out. Denmark has done much with apparent success in luring to the land and in retaining on the land the best of her people. Co-operative associations have brought about business good-will as well as good crops and good prices. Can anything be done to makd social life on our farms more satisfying? Can anything be done to give the women in the homes on the prairies a better chance to rejoice ane be glad that their lot is cast there? Can anything be done to bring about an increase of home industries, not merely for profits, but for contentment and satisfaction through the industrial habits of our industrious people?

How shall we learn how others have learned the lessons of cause and effect and applied these lessons? Should we not in addition to an inventory of our possessions have records and illustrations of the best use that anyone has put them to, in order that a similar, if not identical, use may become the common practice? That is necessary to our people in order that they may be inspired and guided.

We want a record of our wastes, as well as of our conservations. We want such records and illustrations in a museum, national in its scope and service. That would be a useful institution. We want not a place full of dead specimens, but a place for the suggestion and nourishment of living thoughts and new policies. We want records and illustrations of all our resources. Then, by the diffusion of knowledge through various means, we will be led to adopt measures for conservation and for improvements in utilization while we are prosperous. Everybody might then have some guidance from some knowledge of the operations of the best farmers, of the principles of the truest scientists and of the policies of the wisest leaders. In some such way shall statesmanship in agriculture ensure the perpetual well-being of an intelligent people animated by good-will and rooted in land well tilled and beautiful. That, I think, might be to us a vision, as it should be an incentive to help in the making of the new earth wherein dwelleth righteousness.

WEDNESDAY AFTERNOON

At the opening of the meeting in the afternoon the Chairman, called to the chair Hon. Ward Chipman Hazen Grimmer, Surveyor General of the province of New Brunswick.

HON. MR. GRIMMER: The proceedings this afternoon should be of very great benefit along the lines to which the gentlemen who are to speak will address themselves. The gentlemen who spoke this morning covered by their addresses only a small branch of what is to be done as the work of this Commission, but what they said shows the importance to Canada of our work.

The Chairman then called upon Dr. Eugène Haanel, Director of the Mines Branch, Department of Mines, Ottawa, who read a paper on

POSSIBLE ECONOMIES IN PRODUCTION OF MINERALS OF CANADA

DR. HAANEL said:—

There is this difference between mineral resources and other natural resources, that while a forest cut down may be replanted, an exhausted soil, refertilized and a river or lake depleted of fish, restocked, an ore deposit once worked out can never be recovered.

We allow ourselves great latitude of language when we speak of this or that deposit as being inexhaustible. The economic mineral deposits accessible to man are finite in quantity, and the time required for their exhaustion depends solely upon the rapidity with which they are exploited.

The immense pressure exerted by the acquired needs of modern civilization, reinforced by the commercial spirit of the age, will render futile any effort that might be made to curtail the exploitation of the mineral resources of the world. We can pass no laws for a close season in mining, during which mines or smelters should cease operations. All that we can do is to employ such methods in mining that no waste shall occur. The mine must be worked out; nothing valuable must be left behind. Existing methods require to be perfected, or new ones invented, to enable us to discover new mineral deposits at present buried out of sight. The problem of successfully substituting for certain vanishing resources others which are still abundant and capable of taking their place, will have to be solved. Metallurgical investigation must be directed to the invention of processes which are capable of handling economically lower and lower grades of ore. Much is being done in these directions, as will appear later.

Only a few years ago ironmasters on this continent would hardly look at an iron ore if it contained less than 62% of metallic content; now an ore of 50% is gladly accepted.

Iron—The question of the world's supply of iron is of such grave importance that the International Geological Congress has invited some twenty-six different countries—Canada among the number—to prepare estimates of their respective iron ore resources to be presented at their meeting at Stockholm next summer. This action of the International Geological Congress is an indication of the general anxiety and uneasiness created by the enormous demand upon this resource, for which there is no substitute, and without which modern civilization cannot continue.

But, whatever the fears regarding the world's future supply of iron ore, this pessimistic outlook does not apply to Canada, for at the present time, we are dependent upon other countries to supplement our own product by importing of their iron in the crude and manufactured state to the value of about $62,000,000 annually. In 1908 it was $61,819,698. We thus see that conservation of Canada's own iron ore resources has, unfortunately, been practised only too successfully. We are, and will continue to be, industrially handicapped until our iron industry is developed sufficiently to meet the demands of our own country and render us independent of outside sources for this all-important metal.

What we need is not conservation of our iron ore resources, but vigorous development of our iron industry. The very fact that the Government has been, and is, giving a bonus on pig iron and steel produced in this country shows how great is the need for such an industry.

By the methods hitherto employed in the production of pig iron and steel, cheap metallurgical fuel was a necessity; hence blast furnaces could only be erected and do a successful business where iron ore, coal and flux could be cheaply assembled. This is possible, however, only in the extreme east and west of the Dominion.

The middle provinces, though possessing iron ore deposits and fluxes, lack the needed metallurgical fuel. The development of a vigorous iron industry, with coke at $5 00 to $6.00 per ton, could not be looked for in these provinces, if it was necessary to depend on blast furnace methods.

The comparatively recent investigations of the electro-thermic process for the smelting of iron ores have demonstrated that only one-third of the carbon necessary in the blast furnace is needed in electric furnaces. This brings the cost of the metallurgical fuel required for smelting down to a reasonable figure. The adoption, therefore, of this process would lead, not alone to the utilization of our domestic iron ores in the provinces of Ontario and Quebec, but would greatly conserve our fuel supply by substituting hydro-electric energy for the heat energy of two-thirds of the carbon required in the blast furnace.

It may be interesting to state briefly what has been accomplished up to the present time in the development of electric smelting processes. It is only five years since the Commission appointed by the Dominion Government to investigate the different electro-thermic processes for the smelting of iron ores and the making of steel, which were in operation in Europe, presented its report. There were then only five small electric steel furnaces in existence, and only two of these were seen in actual operation. To-day seventy-seven are in operation in Europe, and a number have recently been erected in the United States, some of which are of fifteen tons capacity. Indeed, electric steel is rapidly pushing crucible steel out of the market. Italy and France have the honour of having been first in the field to apply electricity to the commercial production of steel. Germany, which had no part in the original invention of the electric steel furnace, has recently been especially energetic in the adoption of the electro-thermic process for the production of steel and in the modification and improvement of existing patents.

While engaged in superintending the electric smelting experiments at Sault St. Marie in 1906, I noticed that the yard adjacent to the rolling mill was covered with many tons of the waste ends of the Bessemer steel ingots used in the manufacture of rails. No use was made of them at the time, and they were allowed to accumulate and eat up interest. An electric steel furnace set up in the works of the Lake Superior Corporation—for which every facility existed—could profitably have converted this waste into high priced tool steel. I understand that these waste ends are at present being utilized in the open hearth furnaces lately erected.

A process that removes from steel, more perfectly than any other, those deleterious ingredients which render it fragile under shock, and deprive it of its lasting qualities, is manifestly the more economic process. This purification is more effectively accomplished by the electric steel furnace than by any other metallurgical process; its introduction in steel plants is, therefore, in the interests of economy.

It has, within recent years, been demonstrated that, in steel manufacture, carbon is not the only substance which imparts valuable properties to the iron; but that tungsten, chromium, vanadium, nickel, molybdenum and manganese add special economic qualities to iron; and for some purposes, either separately or in combination, are far superior to carbon alone.

A tool made from these alloy steels, which will hold its edge longer under severe stress and do a greater amount of work than another, is the more economical tool. A rail which can stand up longer under severe shock and resist better than another the constant wear and tear of heavy traffic is undoubtedly the more economical rail. It is manifestly in the interests of economy, not alone to employ these alloy steels for the purposes for which they are best fitted, but to manufacture them in furnaces best adapted for their production, namely, the electric steel furnace.

The progress made in the application of electricity to the production of pig iron has been much slower than in the manufacture of steel, since it was feasible only in countries possessing water-powers which could be developed at a reasonable figure. The central provinces of Canada are in this position because they possess the ore, the fluxes and the needed water-powers.

With a view of testing the feasibility of introducing the electric smelting of iron ores into these Provinces, the Dominion Government authorized the making of experiments with Canadian ores. It was not alone proven by these experiments that excellent pig iron could be produced in the electric furnace, but the remarkable discovery was made that, from a refractory ore high in sulphur, a pig iron containing only $0\cdot005\%$ of sulphur could be produced. This is an exceedingly important result, since, by this new process, the large number of sulphurous magnetite deposits which abound in Canada, and which have hitherto been useless, are now rendered available for the production of high grade pig iron and steel. The world's supply of useful iron ores will thus be greatly increased by this electro-thermic process of smelting. The experiments made under the auspices of the Dominion Government at Sault Ste. Marie have been productive of another important result. Roasted nickeliferous pyrrhotite, carrying 2% of sulphur, has been smelted in the electric furnace into a pig iron virtually free from sulphur and containing from 3 to 4% of nickel. About 165 tons of this nickel iron were produced. This is the first instance in the history of metallurgy where the iron content of the pyrrhotite has been saved. Iron pyrites cinders—the sulphurous iron residue of the roasting of iron pyrites in the manufacture of sulphuric acid—which so far have been useless, may now be smelted by the electric process into excellent pig iron. These two instances are brilliant illustrations of the conservation of our iron ore resources.

Immediately after the publication of the results of our experiments at Sault Ste. Marie, Sweden—which has abundance of excellent iron ore and numerous water-powers, but, like Ontario and Quebec, lacks metallurgical fuel—was not slow to perceive the advantage which the introduction of electric smelting would prove in the development of its iron industry. Hence, without hesitation, it proceeded to take an active part in perfecting this method by the invention of a commercial furnace. In the report on the experiments at Sault Ste. Marie, definite suggestions were made as to the lines upon which a commercial furnace should be constructed; and these ideas were incorporated in a furnace designed by three young engineers of the Aktiebolaget Elektrometall of Ludvika, Sweden, who succeeded, after repeated trial constructions, and an expenditure of $102,000 in building a furnace which has proved satisfactory. To anyone who has seen a blast furnace, the construction of this furnace will easily be comprehended. The general design is similar to that of a blast furnace, with the tuyeres replaced by electrodes.

The fact that the output per electric horse-power year with the Swedish furnace did not reach our best results at Sault Ste. Marie is not due to faulty construction, but to want of the proper amount of energy. The capacity of the furnace was at least 1,200 H.P., whereas only about half that amount was available.

Several very important facts have been demonstrated during the summer run with this Swedish furnace. It has been found that it was possible to make an iron containing only 2% of carbon. The essential difference between pig iron and steel is that the former contains up to 4% of carbon, while any iron classed as steel contains from 0·6% to 2·3% of carbon. It will be seen, therefore, that the Swedes have succeeded in producing in the Domnarfvet furnace a high carbon steel direct from iron ore. It has, moreover, been demonstrated that, in the electric furnace, the process for producing iron of different compositions is under more exact control than in other processes. Mr. Yngström, Vice-President of the Copparbergs Aktiebolag of Falun, and a distinguished ironmaster, in his report on the performance of the Swedish furnace after a three month's run, declares that, judging from the tests made at Domnarfvet, the production of iron from iron ore in electric furnaces is successfully accomplished, both technically and economically.

Shortly after the publication of my report on the investigation of an electric shaft furnace at Domnarfvet, Sweden, in December, 1908,

I was informed that, at Tysse, Norway, a contract was let for the establishment, on a commercial scale, of an electric smelting plant consisting of two electric shaft furnaces of 2,500 H.P. capacity each, two steel furnaces of 600 H.P. capacity, and a rolling mill. This plant is to be increased by two additional shaft furnaces and two steel furnaces.

Some two months ago the Jernkontorets, an association of the ironmasters of Sweden, acquired the patents for the electric shaft furnace of the Domnarfvet type, and are erecting a 2,500 H.P. furnace of similar design, with a probable output of 7,500 tons annually, at Tröllhatten, Sweden, for the purpose of demonstrating to the iron ore owners and ironmasters the class of iron which can be produced from the different Swedish ores, and at what cost.

Mr. Boholm, of Trondhjem, Norway, writes me that he is desirous of erecting iron and steel works in Norway, and asks my Department to furnish him with an electro-metallurgist to take charge of the plant.

Canada has done all the pioneer work in connection with the process of electric smelting of iron ores, only, however, to benefit other countries, who have not been slow to perceive the advantages of this process. Italy, Hungary, Russia, Brazil, India, South Africa, Mexico and California—conditioned similarly to Ontario and Quebec as regards the iron industry—are becoming increasingly interested in the subject of electric smelting, judging from the persistent applications made to my Branch for reports and information.

Before leaving this subject, I would like to call your attention to a special method capable of wide application in the delimitation of magnetic ore bodies, which constitute our most abundant iron ore deposits. This method is described and explained in my report upon the location and examination of magnetic ore bodies by magnetometric measurements, published in 1904. By means of this system we are enabled to locate magnetic ore bodies buried out of sight by soil and to determine their general extent and inclination to the horizon. This latter information is especially valuable, since it enables the mining engineers to locate accurately their bore holes for the purpose of proving the deposit. Under favorable circumstances, if the ore body consists of compact magnetite and the surface is fairly level, it is also possible by this method to determine the extent of the ore body beneath the surface and the depth to which it descends into the earth.

This method has been applied by members of my staff for the past seven years, and has been of great service in determining the extent and probable value of the magnetite deposits examined. In one instance a deposit which had been condemned as of no value, proved, on examination by the magnetometric method, to be of considerable extent. Bore holes were located by our engineer, and it was found that the deposits, on the most conservative estimate, contained some eight million tons of ore.

The publication of our magnetometric survey maps has attracted the attention of iron ore experts in other countries, notably Dr. Leith, of the United States Geological Survey, and Dr. Phillips, of the Bureau of Mines of the University of Texas. Both these gentlemen have made application to the Department for the services of one of our experts to instruct members of their staff in the application of the magnetometric method. As this system becomes more generally known and practised, valuable magnetite deposits, which now lie hidden beneath the soil and forests, will be added to those already known, and will thus tangibly increase the general stock of this all-important metallic mineral.

When in the vicinity of magnetic ore deposits, the magnetic needle of surveyors' compasses is always disturbed, and its action becomes erratic. Such occurrences, whenever met with by the surveying staffs of the Government, should be reported to the Department of Mines, for there magnetometric surveys might be advantageously made.

Zinc—For some years the zinc ores mined in British Columbia found a ready market in the United States. The recently erected tariff of the United States has, however, virtually closed this market. If the ore mined is not to lie profitless on the dump, some method requires to be devised which will successfully treat these ores and enable the mine owners to export the output of their mines as a finished product, either as spelter or zinc oxide. In the hope of accomplishing this much desired result, a zinc smeltery was erected in Alberta, but proved unsuccessful. This failure was not altogether due to the character of the ores treated, but was due to inherent defects in the plant, introduced by the designer in an endeavour to improve upon the Belgian model. Prior to the erection of this plant, Mr. F. T. Snyder obtained a patent for an electric process and a furnace designed to treat these zinc ores. The first electric furnace was erected in Vancouver, but proved unsuccessful. The matter was not allowed to drop, however, for with commendable pertinacity a furnace of new design was erected in Nelson, B.C., and the experiments recommenced, but, up to the present time, they have been without success. While the parties interested in these experiments deserve much praise for their perseverance in trying to overcome a real difficulty, consuming valuable time and costing much money, it is to be regretted that the parties interested did not, first of all, investigate the electric process invented by Dr. de Laval, which has been in operation for some years in Tröllhatten, Sweden. The only proper course in experimentation, the only one likely to lead to success, requires that information be obtained not by reading patents, but by investigation and actual observation on the spot of all that has been accomplished in the direction in which improvement is sought to be introduced.

There are, at present, four processes invented in Europe for the production of metallic zinc or zinc oxide from complex zinc ores, which promise economic results:

(1) The De Laval process, in operation at Tröllhatten, Sweden, already mentioned;
(2) The improved De Laval process, a demonstration plant for the operation of which is being erected in London, England;
(3) The Côte-Pierron process, invented in France, and
(4) The bisulphite process. A demonstration plant to operate this process is being erected in Wales, Great Britain.

The first three systems are electric smelting processes; the last is a wet chemical process with a final product of zinc oxide.

Arrangements have been made by the Department of Mines for the investigation of these processes in the interests of the zinc miners of British Columbia.

If any one of the first three processes proves successful and can be introduced in Canada, the interests of economy will be served in a double sense: (1) because the electric process saves fuel, and (2) because the exportation of raw material and reimportation of finished product increases its ultimate cost. This unnecessary expense would also be saved.

Nickel—Whenever we speak of our mineral wealth we grow eloquent in describing our vast nickel resources, and we may well be proud of possessing the deposits of the Sudbury region. But really, of what particular and special benefit are these deposits to our country? We mine the ore, smelt it into matte and send it as such out of the country. If we want nickel or nickel steel we have to import it. The employment of an inconsiderable number of men is all we get out of these splendid deposits. Not alone are they of little material benefit to the country, as at present exploited, but the method practised is exceedingly wasteful. Anyone who has been in that region and examined the method of heap-roasting employed must have been struck with the wastefulness of this method. Part of the oxides of copper and nickel of the ore are, during roasting, converted into sulphates, and when rain falls some of these valuable contents are leached out. I have seen large pools, greenish-blue with dissolved sulphate of copper and nickel, which finds its way into the soil and is lost; while the valuable sulphur dioxide destroys all vegetation in the vicinity. In addition to these losses, the iron contained in the ore is slagged off and lost also.

A more rational process, saving all the contents, would be crushing and concentration of the iron and magnetic nickel contents by magnetic separation. The tailings would contain the copper, non-magnetic nickel compounds and all the precious metals contained in the ore. Roast the iron concentrates; save the sulphur dioxide as sulphuric acid; smelt the roasted nickeliferous pyrrhotite into nickel pig in the electric furnace; treat the tailings after roasting by the electrolytic method as it is practised at present in dealing with the matte; convert the nickel pig into nickel steel in the electric furnace; dilute with pig iron, if necessary, to bring the nickel content down to the required percentage, and add nickel, if required, to raise it.

Experiments are now being conducted for the Mines Branch to determine how much of the nickel remains in the concentrates and how much passes into tailings.

The introduction of such a process, which would treat tailings containing the copper and part of the nickel by the electrolytic process in operation at Fredericktown, Missouri, U.S.A., and patented by Mr. N. V. Hybinette, would be in the interests of economy. A refinery established in the Sudbury region on the plan outlined, would enable Canada to export finished products instead of the matte, as is now done.

Cobalt-Silver Ores—In the case of our Cobalt-silver ores, the miners receive little more than the values of the silver contents in the high grade ore (small allowances are made on cobalt over 6%), and only a percentage of the silver contents in the low grade ore.

All low grade ore is shipped to the United States, where it is used as a silicious flux in the large lead smelters. The lead acts as a collector of the silver, and the cobalt and nickel is slagged off. It is impossible to treat economically the low grade ore in Canada, on account of the absence of large lead smelters in the vicinity of Cobalt.

The mine owners at Cobalt are handicapped by the following conditions:—

1. The smelters being situated some distance from the mines, high freight rates are charged by the railways for the transportation of the ore from the mines to the smelters.

2. The freight rate on coal is high. Coal costs $6.00 per ton at Cobalt. Of this, $3.25 represents freight rates from Black Rock to

Cobalt, a distance of 448 miles. The *cost of the coal*, with *freight rates* from Pittsburg to Black Rock, a distance of 270 miles, is $2.25 per ton. This shows that the freight rates from Black Rock to Cobalt are disproportionately high.

3. Small payments are made for the cobalt contents of the ore, on account of the limited demand for that mineral.

4. The arsenic is of little value after being refined, on account of its being produced some distance from the market (the market is east of Chicago in the United States), and the United States railways give a very much lower rate on arsenic produced in the Western states than the rates obtainable in Canada. Arsenic shipped from Canada is charged a fourth-class rate, while arsenic from Utah and Montana is charged 83.33% of the sixth-class rate. The latter rate is about one-half of the former.

I might say in this connection,, that, if the miner approached the Dominion Government and asked for assistance, much might be done to solve these difficulties and to help the mining industry in general. It would be of great benefit to Canada if the government would install a fully equipped metallurgical and ore-dressing plant, by means of which new methods could be devised for a more economical treatment of our ores. Each ore is practically a study in itself, and much money is lost annually by the installation of unsuitable plants, and by the necessary change in equipment brought about by the experience gained by the company after operating for a time. This could be avoided by having the government do the primary experimenting.

In the case of complex ores, much could be done towards the economical saving of two or more of the valuable minerals present.

I do not think that there would be any doubt but that the mine owners, as a matter of business, would utilize the methods devised by such a department after they had been shown to be successful.

Peat—In the central provinces of Canada the high price of imported coal, on the one hand, and the depletion of our forests, on the other, with consequent rise in the value of wood, due to its increasing scarcity for constructional purposes, together with the possible suffering which would be entailed in the event of the supply of coal being diminished, or even cut off, by a coal strike, or some other cause, in the United States, makes the question of substituting peat for imported coal one of supreme importance.

The cost in Winnipeg of the poorest quality of wood (spruce and tamarack) is from $6.00 to $8.00 a cord; while coal is $10.50 a ton.

In Ontario, Quebec and New Brunswick, wood and coal are somewhat cheaper, but still too dear for both domestic use and economic manufacturing purposes. And considering the fact that we imported, during the year 1908, coal to the value of $28,500,000, constituting an enormous and increasing drain on the wealth of the country, every effort should be made to retain a portion of this money at home, not only to give employment to our own people, but also to lessen our dependence upon outside sources. This much-desired economy may be largely effected by the establishment of a peat industry on a sound basis.

It has been estimated that the known peat bogs of Canada cover approximately an extent of 36,000 square miles. This area would produce about twenty-eight billion tons of air-dried peat, which would be equal in fuel value to about fourteen billion tons of coal. The comparative fuel value of peat, coal and wood is: 1 ton of the best coal is equal to 1.8 tons of peat or 2.5 tons of wood.

The attempts made so far in Canada to manufacture a commercial peat fuel have been failures, and very little peat-fuel is at present available. The chief cause of most of these failures has been in the ignorance of the nature of peat on the part of those who have engaged in the production of peat-fuel. In several instances the bogs chosen for the work have been unsuitable for the purpose in view. A proper investigation of the bog previous to the commencement of operations was seldom made; consequently, methods entirely unsuitable for the utilization of the bog in question have been employed, and the result has been failure. These failures, involving as they did considerable loss of capital, have created a profound distrust of everything connected with peat and the utilization of peat bogs, with the result that, at the present time, the peat industry in Canada is practically dead. With a view to assisting Canadian manufacturers of peat products, a member of my staff was commissioned to proceed to Europe to investigate and report upon the peat industry in those countries in which it is in successful operation. Armed with the practical knowledge thus gained, the Mines Branch is attacking the peat problem in this country, and a systematic investigation of the Canadian bogs has already been started with a view to ascertaining the quantity and quality of peat contained in them.

Up to date about twelve bogs have been examined, mapped and reported upon. Any person desiring to start a peat plant can, upon application, have his bog investigated, and it is hoped that such failures as have been due to the choosing of bogs unsuitable for the purpose to which the product was to be applied, will, in future, be avoided.

Another object of this investigation is to protect the public, as far as possible, by preventing the expenditure of capital in the exploitation of worthless bogs.

It was conceived that the most practical manner in which to awaken public interest in the utilization of our peat resources would be the establishment of an experimental plant where peat-fuel could be manufactured on a commercial scale and by methods which have already proved successful in European practice. At such a plant, interested parties would have an opportunity of ascertaining for themselves the working of the bog, as well as the suitability of the peat-fuel produced.

With this object in view, the Government has acquired a peat bog of 300 acres, located at Alfred, near Caledonia Springs, Ontario, having an average depth of eight feet. Actual work was begun during last summer in surveying, levelling and draining the bog. About five miles of ditches have been dug; a storage shed to hold 300 tons of air-dried peat, a blacksmith's shop and an office have been built, and the necessary tracks and auxiliary machinery for supplying the Anrep peat machine have been installed. It is the intention to begin work in the manufacture of peat at the end of next April.

The recent improvement in gas producers and gas engines has opened up a new field for the use of peat and lignite. It is a well established fact that the most efficient steam plant utilizes only about 15% of the calorific value of the fuel, while a gas producer-plant utilizes about 18 to 22%. The saving in fuel effected by the gas producer has not, hitherto, been duly appreciated in Canada. A power plant located at the peat bog and using producer gas derived from peat can furnish electric energy which may be transmitted to the market in the same way as electric energy generated by water-power.

A Government fuel-testing station has already been built in Ottawa by the Department of Mines, with the object of testing the efficiency of the various classes of fossil fuel and to determine their adaptabliity for the different uses to which fuel is applied.

The first use to be made of this plant will be to demonstrate that peat containing up to 35% of moisture may be economically employed in a producer to furnish power gas for gas engines.

The machinery which is being installed consists of a gas producer and a 50 H.P. gas engine of the Körting type, a dynamo of 50 H.P. capacity, and a wire rheostat to absorb the power developed. About 70 tons of air-dried peat are in the shed adjacent to the power plant. It is expected that the plant will be in working order by the end of February next, when interested parties may inspect the plant and inform themselves with regard to its operation, efficiency and the cost of the power produced.

Many applications have already been received from parties desirous of visiting the power plant at Ottawa and the peat plant at Alfred.

The transportation to great distances of low grade fuel such as air-dried peat, is not recommended, either for domestic or power purposes. But, inasmuch as the expense for the erection of a peat plant of 30 tons daily capacity would not exceed $7,000, and, since workable peat bogs are scattered throughout the farming regions of Ontario and Quebec, the most economical plan for utilizing this fuel would be the erection of a number of plants at strategic points, to be operated in the interests of the neighbouring communities.

Further, peat-fuel is not only a valuable asset as a substitute for coal, but those classes of peat which are practically useless for fuel are extensively utilized by European farmers as moss litter. In fact, the manufacture of this litter and its by-product, "peat mull," has become a well-established industry in Sweden, Germany and Holland.

Peat mull, obtained as a by-product in the manufacture of moss litter, is an excellent material for packing fruit and plants and for storage and shipping. Its antiseptic properties and great affinity for moisture render it invaluable as a preventive of decay in fruit.

In Norway some 200. and in Sweden between 300 and 400, small plants are manufacturing this material; while in Germany and Holland, where there are a number of large plants, the manufacture of moss litter has become a flourishing industry. Most of the smaller plants are owned by groups of farmers, who work the bogs themselves.

Inasmuch as moss litter is, in many cases, a by-product in the making of peat fuel, its exploitation would materially reduce the cost of manufacturing peat-fuel if placed on the market commercially in conjunction with peat mull. Several shipments of moss litter from Holland have been made to the United States—at $16.00 per ton.

The different Departments of Agriculture in European countries very strongly urge farmers to use moss litter. Seeing that Canada is fast becoming an important fruit exporting country, it is evident that the use of peat mull as a packing material would be a great economic advantage.

Before passing finally to the important question of coal mining, I would conclude my plea for the economical exploitation of our abundant peat-fuel resources, the importance of which cannot be overestimated, by warning my hearers that the introduction of a fuel like peat is an undertaking that cannot be accomplished in a year or two, but will require an aggressive educational campaign in order to demonstrate the value of the products as well as the manner of manufacture.

Coal—In England and Germany every effort is made to prolong the life of the coal mines by the adoption of mining methods which insure a more complete extraction of the coal than do the methods practised in the United States and Canada.

The system employed in England is known as the longwall method.* By this method practically the entire coal in a seam is extracted, leaving behind no pillars and barriers; only the coal of pillars and barriers in the air and passage ways is left behind and sacrificed. The percentage of available coal left in these pillars and barriers is about 2.8%; the amount lost through faults and bad coal, 3%; making a total of irrecoverable coal equal to, say, 6%. Although, by the use of this method, the actual cost of extraction per ton of coal is increased, the productive life of the mine is greatly prolonged.

The method employed in the United States is less expensive and permits the extraction of the largest tonnage at the lowest possible cost, irrespective of the loss of life entailed, or the amount of coal left behind. This affirmation applies also to the methods of coal mining practised in Canada. By this system—the room-and-pillar method—only 50% of the original coal is extracted, leaving 50% to be taken out afterwards by the removal of pillars, which is a dangerous operation and which, both in quality and quantity, entails great loss of coal, amounting, at least, to 15% and sometimes double this figure. If the companies operating the coal mines of North America were forced to pay compensation for loss of life and accidents, as under the English law, they would have incurred an expenditure of $7,656,000 during 1908.† If this amount of money had been expended in more economic and safer

---

* "Our investigations and recommendations relate primarily to questions of safety in mining, but in this connection we have been greatly impressed with another closely associated phase of the industry, viz.: the *large and permanent loss of coal* in mining operations in many portions of the United States.

This is a *serious, permanent,* and *national* loss. It seems to be a natural outcome of the ease with which coal has been mined in the United States, and the enormously rapid growth of the industry.

The active competition among the operators and the constant resulting effort to produce cheaper coal has often naturally led to the mining of only that part of the coal which could be brought to the surface most easily and cheaply, leaving underground, in such condition as to be *permanently lost,* a considerable percentage of the total possible product.

Certainly, much of this loss can be prevented through the introduction of more efficient mining methods, such as the *Longwall* system, more or less modified, and the flushing method." Extract from report of "Foreign Experts" to the United States Government.

† See report by Frederick L. Hoffman, statistician of the Prudential Insurance Company of America, Newark, New Jersey.

methods of mining, the number of lives lost would have been greatly decreased and the available fuel supply greatly increased.

But while the conservation of coal by economic methods of mining is of great national importance, the conservation of human life is of still greater importance. The lamentable loss of life and the occurrence of accidents in our coal and metalliferous mines reflects seriously upon mining conditions in Canada.

In England the average loss of life per 1,000 men employed during the years 1903 to 1907 was

    Coal mines............................... 1.29
    Metalliferous mines 1.08

Contrast with this the average men employed in Canada, per 1,000, for the ten years, 1899–1908:—

    British Columbia: coal mines 9.21
    Nova Scotia: coal mines.................. 2.67
    British Columbia, 1908: metalliferous mines.. 5.93
    Ontario, 1907: copper and nickel 2.19
               silver and iron.............. 7.36

The actual death rate per 1,000 men employed at Cobalt in 1908 is difficult to obtain, on account of many mines not sending in returns of the number of men employed, but it is safe to say that the death rate was about 12 per 1,000 men employed underground, 36·6 per cent. of which was due to explosives.

If, therefore, stringent laws have been enacted for the protection of even the low type of labour employed in the South African mines, surely Canada should lose no time in giving its sanction to a code of laws and regulations that will effectually conserve and preserve the valuable lives of its citizens. Canada at the present time, is without such laws and, in this respect, stands unique, for in every other mining country, laws relating to explosives have been enacted. Legislation on these lines would manifestly be in the direction of the highest economy.

Such is a brief generalized view of some of the possible economies in the production of the mineral resources of Canada. I have set forth the economic advantages to be gained (1) by the adoption of the electric furnace in the smelting of our immense deposits of refractory iron ores; (2) by the introduction of more effective metallurgical processes for the treatment of zinc, nickel, and silver-cobalt ores; (3) by the utilization of peat and lignite as substitutes for coal fuel, especially in gas producers; (4) by the manufacture of peat by-products into moss litter and peat mull, in the interests of farmers and fruit growers; (5) by the adoption of the longwall system in coal mining in order to avoid unnecessary waste; and finally, in the conservation and safeguarding of human life by the adoption of a stringent code of laws regulating the use of explosives.

When these economies have been translated into actual fact, doing away with wastefulness on the one hand, and conserving our national resources on the other: when we shall have succeeded in sending out to the foreign markets finished products instead of raw material, as at present, then, not only will the industrial progress of the country be accelerated, but Canada will have taken its place among the great commercial and industrial nations of the world.

Hon. Frank Cochrane, Minister of Lands, Forests and Mines of the province of Ontario, prepared an address on the natural resources of that Province, but, on account of being called away, was unable to read it. The address, however, was secured in written form, and is as follows:—

THE CONSERVATION OF THE NATURAL RESOURCES OF ONTARIO.

The natural resources of Ontario under the control of the Department of Lands, Forests and Mines are lands, timber, water-powers, mines and minerals. The conservation of the natural resources of Ontario may be said to consist of preserving them from destruction or waste and disposing of them as public necessities may require, subject to such conditions as will, as far as possible, prevent monopoly and ensure their economical development.

Lands—The total area of the province of Ontario, exclusive of the great lakes, is estimated at 140,000,000 acres. Of this, there is surveyed, 46,000,000 acres, leaving an area unsurveyed, of 94,000,000 acres. There has been alienated by sales, locations, etc., 24,000,000 acres, leaving still in the Crown, 116,000,000 acres. Of this, 20,000,000 acres are known to be valuable agricultural lands.

Having seen the folly of opening for settlement, townships that are rough and which contain only a small percentage of good land, the Government of Ontario has provided that, before a township is opened for settlement, it must be inspected by a competent officer to ascertain: (a) the percentage of good land in it; (b) the quantities and varieties of timber; (c) whether it is chiefly valuable for its mines and minerals. If the inspection shows it to contain less than 40 per cent. of good land, the policy of the Government is to keep it closed from settlement for the growing of timber, or, if it has large quantities of pine, to keep it closed until the pine timber has been removed, or, if it is valuable chiefly for its mines and minerals, to exclude all settlement.

In the same connection, we found that, in townships already opened, people took up rough lands for the purpose of obtaining possession of the timber, under the cloak of farming. By this practice, lands were withdrawn from the operation of timber license, so far as timber other than pine was concerned, to the injury of the licensee, and without benefit to the Crown.

We have now instituted the practice of inspecting all lands applied for, and if the inspection shows less than 50 per cent. of agricultural land in the area desired to be located, we do not grant the application, but leave the land in forest. Our desire is, and we are carrying it out to the best of our ability, to keep the lands of the Crown for the use for which they are best adapted.

Timber—Secondly, as to timber. The Government has recognized that the pine timber is one of our most valuable assets, and wherever we have found large bodies of pine we have withdrawn the territory from settlement and put it into what we call "forest reserves," where no settlement is allowed.

The reserves already set apart in Ontario are:

Timagami Forest Reserve containing	.. 5,900 sq. miles	
Mississagi Forest Reserve	" .. 3,000	"
Nipigon Forest Reserve	" . 7,300	"
Eastern Forest Reserve	. 100	
Quetico Forest Reserve	. 1,560	
Sibley Forest Reserve	. 70	
Algonquin National Park	" .. 1,930	

Total .... 19,860 sq. miles.

In each of these reserves these is a chief ranger with a staff of fire rangers under him. These rangers are assigned certain beats which they have to patrol. They are supplied with poster copies of the "Fire Act," printed on cotton, to be put up on portages, etc. and also with pamphlet copies of the Act to be handed to individuals whom they meet, so that no one shall be able to say he does not know the law. In addition to this, these rangers caution parties of the necessity for care in the use of fire and of extinguishing it when they are leaving the locality.

When mining prospecting is going on, as in the Timagami Reserve, prospectors must obtain a permit from the Department, giving them permission to explore in the Reserve, and they must produce the same when called upon to do so by the park ranger.

We do not sell any timber in these reserves except where it is damaged by fire. Of course, in the Timagami Reserve there is the Booth pulpwood concession, which covers spruce and jack-pine, and, in the Algonquin Park, part of the territory is under license for all kinds of timber and part for pine only.

It is estimated that there is on these Reserves about nine billion feet of pine, which is worth now about $90,000,000. We had 202 men on duty in them as rangers last year, and we spent for fire ranging purposes about $76,000.

Then there is an area of about 20,000 miles subject to license. On this area we have a staff of fire rangers. Recognizing that the licensees are the people best qualified to select the ranging staff on their limits, we have accepted their nominations—subject to the right of removing the rangers for incapacity or improper conduct—and appointed the men they desired as fire rangers. These rangers, in the same way as those in the reserves, are furnished with copies of the "Fire Act" to post up in public places and on portages, shanties, etc., and also pamphlet copies to hand to all parties with whom they come in contact, such as tourists, surveyors, prospectors, settlers, lumbermen, etc. The area is divided up into districts, and, in each district, there is a supervising ranger, who has charge of the staff in that district and is responsible for seeing that they are on duty and properly performing the work for which they are appointed. Where the licensees do not apply to have rangers put upon their limits, the Department selects the ranger, puts him on and makes the licensee pay his proportion of the expense.

One half of the cost of the wages and expenses of fire ranging is borne by the licensee and the other half by the Department. This system was inaugurated in 1885 and has grown from year to year, and one effect of it has been to enlist the sympathies of those who have an interest in the protection of the forest, such as lumbermen, settlers, explorers, etc. An additional advantage is this, that if a fire does take place, the rangers are able to report to their employers its locality and the quantity of timber damaged, so that the timber can be cut before it goes to waste. We had on duty on licensed land last year 450 rangers at a cost to the Crown of about $60,000.

Recognizing the great danger to the forest incident to railway construction, the Minister of Lands, Forests and Mines was empowered by the Legislature to place fire rangers along the lines of railways traversing the back country, and to charge the expense to the railway companies.

This has been carried out wherever it is considered there is danger to the forest, such as along the Canadian Pacific railway, Canadian Northern railway, Transcontinental railway and the Timiskaming & Northern Ontario railway. We had on these railways, last season, 175 rangers, at a cost of about $73,000.

In addition to the rangers on the forest reserves and along the lines of railways, we had, in exposed regions, along certain of the larger rivers that are used as highways, fire rangers who pursued the same course in warning parties with whom they came in contact, supplying them with copies of the law and impressing upon them the necessity for care in the use of fire.

Along the line of the Transcontinental railway, extending from the eastern to the western boundaries of the Province, are enormous quantities of wood suitable for making pulp and paper. In this region there is estimated to be about 300,000,000 cords of this wood. The Transcontinental, in its course, crosses the following large streams:—

	Length
Abitibi river	250 miles
Frederick House river	120 "
Mattagami river	250 "
Kakozhisk river	200
Kapuskasi river	200
Opazatika river	125
Missinaibi river	250
Kabinakagami river	150
Kenogami river	250

besides other smaller streams.

The pulpwood in this region will float down these streams to the crossing of the railway and will there be manufactured into either pulp or paper. The construction of the railway has necessitated the placing of a considerable staff of fire rangers in that region, but, as the construction is extended, as it is likely soon to be, a large additional number of fire rangers will have to be placed along it, and the timber in this region will be in great danger, as the foreign labour employed in railway construction is ignorant of the law and careless in the use of fire. We have an asset in our timber, pulpwood, etc., which is valued at between three and four hundred millions of dollars, and we would be grossly neglectful of our duty if we did not use every effort to conserve it.

Recognizing that the people of the Province are entitled to the benefit of the labour incident to the using up of their natural resources, we have provided that all pine saw-logs, spruce pulpwood and hemlock must be manufactured in the Dominion, into lumber, pulp or paper. The effect of this has been to increase the demand for labour and give a market for all kinds of supplies used for lumbering purposes.

Waters—The protection of the flow of our rivers is a question of great importance, and this was one of the objects kept in view in the setting aside of parks and forest reserves.

In the Algonquin Park the head-waters of the following important rivers are to be found: Petawawa, Madawaska, Muskoka, Amable du Fond, South and Maganetawan.

In the Timigami Forest Reserve are to be found the head-waters of the Montreal, Matabitchuan, Timagami, Sturgeon, Vermilion, Wanapitei, Onaping and other tributaries of the Spanish, the Frederick House and the Mattagami.

In the Mississagi Forest Reserve are the Mississagi river and its tributaries, the Wenebegon, White and Sauble and branches of the Spanish.

In the Nipigon Reserve are the Nipigon river—the largest stream flowing into Lake Superior—the Black Sturgeon, Gull, Poshkokagan, Pikitigushi, Onaman, Mamewaminikan, Sturgeon and Wabinosh.

In the Quetico Reserve are the head-waters of the Rainy and its branches, the Maligne, Quetico and Sturgeon.

All of these rivers are large and important streams, and the protection of their head-waters is a matter of great public importance and a valuable conservation of natural resources.

Previous to 1898, no reservation of water-powers was made in grants of land by the Crown. If a water-power was situated on a lot or location, and the bed of the river—the actual site of the power—was included in the area of the lot, possession passed to the grantee. In 1898, however, the Legislature of Ontario passed an Act providing for the reservation of water-powers and for the making of regulations regarding their disposal, by the Lieutenant-Governor-in-Council. These regulations provided that all water-powers having a natural capacity at the low-water stage of more than 150 H. P. should not pass with the land, but should be leased, together with a sufficient area adjoining the fall, for its proper development. The lease provided:—

(1) For the payment of an annual rental to the Crown.

(2) For the development of a specified quantity of power within a given time.

(3) For the supplying of surplus power by the lessees to others requiring it.

(4) For the regulation by the Lieutenant-Governor-in-Council of the rates and conditions upon which such surplus power should be supplied.

(5) For the development by the lessees of the full capacity of the power if there were a *bona fide* demand for it, of which demand the Lieutenant-Governor-in-Council should be the judge.

In 1907, these regulations were extended and the form of lease improved, the Hydro-Electric Power Commission being constituted the agent of the Government in dealing with water-powers subsequent to their lease by the Crown.

Under the Act of 1898 and the Regulations pertaining thereto, some twenty water-powers, providing for a minimum development of 26,600 H.P. and a maximum of 53,700 H.P. have been leased. The annual revenue accruing to the Government from these leases is $12,000. Large investments, amounting to several millions of dollars, have been made by the lessees in dams, improvements, and machinery for the development and utilization of these powers.

There can be no doubt that the use of water-power will become more and more general, especially as mineral fuel tends to become dearer and scarcer. The possession of an effective measure of control in the public interest over the water-powers of the Province, is most important. Briefly, the policy of the Government in dealing with this item of the natural resources is to obtain a fair revenue for the public chest, while at the same time encouraging the development and utilization of these powers and guarding against their being monopolized or being held merely for speculative purposes.

The above has reference to water-powers other than the Niagara falls, which has been dealt with in a special way by the Queen Victoria Niagara Falls Park Commission, subject to approval of the Legislature.

Minerals—The application of a policy of conservation to minerals is somewhat more difficult than to water-powers. Minerals lying undiscovered and dormant in the earth's crust are, for all practical purposes, non-existent. Only when they are found and brought to the surface, can they be made subservient to the uses of man. The mechanical and industrial necessities of civilization require a constant and ever-increasing supply of the useful minerals, and it seems difficult, if not impracticable and useless, to put any check upon the production of such commodities as gold, silver, iron, lead, copper, etc. The demand for these primal necessities in the arts and industries of the world is not only urgent but imperative, and the demand must be supplied if the present complex civilization is to remain in existence and develop in the future as it has done in the past.

It must be recognized that the business of mining and extracting minerals is, so far as the deposits themselves are concerned, a destructive industry. A body of ore, no matter how large it may be, is strictly limited in quantity, and when it is taken out of the ground it cannot be restored or replaced or reproduced.

There are some mineral substances exceedingly valuable in their nature which, however, lend themselves more readily to conservation than do the metals. This remark is particularly applicable to the fuels—coal, petroleum, natural gas, peat.

Ontario is practically the only province in the Dominion which produces petroleum. Natural gas is found also in Alberta, as well as in this Province. The requirements of the home market are not now met by the domestic production of crude oil in Ontario, for a quantity equal to the home production is annually imported for refining purposes, and this, notwithstanding the bounty of $1\frac{1}{2}$ cents per gallon paid by the Dominion Government on domestic crude. The production of petroleum in Ontario is, at present, declining, but there is good reason for believing that other sources of supply may be discovered at any time, since the formations in which the present fields exist are widespread in southern Ontario. On the northern slope of the height-of-land there is a large area of rocks similar in age and character to those in the southwestern peninsula, and it is reasonable to suppose they will be found to contain the same mineral substances, namely, petroleum, natural gas, salt, etc.

Natural gas is a fuel which has many advantages. It is cheap, efficient and clean, gives no smoke, leaves no ashes, can be turned on and off at will. The production of natural gas in this Province is annually and rapidly increasing. In 1907, the value at the wells, at a low rate of valuation, was three-quarters of a million dollars; in 1908, almost a million. In the production of natural gas, and especially in the opening up of new fields, there has, in the past, been enormous and shameful waste. In the United States, gas wells have been allowed to blow off into the air millions of dollars' worth of gas, or have been lighted and allowed to burn night and day for weeks and months. There have been similar scenes in our province. Steps have been taken by the present administration of Ontario to check such wanton extravagance. A tax of two cents per thousand feet has been levied on natural gas, with a rebate of 90 per cent., when the gas is used in Canada. A gas well giving off a million cubic feet of gas per day is not a very large well, but if the owner allows the gas to escape, he is presented with a bill of $20 per day for every day of waste. Very few wish to indulge in the privilege of wasting gas and pay $20 a day for the pleasure. The result has been that, since the Act was passed in 1907, there has been an almost entire stoppage of waste of gas in the gas fields of Ontario.

A further step in the direction of economizing this valuable fuel would be to restrict its use, if possible, to domestic purposes only. Large quantities are now used in generating steam and in the coarser industries, such as burning lime and making brick. At least fifty thousand people are enjoying the advantages of natural gas in Ontario to-day, and, if it could be confined to household purposes only, they might continue to enjoy its advantages for very many years. At present, the outlook is for a much earlier exhaustion.

If natural resources, including minerals, cannot be withheld from the urgent requirements of the present generation, to serve the necessities of posterity, they can, at least, while being utilized, be made to yield a revenue for the public good. Accordingly, the Legislature in 1907, imposed a tax of 3 per cent. on the net profits of mining companies when such profits were in excess of $10,000 per annum. All legitimate expenses, depreciation, etc., are allowed for, and the percentage computed only on actual profits. During the three years this Act has been in operation the amount received from this source has been $156,900.

The Hon. Adam Beck, M.P.P., Chairman of the Hydro-Electric Power Commission of Ontario, was then requested by the Chairman to read a paper on

THE CONSERVATION OF THE WATER-POWERS OF ONTARIO

Mr. Beck said:

I count it an honour and a privilege to address the Commission for the Conservation of Natural Resources. I do not think I will err in ascribing your generous invitation to the fact that I have been associated in my own Province, the province of Ontario, with the effort which has been in progress there for some years back to conserve, as far as possible, but with due regard to its vested interests, the valuable water-powers of that Province.

The object lesson which the policy of the Government of the province of Ontario has furnished in the conservation of natural resources has attracted considerable attention throughout the world, and it is, perhaps, fitting that, at the beginning of the career of the National Commission, whose duties are of the highest and most responsible character, I should endeavour to set forth, in some brief but orderly fashion, the basis and progress of a similar movement, on a smaller scale, in my own Province.

I will ask you, therefore, to accompany me in thought while I sketch, as briefly and clearly as the character of my subject permits,
(1) The antecedents and origin of the Hydro-Electric Power Commission over which I have the honour to preside;
(2) The scope of the legislation creating the Commission;
(3) The scope, progress and value of the undertaking with which the Commission is charged;
(4) The effect upon vested interests of the work of the Commission; and
(5) The probable future of the Commission.

I.—Antecedents and Origin of Power Commission—The Hydro-Electric Power Commission of Ontario was born of a wide-spread public demand that steps should be taken by the Province to preserve and develop the people's rights in the provincial water-powers, and to protect them from the baneful effects of monopoly prices. The harnessing of Niagara Falls had been the dream of engineers for a long time. Like other dreams of the leaders of thought and progress among the people, on questions of national import, it interested the public by slow degrees. The various efforts that were made from time to time to form companies for the generation of electric power at the Falls stimulated interest, and when, at last, the manufacture of electrical transmission apparatus had sufficiently advanced to permit of the commencement of large hydro-electric installations, the economic possibilities of the Falls took a stronger hold upon the public mind. The value of cheap electric power to a province dependent upon the coal-fields of Pennsylvania and its trusts was, and is, sufficiently obvious.

One of the first definite expressions of public interest in the question occurred in the spring of 1900, when the Toronto Board of Trade appointed a committee to investigate and report upon the power question. The committee, which was presided over by the late Mr. W. E. H. Massey, reported that the manufacturers' hope for cheap power in the south-western portion of the Province depended for realization upon the utilization of the resources of Niagara falls. The report of this committee was followed by increasing public interest, and, in the early part of 1902, voluntary meetings were held in many cities of the Province, which, together with the support of the Canadian Manufacturers' Association and of numerous Boards of Trade, served to rivet public attention on the matter.

A meeting of manufacturers was held at Berlin in June, 1902, at which representatives from Toronto, Galt, Guelph, London and a number of other centres were present, the object being that of discussing and furthering the best method of securing electric power for manufacturing and other purposes from Niagara falls. Early in 1903, the city of Toronto made application to the Legislature for authority to generate and transmit Niagara Falls power for the users of the city. The application, however, was refused.

To pass rapidly over intervening events, it is sufficient to say that, as a result of the decisions of, and action initiated by, the aforementioned and subsequent meetings of manufacturers and municipal representatives, an Act was passed by the Ontario Legislature the following year (1903) which authorized Ontario municipalities to appoint a Commission to inquire into the desirability of securing the establishment and operation of municipal light, heat and power works and to establish the same. Immediately after the passage of the Act in question the municipalities of Toronto, London, Brantford, Stratford, Woodstock, Ingersoll and Guelph exercised their powers and appointed a Commission to inquire into the best method of developing power for their needs and to estimate the cost thereof. The Commission was composed of Mr. E. W. B. Snyder, of St. Jacobs, Mr. P. W. Ellis, of Toronto, Mr. W. F. Cockshutt, of Brantford, Mr. R. A. Fessenden, a Canadian electrical engineer then residing in Washington, D.C., and myself. Mr. Snyder was appointed Chairman of the Commission, and Messrs. Ross and Holgate, of Montreal, the well-known and highly capable firm of electrical and hydraulic engineers, were appointed by the Commission to investigate and report upon the engineering aspects of the whole matter. Incidentally, it may be observed that the Commissioners served from a sense of public duty, neither seeking nor accepting any remuneration for their services.

The report of this Commission was issued on the 28th of March, 1906, and, by general consent, it set forth, for the first time, an authoritative and exhaustive exposition of the whole question of the commercial value to the province of Ontario of its great natural water-powers, when utilized for the generation and transmission of electric power. It contained, among other things, a reliable estimate of the power consumption of the district embraced, the cost thereof when produced from coal and steam, the capital and operating costs of a large generating plant at Niagara Falls combined with the necessary transmission lines throughout the district in question, and the enormous financial savings and economic stimulus that would result from the carrying out of such a plan of generation and transmission as was therein recommended.

It became evident during the later stages of the work of this Commission, and also in the discussions which followed the publication and distribution of the report among the municipalities, that certain serious difficulties of procedure were inherent in any plan which depended for its final accomplishment upon purely municipal initiative. The Government of the, then, Hon. Mr. Whitney, which, in the meantime, had been formed, recognizing these difficulties, appointed, partly in obedience to the public opinion of the time, and partly from a spontaneous recognition of the importance of the water-power question, a new Commission to make still further inquiries. This Commission was composed of Mr. Geo. Pattinson, M.P.P., of Preston, Mr. P. W. Ellis, of Toronto, and myself. Subsequently Mr. Ellis retired because of ill-health, and Mr. John Milne, of Hamilton, took his place.

Further investigations were made into the location and value of the provincial water-powers by this Commission, the effect of which was to add greatly to the general fund of reliable information on the subject. As a final result of all the inquiries, reports, discussions and public agitation, the Hydro-Electric Power Commission of Ontario was, in obedience to, and with the full force and sanction of, an overwhelming body of public opinion, formally created by statute on the 14th of May, 1906, its powers, however, being revised and amplified by a subsequent Act passed on the 20th of April, 1907. This Commission was originally composed of the Hon. J. S. Hendrie, of Hamilton, Mr. C. B. Smith and myself. Subsequently Mr. Smith resigned, and Mr. W. K. McNaught, of Toronto, was appointed in his place. To the Commission thus constituted, with Mr. P. W. Sothman as chief engineer, has been confided the task of carrying out the great scheme which I shall presently describe more fully.

It will be observed from this brief and rapid outline sketch that the Hydro-Electric Power Commission—whether it be, as is so often represented, on the one hand a priest and prophet of evil, or, on the other hand, as less frequently represented, but perhaps more deeply felt, a great and potent agency for the public good—does not represent a policy which is the sole and exclusive creation of any single man or Government, but rather a policy which embodies the judgment of an intelligently instructed public opinion, the cumulative force of which made itself felt through all the organs of the public voice upon the general mass of men without distinction of party.

I ought, however, before leaving this branch of my subject, to note that the great potentialities of Niagara falls as a power reservoir had, at an earlier stage, fastened themselves upon the imagination of the Government of the Hon. G. W. Ross, which endeavoured by a system of regulation, to do something for the public welfare in regard thereto. The legislation of that Government, however, proved inadequate. It was intended, among other things, as between the companies then in existence, to protect the public interest by prohibiting amalgamations, pooling and the carrying out of arrangements to maintain or increase prices. Not only were the Government proposals incapable, by their very nature, of effective application, but they failed to make provision for the prevention of a system of subdivision of territory between the companies, which, whether ordered by nature or effected by arrangement between them, made the Electrical Development Co. and the Hamilton Cataract Power Co. the master monopolists of electric power in the Niagara peninsula.

I do not wish to be understood as endeavouring by these remarks to make any political capital out of this matter. Nothing is further from my thoughts. No government can safely and effectively prevent amalgamation taking place under some one or other of the variety of forms in which it may be incorporated, nor effectively prevent the making of arrangements designed to maintain certain price-levels when the parties thereto are few in number. There is no satisfactory and infallible method of proving "parole" or "gentlemen's" agreements, and therefore there is no satisfactory method of preventing or penalizing them.

II.—Powers of the Commission—The powers conferred by legislative authority upon the Commission may be broadly described as follows:—

It is duly authorized to investigate and report to the Lieutenant-Governor-in-Council upon any and all hydraulic, hydro-electric and other power undertakings, whether developed or undeveloped, throughout the Province; to inquire and report upon the Ontario branches of power undertakings originating outside, but bringing power within, the boundaries of the Province; to inquire and report upon the power and lighting needs of the Province in all its parts, and, upon the authority of the Lieutenant-Governor-in-Council, to purchase, lease, expropriate or otherwise acquire lands, water-powers and water privileges; to purchase, lease, expropriate, construct or otherwise acquire generating, transmitting and distributing plants and works and to operate the same; to expropriate the power product of, or to contract with, any person, firm or corporation for a supply thereof; and to enter into all necessary arrangements with Ontario municipalities or other corporations, including railway and distributing companies, for the fullest exercise of these powers, with the object of providing adequately for the supply of the power and lighting needs of the Province at the lowest possible cost. Authority is also given to the Commission to control the rates charged by municipalities upon the sale of power purchased from it, with the object of preventing excessive charges to the public or the veiled bonusing of favoured undertakings, and to the Lieutenant-Governor-in-Council to borrow on the credit of the Province all moneys required to carry on the various objects of the Commission.

It became necessary, however, during the legislative sessions of 1908 and 1909, to procure some auxiliary powers in order the better to proceed with the undertaking; and to secure the ratification of certain contracts, including some municipal contracts in regard to which systematic efforts were being made to prevent their completion, and to block and jeopardize thereby the whole undertaking.

These powers, thus briefly summarized, are wide and important, and cast upon the Commission a high degree of responsibility. Properly used, they will greatly develop the latent wealth of the Province and distribute its benefits among the mass of the people. The legislation has provoked much antagonism, and, in certain quarters, it has been strongly and persistently criticized as an improper exercise of legislative authority.

It has been contended that, in certain parts, it is *ultra vires* of the Legislature of Ontario; that, even though *intra vires*, it is, as a whole, indefensible from the standpoint of public morality, which calls for adequate protection of vested interests and sanctity of private contracts, and that, in any event, governments and their creature commissions are inherently incapable of operating business undertakings in a business-like way, and, therefore, from the economic point of view, it is unsound and involves the penalizing of the public in the very service it was designed to promote.

I am not concerned here to argue the constitutional question. That may be left to lawyers. It is improbable that the profession will become extinct or that the law courts will be closed in the immediate future through unanimity of legal judgment on this or any other constitutional question. Suffice it to say that we are advised the legislation is well within the rights of the Province, and, on that view, we are disposed to maintain it.

I would like, however, to consider shortly the moral aspect of the question. The essence of this criticism, which has been chiefly provoked by the building of a transmission line in the southwestern portion of the Province, touches two main points, viz., the right of the Government to employ public moneys in constructing and operating undertakings which may compete with those established by private enterprise, and the right of the Government to stay actions and to validate contracts. Now, on these questions, I would, first of all, point out that the Government of Ontario in authorizing the Commission to construct these electrical transmission lines, has, in reality, appointed the Commission an agent for certain municipal corporations, at their own request. The undertaking, which is in course of construction, is, for reasons of economy and expedition, being built, and will, on completion, be operated by the Commission on behalf of certain municipal corporations who will also pay for it. The Government is practically making a secured loan to the municipalities for the amount of the cost of the undertaking, which, with interest, is to be repaid by the municipalities, by annual instalments, within thirty years. Meantime, of course, the operating expenses are in the form of rentals, likewise payable by the municipalities. Neither the Commission nor the Government, as such, makes or accumulates one cent of profit or revenue out of the undertaking. It is wholly and only conducted for the benefit of the municipalities. I make this point clear in the interest of clear thinking. It is a municipal enterprise conducted by the Commission at the request of, and as the appointed agent of, the municipalities, and at their cost and risk. It is not a direct Government undertaking organized and conducted on behalf of, or for the benefit of, the Government. In the second place, I would observe that, so far as my knowledge goes, the contention that governments are barred from employing public moneys for the furtherance of undertakings that may conceivably compete with those of private enterprise, has no such sacred sanction as its exponents pretend. I do not understand that any revelation has ever been made from Heaven to the effect that a democratic government commits the unpardonable sin when it assists in the establishment of great and necessary public works for the well-being of the people, of whose interests it is the trustee.

I am not aware that the people of the Dominion of Canada violated any moral law in building the Intercolonial railway, or that the people or Government of the province of Ontario did so in building the Timiskaming railway. It is true that the history of the Intercolonial railway has not been a continuous history of increasing surpluses. I have heard it said that there has sometimes been a deficit, and of course it may be contended that the deficit itself is an evidence of such violation. I do not think, however, that such reasoning will stand in any atmosphere except that of a political election. The best of men, as well as the best of projects, often meet loss in this world. The fact of the matter is, that theories of private property and of the limits of State interference are as plentiful as the generations and as varied as the schools of men, and it is grotesque that a single class of people should select that particular theory best suited to their exclusive interests, clothe it with the sanctity of a religious system, set it up for worship among men, and then proceed to ostracize a government which ventures to give a prior place to the authority of reason and the principles of justice in the shaping of measures for the well-being of the people at large. The collective holding and the nationalization of certain forms of property rest upon a moral basis quite as secure as that of private ownership of property. No man in his senses believes that it is wrong to prevent the people being injured by monopolies, or to develop public resources with public money for the public good. As a matter of fact, however, the Commission does not compete with private companies in the generation of power, and, while it is true that the transmission lines of the Electrical Development Company are being duplicated between Niagara Falls and Toronto, that Company has long term contracts with the Toronto Electric Light Company and the Toronto Railway Company, its sole Toronto customers for power, and these contracts are not being disturbed in the least degree. In no other part of the Province is there any transmission line worthy of the name, owned by private enterprise, with which the Hydro-Electric Commission will compete. There has, therefore, been no interference with existing contracts. It has been said that the project violates a covenant given by a prior government. The reply is simple—it does not, for no such covenant has ever been given.

The Commission has contracted to purchase the power it requires at reasonable rates either at the generating stations or at the termini of the transmission lines of certain existing private companies, and it is thereby taking the position of a customer and supporter of such companies rather than that of a competitor and assailant.

In the third place, I would observe that the special legislation to stay certain actions which were intended to block the expressed will of the people and to validate certain contracts were, notwithstanding assertions to the contrary, normal exercises of the legislative power. If it is competent to the Provincial Legislature to prescribe the procedure by which municipal councils may ascertain and give effect to the wishes of the people, it is equally competent to the Legislature to vary the procedure when it is being employed by unexpected methods to block the wishes of the people, and, in this case, it was done at the request of the municipalities concerned. If you will take the trouble to read the masterly report prepared by the Hon. Mr. Foy, Attorney-General of the Province, upon the actions stayed and the contracts validated, and which has recently been transmitted to the Federal Government, I think you will agree with me that this particular complaint rests upon a very insecure foundation.

I pass now to the consideration of the next ground of complaint, viz., that governments and their creature commissions are inherently incapable of efficiently conducting business undertakings, and that, in consequence thereof, the public will be penalized instead of benefited by the effect of the legislation in question. If this is the general rule of government experience, then in the province of Ontario we must have an exceptionally capable Government, because we do not admit for one moment that we have had any such experience, or that there is the slightest foundation for these charges of the prophets of evil. As a matter of fact, however, broad generalizations on questions of this sort are of no value. It is absurd to contend that effective and economic corporate action cannot be procured among men. The highest degree of administrative skill is found among corporations. Government action and Hydro-Electric Power Commission action are forms of corporate action. It has not been decreed that one form of corporate action shall exhibit all the virtues and powers and another form all the vices and imbecilities of men. The quality of corporate action depends on the character and calibre of the men and not upon the type or purpose of the corporation. History sustains the theory of effective government management quite as strongly as it sustains the theory of ineffective government management.

As a matter of fact, under our modern democratic system, which ensures the constant employment in the service of the State of a large part of the best brains of the country, it is ridiculous to assert that such brains are barred by the mere atmosphere of the service of the State from that efficiency of conduct which would characterize them in the atmosphere of private life.

In this particular project, however, it is to be noted that the enterprise is of the highest technical type, both by reason of the nature of hydraulic and electric problems and by reason of the scale upon which the Hydro-Electric Power Commission is dealing with them. The scheme of transmission is the largest in the world, and electric power will be transmitted at the highest voltage known to the art, viz., 110,000 volts. I do not think that there is any other power transmission undertaking in operation in the world to-day at 110,000 volts. It is, however, possible that by the time this project is completed, there will be one other 110,000 volt transmission plant in existence. Whether or not, however, I am strictly correct on this point, it is clear that the operation and installation of the undertaking calls for the employment of engineering talent of the highest order, and of the most highly specialized type. An executive staff of the necessary high and rare capacity may be relied upon to work on a corresponding level of efficiency, whether in the employment of the State or in the employment of the private individual.

To sum up: the objections that have been taken to the legislation in question, and which are dignified with the high sounding names of "constitutional," "moral," and "economic" objections, are all, according to my humble way of thinking, explicable on a very simple principle. It seems to be a universal characteristic of human nature that where 5% is being made, 6% should be striven for, and when 6% is earned, 7% should be aimed at, and so on in an increasing, but never diminishing, ratio. Under the influence of this principle of human action, it is natural for those interested in any department of commercial activity to object to anything and everything that would curtail, or threaten to curtail, their immediate or prospective returns, and all these high-sounding objections, or nearly all of them, could probably, if one had the time or the inclination, be traced to the motive of self-interest in the class or classes affected.

III.—The Scope, Progress and Value of the Undertaking—The field for the activities of the Commission comprises the whole of the province of Ontario. It is, however, proceeding with its enormous and responsible task in a rational way. It was the public recognition of the great needs of the manufacturing districts of western Ontario and the vast untapped reservoir of Niagara falls that led, as as has already been explained, to the creation of the Commission, and it was, therefore, natural and proper that to this particular part of the field the attention of the Commission should first be directed.

Before sketching the physical project which is in process in the district named, I should, however, mention that contracts have been made for the purchase of power from existing companies at Ottawa and at Port Arthur, and for the sale thereof to the municipalities of Ottawa and of Port Arthur. These have been productive of great satisfaction in these municipalities.

In the city of Ottawa, for years prior to 1901, the following rates were charged by the Ottawa Electric Company:—

> House lighting, 15 cents net, per kilowatt hour;
> Street lighting, $65.00 per arc lamp per annum;
> Motive power, $40.00 and upwards, per H.P. per annum.

During this time, I am informed, the Company paid no dividends. In addition to settling an acute triangular struggle within the city of Ottawa, the particulars of which it is not necessary to repeat to this audience, the Commission contracted, in July, 1907, for the purchase of power from the Ottawa and Hull Power and Manufacturing Company, whose generating works are in the province of Quebec, for a period of ten years at the price of $15.00 per H.P. per annum, and for the sale thereof, on the same terms, to the city of Ottawa.

Prior to this, the city's right to purchase current direct from a power company had been successfully assailed in the courts, and it was, therefore, left with a distributing plant on its hands but without any source of supplies. As a result of the mediation of the Commission, the city has, since 1907, been enabled to procure an abundant supply of power at a price which, in turn, has permitted the continuance of a schedule of prices as follows:—

> House lighting: $7\frac{1}{5}$ cents net per kilowatt hour, or a reduction of 50% on the prices of 1901.
> Street lighting: $45.00 per arc lamp per annum, or a reduction of 31% upon the prices of 1901.
> Motive power: $25.00 per H.P., per annum, or a reduction of $37\frac{1}{2}$% from the prices of 1901.

The reduction in prices has so stimulated consumption that, together with the increased demand which has accompanied the growth of the city, the business both of the city and the Ottawa Electric Company has greatly increased, the Company now paying 5% dividends on its outstanding capital stock of $1,000,000, and having, in the year ended 31st December, 1908, added an ample surplus to its reserve account. The gross revenue of the city electric plant for 1908, was over $106,000, with a net profit of over $17,000 after paying interest and making provision for an adequate sinking fund to retire the capital invested.

In the city of Port Arthur a most unsatisfactory state of affairs between the municipality and the Kaministiquia Power Company has been terminated by similar mediation on the part of the Commission. As a result thereof the Commission has contracted to take its supply of power from the Kaministiquia Power Company and to sell the same to the city of Port Arthur on terms which are eminently satisfactory to both the vending power company and the purchasing municipality.

It may also be worth while describing a very interesting situation which developed in Hamilton, and the result thereof. The Commission did not, at the outset, expect to render much service to the people of Hamilton, by reason of the Hamilton Cataract Company's control of the De Cew Falls power, which is situated quite close to the city, and which is the cheapest development in the Province, its original source being the Welland canal. To take other power into Hamilton was like taking coals to Newcastle. It was found, however, upon investigation, that prices in Hamilton for power and lighting services were higher than in Toronto, where the power was generated from steam plants. The scale was as follows:—

SERVICE	HAMILTON	TORONTO
House lighting	10 cents k.w.	8 cents k.w.
Commercial lighting	15 cents k.w.	12 cents k.w.
Arc lamps	$84.00 per annum	$69.35 per annum

Upon the expiry of the city lighting contract, tenders were called for and submitted on the basis of $80.00 per arc light per annum, with a ten-year franchise, or $85.00 with a five-year franchise. The City Council then asked the Commission to submit prices, whereupon it estimated the cost of arc lamps as $43.00 per annum. The Company then came down to a $47.00 rate, and got the contract for five years. Subsequently the city called for prices on power for water-works and sewage disposal, and tenders were submitted by the Cataract Company at $45.00 per H.P. per annum, while the Commission estimated the service as being worth $17.50 per H.P. per annum.

The Cataract Company then offered to supply the city at rates 10% less than those charged by the Commission to any municipality. Both offers were submitted to the ratepayers, and, as a result, a contract with the Commission was duly authorized and executed.

It is worth while noting at this juncture that the advent of the Hydro-Electric Power Commission to the electric power councils of the cities of Hamilton, Ottawa and Port Arthur has not been productive of that destruction of private interests that has been so freely and recklessly predicted. On the contrary, in these municipalities the offices of the Commission have resulted in strengthening, but on a sound and healthy basis, the position of the private power companies, while securing material benefits to the public consumers of light and power.

Coming now to the Niagara peninsula and western Ontario, I will proceed to outline, as rapidly as possible, the main features of the project. The Commission has entered into a contract with the Ontario Power Company to purchase not less than 8,000 H.P., and as much more as it requires, up to 100,000 H.P., for a term of ten years, with provision for three extensions for additional periods of ten years each, at the price of $9.40 per H.P. per annum up to 25,000 H.P., and $9.00 per H.P. per annum if the quantity taken exceeds 25,000 H.P. The power is to be delivered by the Ontario Power Company to the Commission at Niagara Falls at 12,000 volts, and the prices cover a twenty-four hour continuous service.

The physical project begins with a transformer station at Niagara Falls to take the power on delivery at 12,000 volts. Thence a 60,000 H.P. double transmission line operating at 110,000, volts conveys the current to a controlling station at Dundas, whence the line is continued east to the city of Toronto without—in the meantime—any intermediate station. From the controlling station at Dundas a double line of the same capacity and voltage is continued *via* Woodstock and London to St. Thomas, with local transformer stations at these points. From the same central controlling station at Dundas a similar line proceeds north and west *via* Guelph, Preston, Berlin, Stratford, St. Marys and on to London, with local transformer stations at each of these points, the whole high-voltage line thus described comprising about 300 miles. At each of these local transformer stations the voltage is reduced to 13,000 for the purpose of supplying, by additional local feeder lines, the different municipalities in the vicinity thereof. The effect of this method of distribution is to make it possible from the high-voltage circuit above described, in combination with the low-voltage local distributing lines, to supply the needs of practically every municipality within the district at the four corners of which are Toronto Niagara Falls, St. Thomas and Stratford.

The ultimate termini of the said high-voltage transmission lines as determined by economic limits, will be Windsor in the west and Kingston in the east, the additional territories to be tapped by such extensions to be fully fed in turn by a continuance, where necessary, of the local low-voltage distributing lines. This will cover the whole of the south-western portion of Ontario from Kingston to Georgian bay and south, leaving the north-eastern portion of Ontario from North Bay to the St. Lawrence river to be covered by a similar system which, in due time, will doubtless be established at the most appropriate generating points within the district.

The Commission of Conservation
Canada

HYDRO-ELECTRIC POWER COMMISSION, ONTARIO

TRANSMISSION LINES
NIAGARA DISTRICT
Scale, 35 miles to 1 inch

Legend

Transformer stations
Horse-power capacity of transformer stations shown thus....4500
Red circles indicate radii of 10 miles
High Tension Lines
Low Tension Lines
Projected High Tension Line, St. Thomas to Windsor

The present arrangements of the Commission include the supplying of fifteen municipal corporations with their respective power needs up to an aggregate of approximately 27,000 H. P., over the lines described and now under construction, viz:—Toronto, 10,000; London, 5,000; Guelph, 2,500; St. Thomas, 1,500; Woodstock, 1,200; Galt, 1,200; Hamilton, 1,000; Stratford, 1,000; Berlin, 1,000; Waterloo, 685; Preston, 600; St. Marys, 500; Ingersoll, 500; Hespeler, 400; New Hamburg, 250.

Provision has been made for the supply of larger quantities, from time to time as they are required, and also, for the extension of the service to all the municipalities within the area which it is proposed to feed from Niagara Falls.

The municipalities have agreed to pay the Commission for the power in question on the following basis, viz.,—

(1) The contract price of the Ontario Power Company at Niagara Falls, plus
(2) 4% per annum upon that part of the construction cost which is properly applicable to each participating municipality, plus
(3) An annual amount sufficient to create a sinking fund which in thirty years, shall completely pay for that portion of the construction cost which is applicable to each municipality, plus
(4) That proportion of the line loss and the general operating and maintenance charges which is properly applicable to each municipality.

The annual inclusive rates, so computed, payable by each municipality, have been carefully estimated and reduced to the following H.P. scale viz.,—

Toronto	$18.10	per H.P. per annum
London	23.50	" "
Guelph	24.00	" "
St. Thomas	26.50	"
Woodstock	23.00	
Galt	22.00	"
Stratford	24.50	" "
Berlin	24.00	
Hamilton	17.50	"
Waterloo	24.50	"
Preston	23.50	" "
St. Marys	29.50	
Hespeler	26.00	
New Hamburg	29.50	" "

These rates are for power delivered at the municipal sub-stations at 13,000 volts. Each municipality assumes the responsibility for acquiring or providing the necessary local distributing system, and the maximum cost to the consumer on the above consumption will be the above prices, plus the respective local distributing costs.

While the intricacies that enter into any comparison between the costs of hydro-electric and steam power of the varied character and on the scale dealt with herein, are such as to make those most familiar with the question particularly chary about instituting them, it would be a pity to leave this branch of my subject without endeavouring to state, in at least roughly approximate figures, the monetary value to the community of the savings effected thereby, as compared with a corresponding supply of electrical power derived from coal and steam plants located at the sites of the respective corresponding municipal sub-stations. While, therefore, I do not put forward the figures I am about to submit as an exact estimate of the difference, I do submit them as an approximate statement of the difference, and, therefore, of the economic value of the undertaking as limited to meet *only the stated needs* of the municipalities referred to. The exact quantity of power contracted for, amounts to 27,350 H. P. which, at the various rates given, averages, as nearly as possible, $22.00 per H. P. per annum. This, you will bear in mind, is the cost of power available for continuous consumption during the whole round of 24 hours daily. Now if coal and steam plants were erected on the proposed sites of the various municipal sub-stations for the purpose of developing the same quantities of electric power for a continuous 24 hour full load service, the average cost of such would amount to certainly not less than $60.00 per H. P. per annum. (A monopoly would fix the price of electric power at just under the coal-steam cost, or whatever the traffic would bear). The difference is $38.00 per H. P. per annum, which on a consumption of 27,350 H. P. amounts to $1,039,300, or, say, $1,000,000 per annum. As the consumption increases, the unit cost, of course, decreases with the effect of greatly swelling the unit and aggregate savings. The capitalized value at 5% of savings amounting to $1,000,000 per annum is $20,000,000. That is to say, that, if the consumers in question desired to exchange their annual savings of $1,000,000 for a present single payment in hand, they would receive from anyone wishing to make a 5% investment therein the sum of $20,000,000 for them.

The true economic value of these savings cannot however be calculated, because they will be employed from year to year in extending the trade, and in increasing the competitive efficiency of all engaged therein. The investment and reinvestment of such increasing income-bearing advantages cannot be stated in monetary terms. But it is obvious that, in these days of increasing international industrial competition, their value, when made available for the people of the whole Province, is of incalculable consequence; and the conception of which they are begotten is of corresponding dignity.

I should also note that, had this matter been left exclusively in the hands of private companies, their tendency would have been to get the easiest market for their output by inducing manufacturers to settle within easy distance of Niagara Falls, and by selling in large blocks to large users. Under the policy of the Commission, the benefits are being distributed throughout the Province to large and small users alike, thus contributing to a well balanced and general development, rather than an abnormal expansion of one district at the expense of others.

The progress of the work to date may be rapidly described. The sub-stations are all practically completed, so far, that is, as the buildings are concerned. Of the transmission line towers, about one-half are erected, and the balance will be erected within five or six months. The electrical equipment is under construction, and should be completed and installed within six months. Power service will be furnished each municipality in order of completion, and all should be supplied within six months. By these means, it will be possible to compare accurately the relative efficiency of each municipality and develop in the fullest degree the art of competitive efficiency. All the local municipal distributing plants are likewise under construction. Mr. R. A. Ross, of Montreal, has acted throughout as the consulting engineer of the Commission, and it is only right that I should acknowledge in the most ample way the great value of his services.

Meetings of the municipal engineers concerned, have been held at frequent intervals during the past year, with the object of standardizing all possible features of the undertaking; e.g., the establishment of a uniform scale of power and lighting rates, subject only to different discounts to provide for differences in general conditions, is being aimed at, together with a uniform system of accounting and the standardization of the technical equipment of the municipal distributing systems.

I should also add that the total estimated cost of the finished project was $3,500,000, and that the actual cost, as determined by the contracts let, comes well within that figure. From this, it follows that the estimated H.P. rates given the municipalities are safe and assured.

IV.—Effect Upon Vested Interests—I have already made passing reference in two or three places to the effect of the work of the Commission upon vested interests. I shall briefly summarize these and add one or two additional remarks.

At Port Arthur the Kaministiquia Power Company's interests have been distinctly steadied and improved by the mediation of the Commission between that Company and the municipality of Port Arthur. The same effect has been secured at Ottawa.

In the Niagara peninsula there are four Canadian companies, viz., Canadian Niagara Company, Ontario Power Company, Hamilton Cataract Company and the Electrical Development Company. The Canadian Niagara Company has not been affected at all by the work of the Commission. Its activities are entirely on the United States side of the river. The Ontario Power Company has been strengthened by the acquisition of a contract to supply the Commission with from 8,000 to 100,000 H. P. Its position has been distinctly and greatly improved by this contract. The contract was made at a low and very favourable rate for the Commission, but it constituted for the Ontario Power Company purely additional business, which enabled it to improve its position even by the acceptance of a low price. The Hamilton Cataract Company is still carrying on, as heretofore, a large and successful business.

The smoke of battle has gathered mostly over the head of the Electrical Development Company. It was offered—but it declined— the privilege of supplying the Commission with a part of its requirements. It remains in full possession of its Toronto line, its Toronto customers and its Toronto contracts, and it will, doubtless, sell at profitable rates, for all time, as much power as it can produce. All the talk of the injury inflicted upon this concern may be brought to a very simple test. Have its securities appreciated or depreciated in value? The lowest price of its bonds in 1907 was 72 and the highest, 84. In 1909 the lowest price rose to $82\frac{1}{4}$ and the highest to $90\frac{1}{4}$. If this Company had been injured in any degree by the Commission, the market prices of its bonds would have reflected the injury. On the contrary, they have steadily improved in value.

To sum up: The Commission is not engaged in the generation of power in competition with existing companies; it has violated no contract, nor has it employed coercion in its dealings with them; instead, it has strengthened several such by purchasing from them large quantities of power and establishing them on a firmer contract basis.

By the construction of its transmission lines, it proposes to distribute much of the power so purchased throughout parts of Ontario that no existing company is in a position to serve. The wreckage of vested interests with which—according to many newspapers—Ontario is covered, is not visible to any search party that I have been able to organize. As a matter of fact, while the public has already received great—and will yet receive greater—benefits from the work of the Commission, vested interests of private companies have been justly dealt with and have been greatly strengthened.

V.—The Probable Future of the Commission—If the construction project, now nearing completion, answers, as I have every confidence it will, the expectations formed of it, the future of the Commission will be devoted to the completion of the work begun. The Government is not a trustee for the interests of any particular group of municipalities or any particular part of the people to the exclusion of the rest. Its obligations are the same to all the people and to all their municipal institutions. In prosecuting this work, however, just as it will not be deterred by slander, neither will it be hurried by impatient clamour. It will proceed cautiously and prudently, step by step, testing and proving its way, that its progress may be real and enduring. An abundant supply of motive power is to the manufacturing arts what blood is to the human body. It is their very life. And upon the progress of the manufacturing arts depends the future of this country in the international markets of the world. Supremacy in these arts gives employment and prosperity to the people at home, influence and power to the country abroad, and, in combination with the unbounded granaries of the west, it assures to the Dominion a beneficent as well as an honourable place in the civilization of that, as yet unshaped, Imperial future to which we all look forward. Nor would I forget the patient toilers on the land. Back of, and sustaining, the manufacturing arts are the great agricultural classes, the keepers of the granaries of empire, the ultimate source and foundation of moral and political strength, as well as of material greatness.

To raise the standard of living, by multiplying and cheapening the comforts of life, for these great classes is one of the prime objects of the Commission. That it will ultimately be accomplished I have no doubt whatever. This is the task to which I have set my hand. This is the task to which I shall devote my public life. It is no ignoble work. I am not ashamed of it. I am well assured that the vilification of the present will give place to the vindication of the future. Its consummation will contribute to national strength and national greatness. I hope and believe that the work so initiated in my own Province will be carried forward by the National Commission in all departments of our national heritage.

HON. MR GRIMMER: Mr. Kelly Evans has acquired a national reputation in his line of work. In New Brunswick we have heard his oratory and enjoyed it and derived much benefit from it. I have much pleasure in introducing Mr. Kelly Evans, who, I am sure, will not fall short of the reputation he has justly acquired.

Then followed an address by Mr. Kelly Evans, Commissioner, Ontario Game and Fisheries Commission, on

FISH AND GAME IN ONTARIO

MR. EVANS said:

As the Chairman has stated, I have been engaged, for the last four years, in endeavouring to arouse public opinion to the importance of conserving one of our great resources. But, in addressing this meeting, I feel very much as a lawyer might who had been accustomed all his life to addressing juries and who, for the first time, had an opportunity to address the Supreme Court composed of a bench of judges. I realize that you all have a great deal of information in reference to the general proposition of the conservation of our resources, and instead of preparing a paper in advance, I waited till I had an opportunity of listening to the splendid address of the Hon. Mr. Sifton in order that I might be able to draw from it certain lessons which I thought would bear upon the particular resources I have most at heart. The Chairman of the Commission mentioned that a lifetime could be spent in the study of the most minor of our great resources, and, even then, we would not know all about it. In that statement he gave me an opportunity to still further amplify that thought by making the remark that, even in the least of our resources, there may be, as it were, some small bayou which might take a lifetime to explore. Take, for instance, the matter of fish culture and fisheries. There is a professor in a great university in the United States who has been, with a corps of students, more than four years studying the one subject of the oxygenation of water and its effect upon fish life and fish culture.

I should like, with your permission, to give some slight illustration of what waste has been going on, especially in the fisheries of our inland waters in the province of Ontario. It so happens that the blue books give us the value of the Fisheries of Ontario for a considerable period of years, but, in these statistics, while great stress is laid upon the value of the fish, no stress whatever is laid upon the quantities of fish taken. Food being in question, I think it is pertinent on this occasion to draw the attention of the Commission to the diminution of the food supply of the people in connection with our fisheries. Yesterday, I had an opportunity of looking over the report of the Department of Fisheries for the year 1873, and I found that certain alien corporations, known popularly as the American Fish Trust, have been most interested in the extirpation of the fisheries of our inland waters. It is not pleasant reading for them that I should give the figures I intend giving to you because they have been endeavouring to circulate the idea among the people of this country that the value of our fisheries is not decreasing. It is true that, if any of the members of this commission examine without analysis, the blue books as they appear before you, the conclusion would be arrived at that there was no need for alarm. As a matter of fact, what is shown in the blue books would lead you to believe that, in reality, there was very little diminution in the number of fish taking place.

Just as those who first exploited the forest wealth of this country took the most valuable species of wood, the pine, so those exploiting the fisheries of Ontario took the most valuable of our fish, the whitefish. Let us consider the position with regard to this: the total catch of whitefish, in 1873, was nearly five million pounds and to-day it is less than two and a half million pounds. The decrease appears to be in round figures about 2,350,000 lbs., but remember that the engines of capture have been greatly improved since that time and many more men are engaged in the work. In valuing this food diminution at its present price, it would show that, in the value of whitefish alone, a decrease has taken place to the extent of quite $250,000 a year which, capitalized at 5 per cent., would show that the capital value of the whitefish alone has decreased, between 1873 and 1907, by $5,000,000. There has been really no necessity for this alarming decrease having taken place. In 1892, a Government Commission, after taking testimony throughout the provinces, reported to the Dominion Government some alarming facts. Old fishermen who gave their evidence in 1882 spoke of the good old times, when they took as many as 90,000 whitefish at a haul with the net at Wellington beach, and said that, instead of endeavouring to use sewage for fertilizers as the Chairman has suggested, they acted upon the principle of using this valuable human food as manure upon the farm. The quantity of whitefish and other fish then in lake Ontario we have no record of, but that it was immense there can be no gainsaying. That gives an illustration of what might be called waste, and it also impresses upon the Commission the very point the Chairman has brought to its attention, viz: that the Commission may be able to investigate and get information not now at hand, in reference to these natural resources.

But, while the members of this Commission all realize that the commercial fisheries are one of our great natural resources, I do not think it is quite so clear to people generally, that the game fish and the game of the country should be included as a great natural resource. My main object in addressing you to-day is to endeavour to give you certain figures and information which may induce you to believe that the game fisheries and the game should be considered, not only as one of our resources, but as one of our principal resources. Now, to get figures upon this point is rather a difficult proposition. Mr. Byron E. Walker, no doubt, could give us, even from memory, what the returns are from our cereal crops, from our mines, from our forests, and from our economic resources, but I doubt if he could give the members of this Commission the slightest idea as to what money value the game fisheries and the game, say in the province of Ontario, represent. Now, in order that I may give you something that you will readily understand, I wish to take as my illustration in this respect, the state of Maine, in which the conditions are long past the stage of experiment. In the year 1867, the State Government appointed a Commission to enquire into, and report upon, the condition of the game fish and the game of the State, and, when that Commission reported, it stated that the game fisheries were valueless; that there were no moose in the state at all, and that deer could be found in only one portion of the state. Following this report, stringent laws were placed on the statute books of the State, and, in an attempt to enforce them, it is regrettable to find that some of the first game wardens were murdered. But finally, the, importance and the value of fish and game protection gained ground in the State, and what do we find to-day? In 1902, the Legislature of Maine, in order to set at rest some disputes as to what the monetary value of their policy had been, caused a census to be taken of the visitors who came into the interior portions of the State during the year. That summer a census was taken carefully and, when the returns were brought down, the people were amazed to learn the immensity of the traffic; for no less a number than 133,885 persons had come into the interior portion of the State that year. Now, the Government believes that $100 per head is a very conservative estimate of the average amount of money that each man will leave in the State from the time he crosses the border line until the time he leaves. From my own knowledge and experience I may say that, in my opinion, $100 per head is a very considerable under-estimate. But, accepting these figures, you have the gigantic sum brought into the state of Maine, annually, of about $14,000,000. Later on, I took the matter up with Hon. L. T. Carleton, the Commissioner for the state of Maine, to endeavour to find if any change had taken place since 1902. Some of you gentlemen may consider that a man like Mr. Carleton might be enthusiastic and apt to exaggerate the figures touching his own department. But, such is not the case. He wrote me that the Government had no further information to give but that he was taking up the matter with Colonel Boothby, general passenger agent of the Maine Central. My experience of railway men has been that they are hard-headed and long-headed business men as a rule, and Colonel Boothby wrote that, from the statistics in possession of his railway, and from the information he had been able to obtain from other railways, he believed that, in 1907, 250,000 people had come into the interior portion of the state of Maine, to the best of his knowledge and belief, mainly attracted by the excellent fishing and shooting furnished. If you apply the ratio of $100 per head spent by each visitor, you will find that, in that year, $25,000,000 in hard cash was brought into the State from this source, and left there. Now, the state of Maine is about one-eighth the size of the province of Ontario, and our geographical position to take advantage of that particular traffic is just as good as is that of the state of Maine, in reference to the great Mississipi valley, and more particularly in reference to New York state and the densely populated towns immediately to the south of us. At all events, the figures I have quoted will give an idea of the amount of money there is in fish and game properly protected.

It is the attraction to tourists in which the value consists, and I would point out to the members of the Commission that money attracted this way has a peculiar economic advantage to the country that gains it. Can you realize how many sticks of timber it would take to produce $25,000,000 net; how many pounds of minerals, what quantity of cereals, or how much capital? But in this case our fish and game attract the money brought in by tourists. This money is left with you, and represents a net gain, because, in return, you give for it practically nothing more than a little bit of healthy amusement. This is a view I would like you to consider seriously. I would ask you to take that view of it rather than the view which is apt to be taken by some people, that fish and game protection has no economic advantages and that it is all sentiment.

The Ontario Government placed on the statute book three years ago a non-resident angler's tax, and I flatter myself that I was partially instrumental in getting that tax imposed. It was done originally at the suggestion of the Ontario Forest, Fish and Game Protective Association. My particular object in that $2 fee, known as the non-resident angler's tax, was not the revenue derivable therefrom, although I have no doubt that the Provincial Treasurer takes considerable satisfaction in the fact that this year he has received from that source nearly $20,000; but, my principal object in advocating its imposition was that we might have some satisfactory information as to the number of sportsmen who visited us, and that we might show you, gentlemen, and such men as Mr. Byron E. Walker, that there was, beyond doubt, money in the game fish of the province of Ontario. The $20,000 received from that tax, this year, is positive proof that, at least 10,000 persons came into the Province primarily to fish, and, if you figure on an expenditure of $100 per head, as they do in the state of Maine, the Province gets from that source, at least $1,000,000. Now, that tax has only been collected for the last three years, and the machinery for the collection of it is not thoroughly perfected yet. I have other sources of information than the records, and I am quite sure that it is possible to collect at least twice that amount at present, and, if you will take my word for that, you will see that it brings the expenditure up to $2,000,000 for fishermen visiting in the province of Ontario. But it must be remembered that each person who comes in and pays that non-resident tax is not alone, and that many of them are fathers of families and bring with them some members of their family, so that there are a great many more persons actually coming in to the country than those who angle. I think I am safe in saying that there is probably brought into the province of Ontario at least $5,000,000 annually, and this would not come into the Province were it not that we have reasonably good angling.

But I wish again to rely upon that excellent address delivered by the Chairman. I noticed that, in it, he insisted upon the importance of preventing forest fires, and I know that the Hon. Mr. Cochrane takes a great interest in this particular form of protection of our natural resources. Now, it may be possible that this policy inaugurated by the Ontario Government of collecting a $2 non-resident angler's tax may be still further extended. The people have paid that tax very cheerfully, and, speaking as a private citizen, I think it is only fair that those who take advantage of our great public parks, over the management of which Hon. Mr. Cochrane presides, should pay a small registration fee, and in that I would include our own citizens. Part of this fee could go towards the revenues of the Province and towards the employment of more fire wardens. But, above all, the great advantage of such a fee would be that it would enable us to have a record of those persons who go into these regions ostensibly for the purpose of fishing and shooting, but who, often, in their negligence, are the cause of forest fires.

There is another idea which I would bring to the attention of the members of the Commission, showing the advantage of protection of our fish and game. It is this: that very often persons who are attracted to us in that way gain information in reference to the other resources of the Province and make investments here. Some years ago I heard the Hon. Mr. Carleton, of Maine, address a meeting in Boston, and he stated that he knew of two or three investments in the state of Maine which, in the aggregate, would amount to $3,000,000, and the principal directors of these companies had admitted to him that their attention was first drawn to this opportunity for investment when they came into Maine to fish. Strange to say, a year afterwards a man whom Hon. Mr. Carleton does not know at all, but whom you all know, Mr. Wallace Nesbitt, late one of the judges of the Supreme Court, made a statement before the Georgian Bay Fisheries Commission, to the effect that he knew of an investment in the province of Ontario of over $1,000,000, that had resulted entirely from the visit of certain gentlemen to the Province, who had been attracted by sport.

The Chairman of the Commission in his address also referred to the question of public health, and here is where that particular portion of his address coincides with a certain phase of the propaganda I am most interested in, viz., that fish food is a great advantage to the maintenance of public health. It so happens that the province of Ontario is far removed from the seaboard, and the price of sea fish is rather high, and it also happens that, through the machinations largely of the American Fish Trust, about 95 per cent. of the fresh-water fish catch in the province of Ontario goes to the United States. We are, therefore, face to face with a practical issue; the difficulty of obtaining fish in our Province. And, if the contention is correct that fish food is almost a necessity if the people are to be absolutely healthy, the problem is still greater. There are many ways of looking at the value of our food-fish in the province of Ontario—I am speaking now of the commercial fisheries—outside entirely of the approaching depletion of our waters. It is true that, if we sell this food supply to our neighbours to the south, we obtain a certain revenue therefrom, but I should judge that it is one of the objects of this Commission to examine, for instance, whether we are justified from the point of view of the public health in allowing the continued exportation of our fish, especially when we are face to face with the approaching absolute depletion of our supply, and when it is known that this food is going to the people of a country who, after all, are aliens to us. I think that I see, if I am not wrong, somewhere in the distance the question looming up of the prohibition, for a term of years, of the export of all food-fish from the Province of Ontario. I think that question may come up for the serious consideration of this Commission.

In the half-hour at my disposal I have endeavoured to give you some idea of a particular branch of conservation, and, in conclusion, I will point out that the conservation of the commercial fisheries, the game, the game fisheries and the forest, are all inextricably interwoven, and that any action taken with regard to one, must necessarily be action taken with regard to the others. I trust that those who come after us will have no reason to complain that we, of the present generation, have not done our duty in preserving these great assets which Providence has given to us.

WEDNESDAY EVENING

The Commission reassembled at 8 o'clock p.m. in the lecture hall of the Normal School. The chair was occupied by Honourable Francis L. Haszard, K.C., Charlottetown, Premier of Prince Edward Island.

MR. HASZARD: Ladies and Gentlemen,—The first paper on the programme is by Mr. F. T. Congdon, M.P., Dawson, on "Fur-bearing Animals in Canada, and How to Prevent their Extinction." The subject is one of great importance in Canada. Even in the part of the country from which I come we have a class of animals that is becoming highly important, and we hope that, in the not far distant future, it will become more important and much more numerous, as these animals have in recent years been conserved and taken care of. I refer to black foxes, which have been successfully raised in Prince Edward Island, and I have no doubt that what can be done in that Province can be done in other parts of Canada. I shall ask Mr. Congdon to address you.

FUR-BEARING ANIMALS IN CANADA, AND HOW TO PREVENT THEIR EXTINCTION

MR. CONGDON said:

Mr. Chairman, Ladies and Gentlemen,—

I trust that no one will imagine that I am an expert on the subject of fur-bearing animals or on the fur trade, simply because I am making a few remarks this evening. I happened to mention to the Chairman of the Commission a few things that had been communicated to me by those interested in the fur trade in the Klondike, and Mr. Sifton asked me if I would not prepare a short address on this subject for the Commission. My own knowledge of fur-bearing animals is gathered very largely from books, partly from my own experience in hunting, trapping and rambling through the woods and wilds, but most of it, from conversation with hunters, trappers and fur-traders.

The industry was at one time, as you know, the all-important industry in Canada, and at that time, if one may judge from history, it was too rigidly controlled by the authorities. We appear, then, to have passed through a period—and we have scarcely emerged from it yet—in which too little attention has been paid to the fur trade by the authorities in the Dominion of Canada.

The importance of the trade will be gathered from the statistics on the subject, which afford some very peculiar figures. It will be found that our export of undressed fur skins amounted to about $2,443,000, for the year ending March 31st, 1909. Of that, about $1,200,000 worth went to Great Britain, and something over $1,000,000 worth to the United States. I do not know what opportunities the customs officials of Canada have to determine what the export trade in fur is. I know that I have frequently gone out of Canada into the United States from the Yukon territory and have taken furs along with me. Coming from the Yukon, we take the first boat that happens along, whether it goes to a Canadian port or to Seattle, and I do not think I have ever come out myself, or ever known many others to come out, without taking furs, very often, to the United States. I never thought it necessary to make any entry at the Customs. I based my judgment of the accuracy of the figures in regard to the export trade in furs on what I know personally of the trade from the Yukon territory. The Yukon is credited for the year ending March 31st, 1909, with an export of only $19,500 worth of furs. I know of one man who came out during that year with at least $25,000 worth of skins. The reason for this inaccuracy is that no one is required to make an entry in regard to furs taken out of the country. I do not know what means the Government has of determining the amount of furs taken out of this country by the Hudson's Bay Company in its vessels *via* Hudson bay to England. I do know that, both in the Hudson Bay district and in a great part of the north, those who come into the country to purchase furs bring their goods from abroad and take the produce of their exchange with the Indians and trappers out of the country, so that very little benefit, apparently, is derived in Canada from the trade.

A peculiar feature of the statistics on the fur trade is that the export trade in undressed furs from Canada is practically the same as the import in undressed furs into Canada. The export trade in undressed furs is worth $2,443,000, the product of Canada, and the imports of undressed furs are valued at $2,674,418. We import from the United States undressed furs to the value of $1,918,755. If we add together the imports and exports of furs into this country, we find that there is a trade aggregating about $5,000,000, exclusive of the trade in dressed furs. The only explanation of the equality of imports and exports that I can think of, is that we export expensive and import cheap furs.

Thus it will be seen that the fur trade is one worthy of some consideration and attention in the Dominion of Canada. I was very much surprised in reading an article on the subject to-day to find that the export fur trade of the United States is greater than it was in the old days when the buffalo and other fur-bearing animals abounded in that country. The reason is that, to-day, the export trade in skunk, muskrat and fox skins from the United States exceeds in value the export in the old days when furs were much more abundant and when one would naturally expect the trade to be of much greater importance.

I wish to speak of this subject to-night simply in the commercial sense. I do not wish to touch upon the habits of animals or anything of that kind, but merely to treat of the fur trade as a commercial asset of the country.

The most serious losses in the fur trade to-day in Canada are occasioned by three causes: the first, the use of poison; the second, the lack of restraint in trapping; and lastly, the prevalence of wolves. The fur dealers will tell you that very little poison is used, because they will not give the same price for the skins of animals killed by poison as for the skins of those killed in the ordinary way by the use of traps. But I have enquired among the trappers about the matter and they tell me that, when an animal is killed in the cold weather, in the cold northern climate, it makes practically no difference to the skin, and that it is difficult, if not impossible, to tell whether an animal has been killed by poison or by trap. I believe that some claim that the blood-vessels immediately beneath the skin show more blood when poison is used. The use of poison is far-reaching in its evil effects, because, I am informed, that one animal that is poisoned with strychnine, the poison generally employed, will carry that deadly poison through no less than seven removes; that is to say, if an animal eat the flesh of another that has died from strychnine poisoning it will die, another eating its flesh will also die, and so on through seven removes from the first animal poisoned. Thus one may imagine the tremendous destruction caused by the use of poison.

It is difficult, in Canada, to regulate the use of poison, but it seems to me that the strongest and most severe measures should be adopted to entirely prevent its use by those engaged in the fur trade. In the Yukon, restraint on importation of poison could be made very effective. It has also been suggested that trappers should be required to register before entering on the business and also, to report exact particulars of their catches. Imperative requirement of entry of furs sought to be exported, ought to be imposed, as it should be for all exports, if for no other reason than for statistical purposes.

Another serious injury is due to the pressure of the market demand. It is a well established fact that there are cycles in fur production. What the length of the cycle is I do not know, but the occurrence is undoubted. The Hudson's Bay Company has kept records which show the occurrence of cycles during which fur production reaches a maximum, goes down to a minimum, and so on, up and down in fairly regular cycles. The improved modes of trapping now adopted by the trappers, the vast extent of territory formerly uncovered by pioneers, but which is now occupied by them, the immense improvement in traps and in all sorts of weapons create this danger: that when the production of furs is at the low point in the scale, the animals may be extinguished. When the production is at the maximum there is not, of course, the same danger. One difference between hunting by trappers and by Indians is that, while the Indian, whether through laziness or Providence—I would be inclined to attribute it to the former—always leaves a stock of all the fur-bearing animals in a district to continue the species, the white man does not. He goes into a "creek" and absolutely extinguishes all the individuals in it, and therefore makes it impossible that it should be restocked from any individuals left in the district.

Another danger is from the enormous increase in the number of wolves in many districts in Canada. I can see no other way in which that difficulty can be met than by increasing the area over which the bounty is allowed for the killing of wolves. Of course, in doing this great care must be taken to ensure that the killing is not done by poison, but by some other method that will extinguish the wolf and do no injury to other animals. It has been suggested that, if a particular wolf in each district were inoculated with some disease fatal to wolves, he might communicate it to other wolves and so extinguish them. But it is a very rash plan to adopt without further investigation to determine whether other evil effects would not ensue.

A skin that we particularly prize in the north and all over Canada is that of the marten. Other skins are fashionable and popular for a season or two, but I think its excellent quality, beautiful texture, softness of fur and uniform beauty of shading ensure that it will be a permanently valuable fur. A strange thing has occurred this winter in that a fur not highly esteemed in the past, the lynx, has suddenly become popular and valuable. Three years ago lynx could be bought for from $2·00 to $2·50 a skin. I am informed that the only reason for the enormous increase in value has been a discovery by the Germans, the adepts in dyeing, of a process of treating and dyeing that skin beautifully. Moreover, its rounded form gives an air of rotundity to tall, slight ladies that is highly desirable. I think that the popularity of this fur will not endure and that other furs will take its place. Of course, each season shows a popularity of some particular kind of fur, but marten and the richer furs will always be highly valued.

I do not know just what methods should be adopted in eastern Canada for the preservation of game and fur-bearing animals. It seems to me that the greatest benefit to the perpetuation of species would be derived from the creation of reserves over the country. It is a harsh measure to establish a general close season over the enormous extent of land in Canada capable of sustaining fur-bearing animals. By that course you inflict a great hardship upon trappers and pioneers. A widespread measure is difficult to enforce, but it seems to me that, if there were a great number of reserves established in various parts of Canada, these reserves being not too extensive in character and not intended to be permanent reserves, except in certain cases, you might, in that way, greatly encourage the increase of fur-bearing animals.

In the Yukon there are hundreds of square miles where I do not think you could now find a single fur-bearing animal. They have been absolutely exterminated by hunting, trapping, or by the decrease of the food supply which occurred in the years 1904-5. I believe, with regard to these areas, that if small reservations were made, in each of which there was an endeavour to encourage the breeding of some particular fur-bearing animal, a vast amount of good could be accomplished. I think it would be better to make the reservations smaller and limit each reservation to the protection of some particular animal. For instance, one reservation might be specially designed for breeding the marten, another for breeding the fox, and so on. These reserves would furnish a stock which would supply the surrounding country. It would be desirable that these reserves should be maintained for a period and then thrown open and other reserves created elsewhere in their places.

The great cause of the falling off in the number of fur-bearing animals is undoubtedly the disappearance of the rabbit. It is well established that, in some parts of Canada, there is a decrease in the number of rabbits, and in some sections they have almost disappeared. I remember that, up to 1904, every season I came by stage from Dawson to Whitehorse, 300 odd miles, I was never out of sight of rabbits for a hundred miles. You would see them everywhere, sometimes scores at a time. In that hundred miles there must have been tens of thousands of rabbits. In 1904-5 some disease smote the rabbits and they died off by thousands. 1 remember one night at a road-house we saw twenty or thirty rabbits around a stack of hay. Each of us caught one, and we found that they were all on the point of dying and did die before we left. That year the rabbits so completely disappeared that, up to last winter, it was almost impossible, in the extensive regions of the Yukon, to see a single rabbit. In consequence of their disappearance, the animals which fed on them—the fox, (the wolf, which need not be counted) the marten, whose chief food, however, is mice. and other animals—died from absolutely no other cause than starvation, and it does seem to me worthy of consideration, whether, in those large regions which we have in Canada and which can be valuable for nothing except mineral production and fur-bearing animals, it is not desirable to carry on investigations to ascertain whether some means could not be provided by which, on the septennial disappearance of the rabbit, some other food should take its place. I believe the hare, for instance, might be introduced into these regions of the country, and it might so happen that the period of disappearance of the hare would not synchronize with that of the disappearance of the rabbit. Undoubtedly the hare is as suitable for northern climates as the rabbit can be.

What I particularly desired to bring out with regard to this subject was the lack of any considerable study of the subject by any authorities in the Dominion of Canada, and I wish to invite the attention of the Commission to the necessity of investigating these various matters.

I have mentioned one fur, that of the marten, because I deem it the finest of all furs. There are, in addition, the mink, the otter, the fox, the ermine and innumerable other fur-bearing animals in Canada of great value; but I think it would be desirable, in the reservations I have spoken of, to give special attention to the better class of these fur-bearing animals and to endeavour especially to increase and multiply them and make them a source of greater revenue to the people of the Dominion of Canada. The low point of the cycle with regard to the fur trade has been passed. In 1904-5, or, possibly, in the following year, the very lowest period occurred in the fur supply in the northern lands of Canada, and I think this is true of Canada generally. We are now on the upward turn, and it seems to me that this is the time in which an endeavour should be made to stock some of the enormous unused lands in Canada with fur which will be valuable in the future. If it served no other purpose, it would supply a means of livelihood to the Indians, to whom we owe at least something, and it would ensure a larger production of furs in Canada than we have at present.

I would invite the attention of the Commission to one other question, and that is whether Canada could not develop to a greater extent the dyeing, dressing and manufacture of furs. It seems a strange thing that we should export about $2,500,000 of undressed furs and should import undressed furs of the same value, and that we should be able to dress the furs we import and not be able to dress the furs we export. I think that steps should be taken to enquire into the causes governing that, to inquire into this whole trade and to endeavour to devise some plan which will ensure its being of greater advantage to the people of Canada. I do not know that any one can, at present, say what is most likely to develop this trade. It seems to me that the first work of the Commission in regard to this subject, as in regard to many subjects that are now being broached for the first time before the Commission, must be to collect the information which will enable them later to develop and devise intelligent methods for increasing this trade.

In answer to a question respecting the quality of the mink from the Yukon Territory, Mr. Congdon said: I understand from fur dealers that the fur of the Yukon in many lines, mink included, is the very best in Canada. They say that the furs obtained in the Yukon are larger and finer in shape than the furs of any other part of Canada. That is particularly true with regard to the marten. The marten of the Yukon more nearly approaches Russian sable than anything else in the world. I think it is worthy of enquiring whether we could not import Russian sable into Canada. I do not think myself, that it is, in any respects superior to the Yukon and northern marten, but there undoubtedly is a strong prejudice in favour of the Russian sable, and the possibility of stocking parts of Canada with it is worthy of consideration. I need not mention the values of these furs. A marten skin of first class quality is worth $15. If you match it and have ten skins of the same quality well matched, they will bring $500 easily. If we can by any means increase an industry that already yields $2,500,000 annually, it is surely worth attempting.

In answer to a question whether the beaver could live in the Yukon, Mr. Congdon said: Oh, yes, you find them on all the rivers. I would like to take some of you up some of those rivers, because you would find them ideal, not only for fur-bearing animals, but for human beings. You can travel for hundreds of miles on rivers equal to the Ottawa, and I cannot imagine the world affording any more wonderful field for the production of fur-bearing animals. If the Government cannot do anything else for the fur trade in the north country, they can let the land out for pelting farms, and I would be as much in favour of giving a bonus to such an industry as to any other.

THE CHAIRMAN (Hon. Mr. Haszard): The next paper on the programme is that by Dr. Peter H. Bryce, M.A., M.D., Chief Medical Officer, Department of the Interior, Ottawa, on

MEASURES FOR THE IMPROVEMENT AND MAINTENANCE OF THE PUBLIC HEALTH

DR. BRYCE said:

To comprehend adequately the meaning of all that is implied in the term "National Health," it will be necessary to realize that, while the nation's health is primarily measured by the number of deaths in any given population, yet, from a national standpoint, it may further be understood as indicating the maintenance of the largest possible number of effective citizens, viewed from the standpoint of their economic value to the State. Thus, a nomad population in a temperate upland, living in simple fashion with its flocks and herds, may, under such conditions of life, naturally maintain a very high degree of individual health, and yet, from an economic standpoint, be but little comparable in social effectiveness with a busy industrial urban population living under sanitary conditions which have been rendered so good through present day scientific knowledge as to be compatible with the highest individual health.

It is therefore apparent that one must clearly distinguish, as Prof. W. Z. Ripley phrases it, "between the physical environment, which is determined independently of man's will, and that social environment which he unconsciously makes himself and which, in time, acts and reacts upon him and his successors in unexpected ways."

This is well illustrated, in his "The American Commonwealth," by the Hon. James Bryce, the British Ambassador to the United States, who says:—"The very multiplication of the means at his [man's] disposal for profiting by what nature supplies brings him into ever and more complex relations with her. The variety of her resources, differing in different regions, prescribes the kind of industry for which each spot is fitted; and the competition of nations, always growing keener, forces each to maintain itself in the struggle by using to the utmost every facility for the production or for the transportation of products."

Accepting these several dicta as expressing the generally accepted philosophic thought of to-day, we shall find that behind them lies the conception expressed by Dr. James A. Lindsey, M.A., of Belfast, in a paper on "Darwinism and Medicine": "That the organic world is the scene of an incessant struggle, of a keen, vital competition in which the fittest survive—that is, the fittest for the environment—in their capacity to obtain food, resist their enemies and propagate their kind, while the unfit perish, has been recognized as the fundamental law of life."

As Weismann says, this principle has become the basis of the science of life; it "has conquered the world and has become so inwrought in the texture of our thought that it is now practically impossible to think of any biological problem except in terms of evolution."

We can, therefore, clearly see that "The process of life is, as we begin directly to distinguish, a process of development which is, beyond all doubt, overlaid with a meaning that no school of scientific thought in the past has enunciated."*

The consideration of our subject naturally leads us to enquire what are the problems which a people have to consider as affecting their national health. Our people inhabit the northern half of a continent extending from the 42nd parallel to the pole, whose eastern rocky coasts are washed by the waters of the polar current; whose western shores are laved by the temperate waters of a warm ocean stream; whose western portion, with its warm valleys, is ribbed with mountain chains having their slopes dipping eastward to the boundless plains of the interior, which, again, reach to the forested areas of a low-lying rocky range, extending for thousands of miles. Such areas supply every condition for the development of the great basic industries of civilization. In adapting themselves to all these varied conditions of climate and occupation, Canadians, at the same time, have to devise means of preserving their health.

I.—Value of Population as a National Asset—Not until the value of population as a national asset is fully comprehended will any people be prepared to exercise systematically, either as individuals or as a community, those precautions necessary either to maintain or to improve its health to the highest degree possible under its particular environment. To-day France is struggling with a practically stationary population, and finds it necessary to go to its Algerian provinces to recruit its army; while its ancient rival, Germany, sees her population increased from 38,000,000 in 1871, to 68,000,000 in 1908, and her industrial population from 15,000,000 to 40,000,000. In the latter country, so vital to national greatness is population deemed, that the Kaiser has agreed to educate the eighth son of every family in Germany.

To illustrate the fact by a more familiar example, Ontario, which increased its population from 450,000 in 1841, to 1,396,000 in 1861,

---

* Benjamin Kidd, "Western Civilization."

with an increase of revenue from about $700,000 to about $3,500,000, grew but slowly from 1871 to 1900, having an increase in population of only 563,293, the total births being 1,200,000. For all Canada, the population in the several census periods was:—

1871	3,485,761
1891	4,833,239
1901	5,371,315
1906	6,320,000

The intimate relation between population and progress is seen in the trade returns:—

	EXPORTS	IMPORTS
1870	$ 84,214,000	$ 55,181,000
1906	283,282,000	231,483,000

It is interesting to supplement these figures by those for the same periods in the United States:—

POPULATION	TRADE RETURNS
1871—38,558,371	Imports—$ 435,958,408 Exports—$ 392,771,768
1890—62,622,250	Imports—$ 789,310,409 Exports—$ 857,828,684
1906—84,154,009	Imports—$1,226,562,000 Exports—$1,743,864,000

But the most remarkable illustration of the relation between national prosperity and a sturdy and industrious population is seen in that area called the twelve north-central States. The population was, in 1870, 12,981,111; in 1900, 26,333,006; while the value of farms and farm improvements increased from $3,451,000,000 in 1870, to $9,563,000,000 in 1900. The population, which was made up of 60% foreign born or the children of foreign born, produced more than 50% of the total agricultural wealth of the United States in 1900, and had in all the twelve States a death rate lower by 3 in 1,000 than for all the United States.

While immigration is thus shown to be a most potent factor in national development, it is yet more important, as illustrated by German statistics, that the native-born population shall have a normal increase both by a high birthrate, and the preservation of the infants born. Assuming a natural annual increase of 15 per 1,000, within 15 years over one-third is added to any normal population. Further, it is apparent that, within fifteen years from birth, some 35% of such a population would move into the class of at least partial producers and, were the nation's existence at stake, into the ranks of her defenders. But, it is further apparent that the preservation of the lives of the workers in the periods beyond 15 years, and of the mothers of the nation, who go to recruit the population, is equally a part of the programme of conserving the national wealth and resources. In a word, it is apparent that we must attempt what H. C. Patten, M.A., M.H.O., Norwich, England, in a recent article has called "The State Standardization of our National Life." He says: "We say implicitly that it is to the national interest and vital to our social welfare that every child shall receive a miminum amount of education... In all sobriety and earnestness we must think out for ourselves and endeavour to make others realize what are the essentials of a healthy communal existence, what standards in feeding, in housing, in medical assistance, in education, in physical training, in recreation, we are prepared to advise."

II.—The Preservation of Infant Life—Dr. George Newman, Chief Medical Officer of the Board of Education, England, has said that it is "evident that the problem of disease and physical unfitness from infancy to the end of school life is, broadly speaking, one and the same; and that the conditions and circumstances, whatever they may be, which produce a high mortality rate, are also exerting an injurious influence on the childhood of the State much beyond the age of infancy."

To understand the full importance of the statement the following table is given:

DEATHS PER 1,000 FROM ALL CAUSES

	under 1 year	1–5 years	5–10 years	10–15 years	Total ages 1-15
Mortality in England and Wales, 1907	117·62	17·58	3·37	1·97	15·00
Mortality in Ontario, census, 1900	132·00	14·5	3·3	2·3	16·30

The figures regarding infant mortality should be considered in conjunction with the facts that the average death rate in 1901–7 for the United Kingdom was 161 per 1,000, while that for Ontario in 1902 was 126. What Canada loses or gains may be seen in the figures for 1900. A somewhat greater death rate is seen in Germany, where, of 2,000,000 births annually, some 400,000—or 20%—die within the first year of life.

Figures comparable to the foregoing are given in the Mortality Bulletin for 1908 of the United States census. According to it, almost one-fifth of all the deaths were of infants under 1 year, and over one-quarter of the deaths were of children under 5 years, or there were (estimated) 273,000 deaths of infants under 1 year and some 400,000 under 5 years.

Regarding the death rate in England, Newman points out that 30% of the mortality under 1 year of age occurs during the first month, and that the mortality is one-third higher in urban than in rural districts.

The Registrar General classifies the causes as (1) common infectious diseases; (2) diarrhœal diseases; (3) wasting diseases; (4) tubercular diseases; (5) other causes. It is worthy of notice that while the deaths under one year have not, in England, shown any notable decline, those between 1 and 5 years have, since 1860, shown a decline of 40 per cent., due, in large measure, to the municipal control of contagious diseases.

The meaning of these figures from the standpoint of economic loss will be understood when it is seen that, in the population of England and Wales, which is approximately 40,000,000, there are lost to the nation during the first two years of life, 150,000 children; while a very large number, although escaping death, have the seeds of disease. This may be seen in the results of the examination of school children under the new English Act requiring the medical inspection of all school children. Thus, in an examination of 459 school children in a single suburban London district, Dr. George Carpenter, of the Queen's Hospital for Children, found that of 459 presumably healthy children—249 boys and 210 girls between 3 to 7 and 10 to 15 years of age—234 had weak ankles or flat feet, 200 had rickety deformities, 367 had decayed teeth (1,514 decayed teeth in all), 119 had enlarged tonsils, 129 had adenoids, 21 were deaf from catarrh, 9 had discharging ears, 181 had deep cervical glands enlarged, 177, the submaxillary glands enlarged, 337, the superficial cervical, 252 had inguinal glands enlarged, 81 had hernia.

If it is assumed that the population of Canada, while in many respects better born, better fed and better clothed than that of England, has, owing to less generally developed and more imperfectly executed sanitary laws in a more severe climate, an equally high mortality as that of England, it is apparent that there will be an annual loss of 26,250 lives during the first two years of life. Actually, in 1901 the loss to Canada was 81,201 or, in a population of 7,000,000 would have been over 100,000. If, of the total children born in English, American or Canadian cities, some 8% die within the first month from birth, then it is apparent that there must exist conditions as regards either (a) the health of the mother or (b) the post-natal environment of the children, whether poor nursing, or lack of clothing or of fresh air, which are accountable for such a serious mortality. In England and in many European and American industrial centres, it is not an infrequent thing for the mothers of very young children to go to the factory, leaving the baby to be cared for at a crèche or nursery kept by one of their own class. As there is almost inevitably overcrowding, foul air, neglect and artificial feeding, it is not difficult to understand the cause of the high mortality. There is, as yet, but little of this practice in Canada, but, in certain large cities, the practice has begun. So common is the practice in England that systematized attempts to cope with it are being made. This is being done in the "Infant Depots" of Sheffield, which were established with the idea of actually teaching mothers the rules of good nutrition. They thereby tend to prevent, lessen and cure chronic gastro-intestinal disorders and so raise the general standard of the health of infants. This scheme, probably the most important of any public health measure for saving infant life, in order to be successful, demands an efficient staff of trained workers and health visitors to encourage, advise and gain the confidence of mothers by visiting their homes in a friendly manner rather than as officers of an inquisitorial or police surveillance.

The milk depot is to educate mothers how to prepare properly, infants' artificial food. Dr. A. E. Naish, M.A., Sheffield Royal Hospital, says "that apart from the direct benefits, which he shows are abundant in the gain of health and weight of children, this women's school for babies has succeeded in raising a spirit of emulation amongst mothers which it would be hard to reach in any other way." It need hardly be pointed out that the school will extend its lessons to show the necessity of the better care which a mother should take of her own health. From the standpoint of conserving the lives of the future workers it supplies the most logical and potent agency yet developed in public health work. What it means will be understood when it is pointed out that, if 25% of the deaths of children under one year in England could be prevented, it would mean 30,000 lives saved annually and, at the same death rate, some 7,000 in Canada. The marvel is that almost nowhere has a civilized community hitherto organized in any country any official department intended systematically to save the lives of infants.

An organized, if unofficial work which is essentially preventive is that of the social workers of different hospitals, especially illustrated by that of the Massachusetts General Hospital, where there is a regular staff of eight trained social workers with a number of volunteers. It was found that the hospital and dispensary patients treated needed more than medical treatment. Many have no funds to buy even the medicine required. Hence the hospital workers come in touch with many most varied charitable agencies and their work becomes both preventive and curative.

How directly associated with this work is the municipal control of the milk supplied to children will be shown later in dealing with the question of public milk supplies. The work of the Nathan Strauss laboratories in New York city in supplying pasteurized milk at a minimum cost, especially during the summer, has been shown to have been the direct means of saving hundreds of babies. To illustrate only one point, viz., the importance of the care of the food of babies, statistics are given to show that, in some German cities (and similar conditions prevail elsewhere) the cause of deaths of children is due to diarrhœal diseases to the extent of from 36 to 54%. These are caused by milk through the bacteria of fermentation, for it has been pointed out that 51% of artificially fed infants have died, and only 8% of the breast fed; while in France, of the 20,000 infants who died, four-fifths were bottle fed. As applied to the preservation of the lives of the 175,000 children born annually in Canada, the importance of the fact will be fully appreciated, when it is further realized that at Heidelberg, in Germany, some 40% of all cows slaughtered has been found to be tuberculous. It will be understood how the inoculation with this disease, whose effects increasingly appear in later years, may be conveyed through the milk of cows. How potent a factor, even in the case of children, this becomes is seen from the fact that a statistical analysis of the deaths in a single English county (Dr. H. W. Taxford, M.O.H., Holland Parish Council) shows that 8% of the total deaths in the first four years of life were registered as due to tuberculosis, and 9% to disorders of nutrition, most of which were probably tubercular. The other infectious diseases in this county caused 14% of the total mortality and included 7% due to measles, 3% due to whooping cough, 0.9% due to scarlatina, and 5% due to diphtheria, while 1.7% were due to diseases of the respiratory system, such as bronchitis and pneumonia. In all, the deaths amounted to 7 per 1,000 of the total population.

It is of the utmost importance to realize that from 20% to 25% of the total infectious deaths from 0 to 4 years inclusive, in England and in Canada, too, are due to whooping cough and measles alone, both of which, in a special manner, give the bacillus of tuberculosis, if present, its opportunity of becoming the cause of a general infection.

As the death rates in this case were clearly comparable to those in Canada, it will be seen that the percentage of the population from 0 to 4 years is almost 25% of any total population. The reduction of the deaths even 5 per cent. in a population of 7,000,000 would, in five years, add 30,000 native born children to the population. That such is possible may be inferred from the fact that in Ontario, from 1882 to 1902, with an increasing population, the deaths from the acute contagious diseases fell from 4,670 to 1,768.

What prevention in the case of a single disease may mean is illustrated by the decrease in deaths from diphtheria. Thus, there were 4,541 deaths in 1881 in Canada from this disease; 3,536 in 1891; 1,982 in 1901; while the population had increased some 33% in 1901 as compared with 1881.

III.—The Health of School Children—In any ordinary population about one-seventh die within the school ages of from 5 to 15 years. The notable reduction in deaths due to the contagious diseases of childhood has been already noted; and in no department has more public health progress been made, both in Europe and America, than in school sanitation. The progress of this branch has, within the past ten years, been extremely satisfactory, and has been measured by the extent to which the medical inspection of schools has been systematically adopted in our great centres of population. By the act of 1907, medical school inspection was made compulsory throughout England and Wales, while it has been operative in Boston, New York and Chicago for from 10 to 15 years.

In Canada, it is only just beginning. Its first positive benefit is illustrated in the early discovery of initial and mild cases of the acute contagious diseases. The value of the work may be judged from the fact that, under old time methods when no school inspection existed, out of 17,704 cases of scarlet fever in London, Eng.:—

>5,279 cases were under 5 years;
>6,729 cases, from 5 to 9 years;
>3,187 cases, from 10 to 14 years;

or but 29% were under 5 years. In a similar outbreak in Toronto in 1897, 70% of the total cases were in school children, though the ratio of population for the two periods is 11 under 5 years to 6 over that age.

What prompt and effective work in dealing with outbreaks amongst children means, cannot be better illustrated than by a single instance which occurred in the city of Ottawa in 1903. For years Ottawa had an unenviable notoriety in the matter of contagious diseases. In 1902, there were, in all, 609 cases of scarlet fever and 234 of diphtheria. In February, 1903, a new well-equipped isolation hospital was opened, and after March, all cases of these diseases were sent to the hospital. During the first three months of the year, 161 cases of the two diseases occurred, and but 159 in the succeeding nine months, or, compared with nine months in 1902, there was an actual reduction of 75% in cases and a reduction in deaths of 85% in scarlatina and 54% in diphtheria.

Begun in New York in 1897, medical school inspection had been extended in 1906, to 5,007,244 examination of school children, who were inspected in 88,813 school visits by trained physicians. The work is carried on by a staff consisting of the chief medical inspector and 200 medical assistants, together with a supervising nurse and a corps of trained nurses. All cases of suspected contagious diseases are at once excluded, 12,895 being excluded in 1906. Each medical inspector is assigned to a group of schools, which he visits daily by 10 o'clock and examines in a separate room (a) all children reported by teachers as appearing unwell; (b) all children who have been absent; (c) all returning after having been excluded; (d) all referred by the nurse for diagnosis. A routine physical examination is made of each child sent in, and a complete record of each is kept. The inspector gets lists of absentees, and these are visited in their homes. The nurses report each morning at each school at a specified time in order to treat the minor contagious cases which were ordered to report to them. They make weekly visits to the schoolrooms to make a routine examination of the eyelids, hair, skin and throat of each pupil. The Department maintains a hospital and two dispensaries. The total number of complete physical examinations made in 1906 was 78,401. Of these, 37,000 suffered from diseased glands, 17,928 from defective vision, and 56,259 required treatment of some kind. It is at once apparent that it is the diseases of nutrition, especially those indicating tubercular infection of some part of the body, which form at least two-thirds of the total cases.

The work of prevention has been promoted in London, Boston, Germany and elsewhere by having delicate, crippled and mentally dull children brought together in special schools. This work of prevention, especially in England, has been extended to the feeding of school children in the poorer districts. It has, moreover, been found by medical inspectors of schools in one or two Canadian cities that, even here, in not a few cases, where fathers leave home early and mothers go out to work, the school children are often but poorly fed and nourished.

In a report by Dr. R. Crowley, school medical officer, Bradford, England, for 1908, it is pointed out that from 1,500 to 2,665 dinners were given monthly, and in the last three months of the year, from 1,500 to 1,900 breakfasts were likewise given. Schoolrooms of churches or other convenient places, sometimes the school premises, were utilized and meals given at a cost, including all administration expense, of 1·88d. per meal.

Giving the mid-day meal is of great educational value, teaching cleanliness of the hands and person generally, and demonstrating the great need of giving individual attention to poor children. When it is fully realized that the school is the first place where the State, under ordinary circumstances, comes into official contact with the individuals of a community and that, for some time, it largely undertakes the control of the life of the future worker or producer in some branch of industry, it is of the utmost importance that this control should be of the most perfect character, viewed from the physical standpoint. There is probably not more than one child in three who, in some particular, does not require education in physical culture to correct either inherited defects or those acquired in the home or school environment on account of bad lighting, foul air and bad seating. The first daily lesson in every school should be a graded one in physical culture, either as calisthenics or gymnastics. All the benefits of a trained militia can be had without more than nominal cost if we would utilize all our regular militia as drill instructors. It would be of the greatest benefit, both to the health of the pupil and to the discipline of the school. How slowly such reforms in methods have come is seen in the fact that, as long ago as 1859, Sir Edwin Chadwick, the father of State medicine in England, pointed out, before the Social Science Congress, that not only could 40 school boys be trained in physical and military drill for the same cost that it took to make one recruit into a soldier, but further, that it was a training of the physical frame at an age when it was readily influenced before the bony parts were set, and when the mind was responsive to teaching which became a permanent part of the boy's make-up.

IV.—Typhoid Fever—In north temperate climates the prevalence of this disease has long been accepted as the measure of organized municipal citizenship. A new mining camp, a fish-cannery town, or a summer resort place, has, with our *laissez faire* American methods, always been presupposed to run itself in a sanitary fashion, precise governmental supervision never preceding proper municipal organization. The fiction was apparently believed that all the sanitary requirements of a well organized community would spring up full armed like Athene from the brow of Jupiter. So far as I know, there never has been a new settlement started in Canada which has not paid its penalty in lives, in suffering and in expense from an epidemic of typhoid, a disease, of all those which we know, the most directly controlled by an active town council and health board, through adopting and enforcing up-to-date methods of disposing of excreta and supplying good water. Though with but few of such new centres developing in the census year of 1900, Canada paid her debt to filth, stupidity and carelessness to the extent of 1809 deaths and some 20,000 cases of typhoid. The point will impress itself upon us when it is seen that, in 1907, the Ontario returns showed that, in the eighteen cities of 508,510 population, there were but 179 deaths from typhoid, while in a population of 102,797 in Algoma, Nipissing, Thunder Bay and Rainy River districts together, there were 121 deaths, or 1·17 per thousand, as compared with ·35 per thousand, or over three times as many deaths per thousand as in districts where pure water supplies guarded against pollution, existed. That these deaths in the new territories were nearly all among the strength and vigour of our young Canadian manhood makes the economic loss and the story of our administrative indifference, neglect and ineffectiveness all the greater.

I cannot do better to illustrate the situation than by quoting the causes given in a report of the Provincial Health Officer of Ontario regarding a typhoid outbreak in Sault Ste. Marie in 1906. As given these were:—(1) The location of the intake pipe of the Steel plant water supply where it could not fail to pump up water from a polluted source; (2) The location of the city water pipe proper in the power canal, liable for all the months of navigation to pollution with sewage; (3) Many shallow polluted wells; (4) Unprotected and polluted springs and streams; (5) Cesspools and privies polluting well waters; (6) Surface ditches carrying filthy house waters to the street gutter; (7) Filthy premises; (8) Flies carrying pollution from infected excreta to the food exposed in kitchens; (9) Use of polluted water by dairymen; (10) Personal carelessness and neglect to disinfect excreta and linen by those nursing the sick.

The recommendations made were simple: they simply advocated the removal of the ten insanitary conditions enumerated.

At the present moment Cobalt is pointing the moral and Montreal adorning the tale of the unerring vengeance which Nature takes upon those who violate her plainest laws regarding cleanliness in the disposal of organic wastes. This moral was well illustrated when twenty thousand men, or one-third, of Lord Roberts' army were rendered ineffective from typhoid at Bloemfontein, with a death roll of ten per cent.; while a similar toll was paid by sixty thousand volunteers camped in relays at Chickamauga during three months in 1898, where a beautiful park with its pure spring creeks was turned into a plague spot by official stupidity and lack of sanitary organization. The melancholy story of official stupidity and lack of sanitary arrangements in both these cases has been told us in official reports and needs no further reference, except to compare it with the results of the opposite condition in the case of the Japanese army in the Russo-Japanese war, and with the three years' operations on the Assuan dam, on the Nile, where fifty thoussand men were engaged and practically no deaths, either from cholera or typhoid, occurred.

Apart, however, from the Ontario figures, which show typhoid to have steadily declined where 125 water supplies have been introduced during twenty-five years, the decennial decrease in deaths per thousand from this disease in England and Wales was as follows:—

PERIOD	DEATHS PER THOUSAND
1871 to 1881	·322
1881 to 1890	·198
1891 to 1900	·174
1901 to 1905	·110

Similarly, the German cities which, before their water supplies were filtered, showed death rates similar to those of the great American cities, have had the death rate reduced as is seen in the following table:—

Cities	Deaths per thousand
Hague	·049
Rotterdam	·052
Dresden	·069
Vienna	·070
Munich	·070
Berlin	·080

As compared with these, Cleveland in a single year, 1893, had 494 deaths, or more than the total in all Ontario in 1902, while Chicago, up to the year when the drainage canal was completed, had from five to six hundred deaths annually, which rate was reduced by the drainage scheme by more than 50 per cent. To show, however, that the death rate from typhoid is still excessive in many American cities, Pittsburgh may be given as an extreme example, with its 500 deaths in 1904, in a population of 375,000. Dealing with larger figures, from

the United States census of 1905 it is found that in a population in
the registration states and cities there were the following deaths:—

	Population	Deaths from typhoid
States	32,996,989	10,557
Cities	23,724,258	8,200

Or, in the cities during 1901–1904 there was an annual death rate of
nearly 40 per thousand, as compared with 11 per thousand in England,
7 in Germany and 5 in Norway.

To show that scientific supervision, instead of municipal *laissez
faire* and ineffectiveness, operates directly in saving life, the example
of the European cities already quoted may be given; while the further
facts of Japan with 40 million people having, in 1903, but 4,292 deaths
and England with the same population but 4,000 deaths, emphasize
the point still more. Remembering that typhoid is in a peculiar degree
a disease of adolescence and adult life, the economic loss may be compared in American and German cities. When we realize that each life
is worth at least a thousand dollars to the State, we find the loss from
typhoid alone to be $10,000,000 in a year in 32,000,000 population, as
compared with $4,760,000 in a German population of 68,000,000. The
history of Ontario cities and towns, with 125 good public water supplies,
as compared with some of these American cities, proves the enormous
economic advantages of such freedom from typhoid; while the epidemies of Ottawa in 1888, of Winnipeg in 1906, and of Montreal to-day,
give adequate emphasis to the scientific fact now absolutely demonstrated that, given the natural waters of Canada in their native purity,
they are capable of supplying an absolutely safe public and domestic supply of potable water. On the other hand, it is equally true
that, if through individual or municipal neglect they become polluted
with sewage, sooner or later their degree of pollution will be measured
by the typhoid death rate.

V.—Tuberculosis—We have spoken of the deaths due to infant
mortality, to the often serious influences of school life upon health, and of
the deaths due to typhoid fever, the influences at work in all these cases
being, at least in part, such as the individual cannot control. But in
tuberculosis we have a disease which in a peculiar degree becomes the
gauge of individual effectiveness, measured from the physical, ethical or
economic standpoint. Indeed, it has been truly said that we have in nothing else so accurate a measure of the social and scientific plane upon
which any modern community lives as that of its comparative immunity
from tuberculosis. It is the disease of house life, not the disease of the
pioneer shack town; it is the pest of the densely populated city, with

its slums and overcrowded work rooms and factories, rather than of the farm house or rural settlement—albeit a densely populated Indian hut may exist even on the boundless prairie. It is a disease which, while often dependent for its evolution upon an attack of measles in the child or upon the exhausting effects of typhoid on the young man, tells especially the story of poverty, ignorance and dissipation, not alone in the individual himself, but in his parents.

Whether, or not, it is due to ingestion of food or to dust carrying tubercular bacilli, all recent scientific studies point to the fact that the larger amount of tuberculosis is the result of infection in infancy. Dr. R. W. Phillips, of Edinburgh, has recently stated before the British Medical Association that out of several groups of children selected at random in Edinburgh he found no fewer than 30% with undoubted traces of tuberculosis. Drs. Floyd and Bowditch, of Boston, have reported on ten thousand cases examined at the outpatient department of the Boston consumptive hospital and found that 38% showed definite pulmonary lesions and 30% more gave evidence of tuberculosis in some part of the body; while 67% were the children of tuberculized patients.

As the percentage rate of deaths from this disease, whether in Boston or in Edinburgh, is equalled, and even exceeded, in some cities of Canada, it is apparent that the causative conditions exist here much in the same degree as elsewhere. Thus the census of 1901 gives the following deaths:—

Toronto	419	or 2.00 per thousand	
London	43	" 1.19 "	"
Hamilton	97	" 1.80 "	"
Ottawa	136	" 2.30 "	"
Montreal	561	" 2.10 "	"
Quebec	172	" 2.50 "	"
Halifax	149	" 2.80 "	"
St. John	63	" 1.50 "	"
Winnipeg	69	" 1.60 "	"
Vancouver	66	" 2.40 "	"

As is well known, it is not alone that tuberculosis causes more than 10% of the deaths in most of our municipalities, that it is to be dreaded, but that the death itself is but the record of the end link in a chain of circumstances, which, beginning often with the delicate child in infancy, have linked themselves to the struggle for health during adolescence and thereafter, during the years when the individual has had to provide for himself in a losing game year by year, the ability to labour growing less and along therewith the revenues to maintain him or his family constantly decreasing. The most recent figures available for illustration, are those for Ottawa in 1909, which show 137 deaths from tuberculosis in 83,000 population, or 1·65 per thousand, of whom all but 22 were over fifteen years and almost without exception, belonged to the wage-earning classes and lived in the smaller houses in the older wards of the city. When it is remembered that 80% of the population of any ordinary city are included under this class, the loss through the prevalence of this chronic disease or the gain from its diminution, will be realized by all.

Professor W. F. Wilcox, M.D., of Cornell University, has referred to two modes of viewing the effects of tuberculosis economically, the first being the effect upon the average life of the individual and the other its effect upon the earning power of the community. He then adds: "A statement that the elimination of tuberculosis would increase each person's expectation of life at birth by a specified number of months seems to me a truer measure of the weight of that incubus on society than a statement that its removal would increase the earnings of the community by a specified number of dollars. We do not live in order to earn; we earn in order to live or to live well."

Adapting the British Life table to New York, Wilcox quotes Dr. Hayward as saying before the British Congress on Tuberculosis in 1901, that "if there had been no phthisis the average length of life of each individual born would have been increased by two and a half years. With tuberculosis eliminated and all other conditions unchanged, a male child at birth would have an expectation of living 45.9 years, instead of 43.3; a female child at birth would have an expectation of living 49.2 years, instead of 46.7. Owing to the special incidence of tuberculosis on the years of working life, this gain would benefit mainly the adult population. A youth of fifteen years would have an increase of more than three years in the total expectation of life, were tuberculosis to disappear." To give a concrete illustration, we may take the 115 deaths of persons of 15 years or over, who died in Ottawa last year, and by adding three years to the life of each we would be adding at least $350,000.00 to the wealth of the country.

We have already pointed out that in fifteen years at least one-third of the population of any country moves from the non-producing years, under fifteen, into the producing sphere. If a person dies before he becomes a producer, we say, economically, that the parents alone lose their outlay on his maintenance, since he has not yet been a producer; but if he dies after becoming a producer, it is as if he had left the country; or, if he remains at home and his care during illness costs more than he produces, then clearly he becomes an economic loss. Professor Wilcox, taking the figures for New York State, with a population of some eight millions, finds that 27% of the total population was between the productive years of 16 and 65, and that there were 605,519 male wage earners and 98,012 salaried officials, or 701,531 in all. The average annual earnings of all was $657.00 per annum per person. There was a total number of deaths from tuberculosis in this year, 1906, of 16,570, so that, applying the figures regarding the value of the earnings to the State lost in a single year from both men and women, Wilcox puts the loss at $52,233,467. As he puts their loss of service to the State and the further cost of their care and maintenance for at least nine months of sickness, at $2.50 per day, the total economic loss in a single year becomes $63,418,217.00. A similar death rate in Canada, with her estimated seven millions population, would mean some $54,000,000, or, estimating this on the actual death rate in 1901, it would mean a loss of actually $50,000,000 in 1908 to Canada, from deaths due to tuberculosis.

VI.—Deaths Due to Industrial Causes—These are recognized *en gros* when one reads the number of deaths in any year through railway accidents and the number of persons injured; but seldom is the public deeply impressed, unless when an accident, such as that occurring at the Quebec bridge, carries its hundred or more workmen to a sudden death. The distribution of deaths, by occupation, is not easily obtainable, but a few particulars are available. Thus, in 1908, there were, in Canada, 436 persons killed by steam railways and 2,360 injured, and on electric railways, 67 men killed and 1883 injured. In the death returns of Ontario for 1907 the list of occupations gave 9,107 housewives, 4,214 farmers and 2,728 labourers; but in no other class were there more than half as many deaths as those given for accidents on railways. While the deaths due to railway and street car accidents are liable always to become the occasion of suits for damages, and the companies, naturally, seek to minimize them, yet a much larger number of deaths probably result from the lack of ordinary precautions for safeguarding life in occupations of every kind, from coal mining down to departmental stores, through ignorance, indifference or the want of appreciation of the value of a human life. This is seen probably in its grossest form in the rough work incident to new mining camps and railway construction, where the immigrant, often ignorant of the work and of sanitary laws, is too often subjected to conditions or allowed to live under such surroundings as are wholly incompatible with health or life. Legal enactments intended to minimize such evils exist; but such camps illustrate the struggle where life in the rough is between man fighting for an existence and capital fighting for the maximum profits.

But ample illustrations have been given of how, at every stage in the life of the individual, from childhood to old age, as in that of the forest tree, man is beset with dangers. What these are, we know to-day in a very large degree, and in some measure we likewise understand how to avoid or combat them. But, as in the neglect of protecting the forests against parasitic diseases, insects and fire, and against cutting the tree before its prime, so it is too often not so much ignorance of methods as lack of the keen appreciation of the benefits to be derived from them, or a selfish greed for immediate gain rather than a waiting for deferred profits, which makes protective or conservation work ineffective either as regards trees or men.

VII.—Preventive Measures—It seems proper, however, that we should indicate what it is possible to do to protect human life against some of the more serious causes of death which have been indicated.

A—PROTECTION TO INFANT LIFE

Though difficult in their application, the methods to be adopted are quite evident, namely: (1) better housing required. This increases with education in sanitation, morals and in provident living, and is essentially a matter for society, for the municipality and for the State to assist in. (2) Improvement of the food supply. This is primarily a question of a safe and abundant milk supply, and, as the figures given of the deaths of children fed on artificial food show, dominates in importance every other health question relating to children. After studying the problem for twenty-five years and observing the very inadequate results obtained up to date, where the problem is most advanced, I am convinced that not until the State regulates and establishes methods even more exact and scientific for the control of public milk supplies than are already utilized with regard to public water supplies— in other words, not until the State provides a *municipalized public milk supply*—will the children be in any adequate degree protected. When the milk trust obtains control of the food supply, as at present in New York, of about a million babies, and reduces farmers' profits to a vanishing point, it is surely time, if government stands in any way related to the good of the people, that it should undertake to deal both with the quality and the price of this one essential of infant life.

Illustrating the situation from the last annual Boston report, some 300,000 quarts of milk go daily to that city, of which 90% must reach it by rail. Through railway commissions, and under interstate commerce laws, the delivery of milk could be regulated by receiving on trains only such as has been shown to be up to a given standard. It could be kept cool during transportation, as fruit and butter for export are now kept, and it could be distributed by the municipality and paid for as water or gas is paid for. Instead of the pitiable exhibition of a filthy cart dodging from house to house on different streets in a broiling summer day, ladling out almost certain death to little children, cool milk, not altered by the germs of fermentation, would be delivered from door to door on every street, and a charge made sufficient to cover the outlay of inspection and handling. There is no item in the life of a child which has for the State a tithe of the importance which the milk supply has, and to-day a filthy cow in a filthier stable, handled by an ignorant or indifferent labourer, is accepted almost everywhere as a thing to be tolerated even in a progressive community. During cholera outbreaks, sieges and famines, public authorities have hitherto policed the food and regulated the prices; and it seems high time, when nearly 25% of the children born die within the year of birth, that drastic regulations for the handling of milk should be put into force.

Taking up "Public Health," the monthly journal of the medical health officers of England, for January, 1910, just after writing this paragraph, I was pleased to find that New Zealand, that colony with co-operative schemes applied by government, has actually put into practice essentially what has been insisted upon in this address as necessary. In Wellington, N.Z., the city council has the following milk regulations:—(a) There shall be a municipal milk station at which all milk arriving by train shall be inspected and cooled, and only inspected milk shall be allowed to be sold as household milk. (b) All dairies and herds shall continue to be inspected by the Department of Agriculture and all cans and receptacles are to be approved. (c) Within six months all dairy herds shall have been tuberculine tested, and must thereafter be tested yearly. (d) Milk brought in by road need not go to the milk station if it be shown that it is delivered within four hours after milking, and should the vendor undertake to have his milk tested as to quality. (e) All dairies must be licensed. (f) All milk passing through the station must pay a nominal charge for inspection. (g) Milk sent into the city by rail must not be delivered at the station later than four hours after milking. (h) To ensure proper domestic treatment of milk the Town Council encourages the visiting nurse system and, to encourage proper feeding of infants, provides a certain amount of free milk to the poor as recommended by the nurses. (i) All milk shops must be licensed and milk alone sold, and it must be kept in specially ventilated and separated compartments.

B—IMPROVEMENT OF THE HEALTH OF SCHOOL CHILDREN

The methods adopted for inspecting school children in New York and elsewhere have been set forth, and but little more need be urged than the adoption of such methods, excepting that close watch must be kept against overcrowding. Care should also be taken to ensure abundant ventilation, which, in many of our schools, is very partial, and to secure adequate lighting as well. The increase of short sight and abnormal vision has raised the serious question of how such is rendering employees in many lines of work ineffective as regards producing the best results in the industry concerned. Scientific lighting, ventilation and construction of workshops and stores is a matter which, as yet, is wholly haphazard with us, and everywhere eyes are being permanently injured by constant work in dark rooms lighted by the glare of electricity instead of sunlight. The system of school nurses following the children to their homes is in many instances the first forward step toward the sanitary reformation of whole households. Cases of acute or chronic disease are often discovered in this way, and aid is brought to them, while the school class is secured against infection.

C—PREVENTION OF TYPHOID AND OTHER DISEASES DUE TO ORGANIC FILTH

The methods to this end have been indicated in the preceding pages; but it is essential, in discussing such a problem having a national bearing, to point out that, apart from provincial and interprovincial streams in Canada, there are twenty-three international rivers and streams, in addition to the Great lakes, which, in many instances, have already become polluted, and the rest are likely to follow with the rapidly increasing settlement on both sides of the border. To-day the St. Clair, the Detroit, the Niagara and the St. Lawrence are being grossly polluted, and the two great countries have, as yet, taken no steps towards dealing with the problem. The first move made in the matter was at the last session of the Senate of Canada, and it is to be hoped that the principles laid down in the evidence before the committee, which is now being published, will be followed by Federal legislative action. The progress made by European countries in the work of preventing the pollution of streams and in the purification of public water supplies has been abundantly shown in statistics already given; but in Canada, while the provinces have done much in some instances, interprovincial streams, like the Ottawa, await the conjoint action of different provinces or the assumption by the Federal authorities of jurisdiction clearly within their power. Though this is true, it must not be forgotten that the conservation of public water supplies is primarily a municipal consideration, to be supported by Rivers Conservancy Boards, appointed by the general Government to deal with the watersheds of our several streams. There would seem to be no more urgent or appropriate field of operation for the Commission of Conservation than that of undertaking at once the study in detail, from the public health standpoint, of the principal watersheds and river basins of Canada, which already have become populous, and, where the streams, which are the supplies of the people's drinking water, are already polluted and will become increasingly more so if preventive measures are not taken.

D—PREVENTION OF TUBERCULOSIS

To attack the prevalence of this disease—due both to house density and municipal ineffectiveness—is to lay down a programme dealing with milk and meat foods, the housing problem, the school problem, the factory problem, and, indeed, with every sphere of human activity, where competition and the fierce struggle for existence go on. We have especially spoken of wholesome milk for children and good school air. But to lessen the mortality from industrial occupations we must look to Factory Acts to prevent overcrowding and bad ventilation, to the compulsory installation of safeguards to health, as in the grinding industry, where one-half of the employees die of pulmonary tuberculosis and where, as at Sheffield, in a single "gannister" coal mine 64 out of 76 deaths were due to consumption. The education of the workman must also be carefully looked after. With our enormously rapid development of mechanical and manufacturing industries of every kind in eastern Canada, it is most essential that the interests of workmen and their families be guarded against the dangers of trades such as those that have proved so fatal in older countries.

Reference has been made to the housing problem as one of the greatest steps towards the conservation of health. In the great cities of Britain and Germany the steps taken to deal with it in recent years have met with remarkable success; while the problem has forced itself, within the last ten years, upon the great cities of the United States. In New York new tenements, erected under strict building enactments, have been constructed within nine years to house a million people. To the social workers first, who have discovered and made known the conditions, and then to municipal administration giving effect to public opinion, are due some of the most notable results. Following active charity and municipal assistance, the æsthetic idea, to-day illustrated in town planning, has been developed; while finally, the economist is realizing the full meaning of the conservation of human life as a national asset.

We, in Canada, attracted by the magnificent example of national development in the United States, where the population has increased from 53 millions in 1880 to 84 millions in 1905, may have unconsciously overlooked the meaning and value of an effective internal national growth and development. The most remarkable illustration of the discovery of the economic value of the individual citizen has been seen in the growth of Germany since the war of 1870. In the single matter of tuberculosis alone, there have been, within ten years, more than 100 people's sanatoria, with 10,000 beds, erected for the tuberculized workman, who takes advantage of his thirteen weeks' sick benefit from the compulsory insurance laws, to take the "fresh air" treatment. Provision, moreover, exists for insurance of working women by which authorities are empowered to give compensation for loss of time and cost of sickness in maternity cases.

If anyone is inclined to question the value of municipal, provincial or State interference in matters affecting the public health, it would appear that the illustrations taken from England, Germany and even the United States go abundantly to prove that *laissez faire* methods are no more logical in the face of foes active against the public health than they are when a foreign foe in arms attacks our shores. National prosperity in every field is demanding more and more the daily application of the scientific method in every field of human energy which, in a physiological sense, is capable of being weighed and measured as accurately as the number of foot-pounds of work obtainable from the consumption of a given number of pounds of coal, or as the number of kilowatts of electricity from a waterfall of a given height, depth and breadth. Public health is no longer to be classed as an *imponderable* but as a *ponderable* entity, to be dealt with along lines as exact as the building of a railway of minimum grades, or the getting of the highest mechanical efficiency out of a well-constructed steam engine.

Mr. H. T. Güssow, Dominion Botanist, Central Experimental Farm, Ottawa, was then called upon, and delivered an illustrated address on

DISEASES OF FOREST TREES

Mr. Güssow said:

Considerable attention has been paid in the past to the study of forest tree diseases, especially in countries where it was realized that closing one's eyes much longer to the existing dangers would result in serious losses to trade and commerce. This extremely useful study has revealed to a considerable degree the economic importance of the disease-causing organisms which may attack our forest resources.

Unfortunately, as yet, very little attention has been paid to this subject in Canada. Canada's supply of timber has often been said to be inexhaustible, and practically anybody provided with the necessary capital and permission could go and fell trees to his heart's content. There was no question of selecting, of careful consideration or of economy; the future would take care of itself; there was enough forest land to supply the whole world with timber! Yet what is the good of closing one's eyes to the fact that it may take a day to pull down a tree, but many years to grow one?

I forget, however, that I am addressing the members of the Commission of Conservation, all of whom are far more familiar than I, with this method of silent devastation that has been practised for some time. It is my intention to speak on diseases of forest trees, and I have selected from among a large number a few that to me appear to be of the greatest economic importance.

As far as the maladies of other plants are concerned, the public have had their eyes opened and little urging is required to get them to employ the best means for checking the growth of parasitic fungi, which affect the pocket by injuring the crops, or diminish our enjoyment by disfiguring our fields and gardens. But, with regard to forest trees, there is a regrettable indifference, just as if diseases could not possibly harm them, and yet, severe losses do result annually from such fungus epidemics, which are in no way checked in their progress.

Speaking generally, the diseases of trees may be divided into two groups: First, those caused by mechanical or physical conditions; and second, those where parasitic organisms, such as insects and fungi, are the principal agents involved. With some of the more important insects, my colleague, Dr. Hewitt, Dominion Entomologist, no doubt will deal, and hence the present remarks will be confined, for the most part, to diseases of forest trees caused by parasitic fungi.

It is a common observation that different types of soil and climate support different kinds of trees and other plants. The study of this subject has more recently engaged the attention of the Ecologist. But it is not always that we find certain trees growing in certain soils and under certain conditions, for the simple reason that man's efforts introduce trees into environments not peculiar to them. Nurseries and plantations of any kind supply excellent examples of their growing under conditions enforced upon them. Parts of our forests which have been cleared may again be desired to serve for the raising of young forest trees, and it is here where frequent failures are experienced. For we must bear in mind that the natural conditions are now totally changed; where formerly a humid atmosphere was present, we have now more air, and where natural shade prevailed, we have more light. The young plants that may be raised in such open woods are exposed to a marked degree to such physical influences, which would, under the old conditions, exert no injurious influence.

This exposure to physical conditions, however, is not the only factor which may induce disease; the trees are especially exposed to infections from other sources. There is particularly one fungus enemy of young seedling conifers which is known as the "Damping-off fungus." When the young seedlings have grown to a certain size under this new condition, it is by no means a rare occurrence that they suddenly begin to die in larger or smaller patches, and, if no means are employed to check this progress of dying off, soon all the seedlings will succumb, and any that are planted thereafter will fall victims to some mysterious foe. The cause for this sudden failure is now thoroughly understood; it has been found to be due to a microscopic fungus which attacks the young plants at the base and kills them with great rapidity. This disease in young coniferous trees is very serious, and it is fortunate that means have been discovered to prevent it. For although we shall not for some generations experience any shortage of forest supplies, providing, of course, that some method is discovered for fighting that arch enemy, "Forest Fire," we must bear in mind that planting young trees is the next important problem in the conservation of our forests. In some countries the annual planting of certain areas with young forest trees is enforced by legislation, and, on the whole, the lumberman is much checked in injudiciously cutting down timber trees. The best results in preventing the damping-off of coniferous seedlings were obtained by treating the soil several days before sowing the seed, by thoroughly drenching it with a solution mixed in the proportion of one ounce of sulphuric acid to one gallon of water. This treatment was repeated about a week after the seedlings came up. Checkplots were used in these experiments which received no treatment and they had practically no seedlings left, while, in the treated plots, there was a good stand of fine healthy seedlings.

It is possibly due to the presence of this "damping off" fungus and its severe losses that, during recent years, large shipments of young forest trees have been imported into Canada from foreign countries, especially Europe. This importation is partly practised to obtain young seedlings of two or more years of age which are past the stage of infection from this fungus, and partly, because they can be obtained at such cheap rates that considerable time and money are saved. And certainly, nobody could raise any objection to these importations, although, quite recently, together with these seedling conifers, there is reason to believe, that a very serious disease was imported which may develop into a dangerous enemy to our white pine forests. This throws a very different light on the practice of importing seedlings. Unfortunately we have enough diseases of our own and do not want the introduction of new ones, which, like the new "blister-rust" of pines, as this disease is termed, would endanger not only the health of our seedling trees, but attack our own original resources in the shape of old trees, as well.

In the spring of 1909, 200,000 white pine seedlings were imported from Europe into Canada. These seedling plants were stated to be attacked by the fungus causing white pine rust, a disease which has caused great devastation amongst pines in many European countries. Unfortunately the pine seedlings were not carefully examined when imported, and were planted out. However, they are quarantined and are now closely watched. I will show you, later, a few lantern slides, one of which illustrates this disease and gives details of the life history of this parasitic fungus. During one stage of its growth the fungus is easily observed by the presence of numerous orange red powdery cushions growing from a blister or swelling on the stem of the young pine, but which will appear also on the branches and twigs of older trees. The fungus produces a large number of spores. of an orange red colour, masses of which form the clusters already described. Spores of fungi may be compared to seeds of higher plants, because they are capable of germinating similarly to seeds and thus, of course, disseminate and spread the disease. They are very minute, so that a single spore cannot be seen unless examined with a microscope. In consequence of their minuteness the spores are borne easily by the air and on windy days may be carried miles away from the infected areas. The disease, however, perpetuates itself, not only by means of the spores, but also by the rootlike, extremely delicate, microscopic tubes which grow in the tissues of affected plants and which will produce, in the subsequent season, a new crop of spores.

There is another factor peculiar to nearly all rust fungi which increases still more the serious nature of the disease. The spores of rust fungi generally pass through another stage in their life history upon other plants. Thus the white pine rust spores, when shed, are not capable of germination on other pines directly, but they attack all kinds of cultivated and wild plants belonging to the gooseberry or currant tribe. The leaves of these plants are necessary for a further development in the life cycle of this particular fungus. My illustrations will show you the effect of the spores on leaves of currants. Here the spores rapidly germinate, causing many small reddish pustules to appear on the surface of the leaves, and in these pustules another form of spore is produced, which, in conclusion of the cycle of the fungus, is capable of germinating only on pine seedlings. This process repeats itself with every new generation of spores on the pines. Thus we have : First, spores developing on the pine, then passing through the second stage on leaves of gooseberries or currants, where they produce another crop of spores, which return to the pines in continuance of their cycle of life.

I do not intend to describe the damage due to these spores on the berry bushes, but shall just say that the damage there may also be considerable. I have no doubt that you will agree that we have here to deal with a very serious enemy of our forest trees, and that my reference to this parasite will make forest nurserymen careful. Under no conditions should pines attacked by rust be planted, and precautions should be taken when importing young seedlings to obtain them from uninfected areas, or to have them examined on arrival in Canada by a competent botanist who is able to recognize the disease in all its symptoms. Since it is evident that pines and Ribes plants are both necessary to the development of the white pine fungus, the destruction of either kind of hosts must result in the extermination of the rust. Wherever the pines are attacked a search should be made all over the neighbourhood for Ribes and their destruction proceeded with.

A disease which seriously affects the value of timber occurs on our larches or tamaracks. I propose to give you a short account of the disease, which is known elsewhere as "larch canker." The same disease is reported to appear in the larch groves of North America and Canada, although practically no measures are employed on this side of the Atlantic to check it. The symptoms of this disease are the peculiar flattening of the trunk of larch trees, the copious outflow of resin and the more or less complicated cankerous spots on the stems or branches of trees. If these affected parts are regularly examined, there may be discovered at certain times a small whitish cup-shaped fungus, growing on the surface of the diseased bark. I shall, later on, show you a slide or two illustrating the disease and its cause. The fungus caps grow from the roots or mycelium which lives in the bark of the trees, and thus they may be produced, according to the severity of the disease, in more than one place. The small cups may often be observed on all parts of the trees, even to the smallest branches.

When larch canker is present and this fungus spore germinates on the bark, it pushes out its germinal tube into the tissues of the bark, where it rapidly branches and permeates the bark and extends into the active layer below from which the new wood and bark is formed. In consequence of this irritation the bark is killed and the functions of the active layer underneath it are arrested. The fungus grows year after year and the portion killed increases in size. The tree now makes every endeavour to heal these wounds by sending forth from the edges of the wound numerous new cells which try to cover the diseased part. Curiously, this fungus has its active and its passive states; during the latter the tree exerts its powers in producing new tissues intended to cover the wound, which new tissues are vigorously attacked by the parasite during its activity. A natural consequence is the survival of the strongest. This battle may go on for years, but in very few cases, will the tree be the victor. My slides will show you some of the complicated results after a number of years of this battle for existence. The result of such infections of a whole plantation is of serious economic importance; the timber is practically useless as such, and trees frequently break off at the infected places through the weight of snow or by the force of the wind.

To prevent these serious complications the trees should be carefully examined when young, and, when the first symptoms of the disease are observed, the best method to arrest the progress of the parasite would be to cut away with a sharp knife all diseased bark down to the healthy tissues and paint the surface immediately with a coat of white lead paint.

These few examples may suffice to illustrate the seriousness of forest tree diseases caused by microscopic fungi. I will now refer to some diseases caused by the larger fungi which live on timber trees generally. These fungi may grow entirely on living tissues or they may occur on timber after it has been cut down. In both instances their economic importance is considerable. I have brought a specimen, which shows on the stem of a white birch a specimen of the wood destroying fungi with which I intend to deal. The fruiting bodies of these fungi are familiar sights on dead and living trees, on railway ties, on the timber in mines, in houses, etc. I am sure every one of you will recollect having seen them actually growing. In either case, whether growing on dead or living wood, we find the wood cells filled with minute, fine threads which penetrate in all directions. The mycelial threads of the fungi concerned in these attacks secrete a ferment acting upon the contents of the living cell. In a short time the death of the cell results and ultimately of the tree. The mycelium may also be present in trees that have been cut down, or in logs, boards, etc., where it will continue to grow till the wood is wholly decayed, that is, when all substances are dissolved which the fungus uses for food. The decay is very rapid in the so-called sap wood of the tree, which contains considerable quantities of starches and oils, while it makes much slower progress in the heartwood. Not until the threads of the fungus grow out from the wood into the air will it be noticed that a tree is diseased. Up to that time there is no external evidence of disease. The threads which appear outside the bark of a trees give rise, in some cases, to a mere film, such as is shown growing on this specimen, or they may form complicated structures, usually called "toadstools," or those hard, brownish knobs called bracket fungus, a specimen of which I have shown growing on the birch. For a long time these objects were regarded as growing on the rotted wood, and it was not until recent times that we learned that the decay was due to them. From these remarks, you will understand that when you observe any "bracket" or other fungus growing out of the trunk of a tree, it is really badly decayed within. The structure of these fruiting bodies is very varied; my slides will show you the most common ones and also the damage due to them.

That you may understand how the disease of timber trees is spread, I beg your attention for a few moments to review the structure of some of these disease-causing organisms. The specimen on the birch which I have passed round shows on the lower surface a large number of small oval pores. Hence the scientific name of *Polyporus* is given to this particular fungus. When a section is made through this layer of pores one can observe, by the aid of a microscope, a number of very minute oval bodies which are the spores of this fungus. When these spores are liberated they may be carried to other trees, and if they find suitable conditions for their development, they will start the decay which makes progress internally. When it is later discovered that fruiting bodies of fungi appear on the stem or trunk, it is too late to save the tree. The spores prefer for their development a wound that may be present on the bark of trees. In a forest, such wounds are very numerous; branches continually break off, woodpeckers make holes in stems in their hunt for trunk borers, boring beetles themselves puncture the bark, and there may be many other causes. Experience shows that open wounds are dangerous in plants, as they are in animals. Every surgeon recognizes the dangers attending upon wounds in animals, and, before the days of antiseptic treatment, the dangerous, and often fatal, results of operations were due, in many cases, to the infection of wounds by germs from the air. So with unattended wounds of trees. They may easily become infected with fungus spores or other disease germs, and with fatal results.

From these observations, it is evident in which direction salvation lies. And, if the Commission of Conservation would institute some method of inspection of forest reserves and plantations, it would be one of the most important steps in the direction of conservation of one of the most important natural resources of Canada.

In concluding my address I wish to make a few remarks on the relation of insects to forest tree diseases. My colleague, Dr. Hewitt, who will address you on problems of injurious insects of forest trees, will deal with them from the entomologist's point of view. I only wish to say that frequently one may observe fungi like *Polyporus volvatus* growing on branches and trunks of trees in a peculiar sort of arrangement. On careful examination, it has generally been discovered that the fruiting bodies of this fungus issue from the punctures in the bark caused by some bark or trunk-boring beetle. For this reason it is very evident that unless war is declared against the noxious insects, the plant pathologist cannot possibly suggest cures or prevention of diseases caused by fungi which gain an entrance through wounds caused by insects. I conclude my address by showing you some lantern illustrations which will bring home to you the urgent necessity of protecting our forests from the smaller and larger organisms that annually cause great losses, which, if expressed in figures, would amount to a surprisingly large sum.

After Mr. Güssow's paper, Dr. James Mills asked: Are these methods of fighting disease applicable to forests?

Mr. Güssow: Experience in other countries has taught that such is the case, but it is necessary to have a system of inspection such as they have in Germany. The forests are divided into certain districts and each district is inspected annually by officials who have their men knock off every part which is infected, cut off the infected limbs or break off the fungus tops, so as to prevent fructification and consequent infection of the neighbouring trees.

Dr. Mills: Does it occur on the younger growth only?

Mr. Güssow: No, it occurs on all trees, young and old. It is not always the case that these fungi will appear on the branches high up. They are found from five to ten feet from the ground and are broken off with long poles to which weights are attached.

Dr. Mills: You think, then, it is possible to apply these methods to forests?

Mr. Güssow: Yes, but it would be necessary to have some method of forest inspection.

Dr Mills: Would the breaking off of the fungi destroy them?

Mr. Güssow: No, you must destroy them by fire.

Dr. Mills: Should not a tree so infected be marked?

Mr. Güssow: Yes, that is understood. They should be cut down as soon as possible, otherwise new fungus bodies will be produced.

The Chairman called upon C. GORDON HEWITT, D. Sc., Dominion Entomologist, Central Experimental Farm, Ottawa, who gave an illustrated address on

INSECTS DESTRUCTIVE TO CANADIAN FORESTS

DR. HEWITT said:

One of this country's most valuable resources is the forests, which not only cover so large an area of the land, but, in many cases, are the only forms of vegetation possible in extensive areas which cannot be otherwise utilized. Nature has bestowed this source of wealth and of welfare on the nation with a lavish hand, and with an ever-increasing arm have these opportunities for material prosperity been embraced; but this cannot go on for ever. The virgin forest land is not inexhaustible, and, as the supply of such timber as Canada produces, affects indirectly interests so widely separated as mining and printing, and directly affects our material prosperity, it is not only necessary for us to study carefully how we may best conserve this supply, but also, how, by a careful system of afforestation, deforested areas can be reafforested and how conditions in treeless areas can be improved by suitable afforestation.

My present object, however, is not to indicate the importance of forest conservation and afforestation, of which others far more competent than I have spoken, but to consider a very important factor which seriously affects these questions, more seriously than is at first sight apparent. This factor is the injury caused by insects to forest trees. Three factors are chiefly responsible for the destruction of our forests, namely, fires, plant diseases and insects, and these three factors are often closely associated. Fire may precede and make easy the path of total destruction by insects, or the reverse may occur; or, on the other hand, fungi may gain entrance to trees as the result of insect attack. Unfortunately, the extent of insect injury becomes apparent to most people only when the ravages attain some magnitude, the earlier phases of the outbreak having been passed over unnoticed. The result of this is that we frequently have a destructive species of insect firmly establishing itself unobserved by the forester or others in charge, and, instead of being able to take such remedial measures as might be possible in the early stages of the attack, we are confronted with an outbreak of so great a magnitude as to render such measures impracticable and impossible. I shall give you instances of such occurrences. Our great difficulty lies in the fact that these outbreaks occur on a large scale in wild virgin forests, in dealing with which we are almost impotent. If, however, the attack is recognized in its earlier stages, by judicious treatment of the trees in the way of felling at the proper time and other careful forestry measures, it is possible to prevent, in many cases, the destructive species of insect assuming large proportions and the outbreak, a serious character. In dealing with these forest insects, it is essential that the attack shall be recognized in the earliest stage possible. If this is done, the species of insect responsible for the injuries can be determined, and, if necessary, studied, and we may be able to suggest from the results obtained by such a study the remedial and preventive measures necessary. Those measures depend upon the life-histories and habits of the insect concerned, and it is impossible, in the absence of such knowledge, to adopt the best means of controlling or preventing the further spread of the insect. It is apparent, therefore, that the conservation of our forests is greatly dependent upon entomological knowledge, and this dependence will increase with the growth of the national importance of our forests.

The combating of destructive insects is as important as the prevention of forest fires, since the ultimate results of the two are similar, namely, the destruction of large areas of forest. In fact, so similar are the results that the destruction of forest areas which has been due to outbreaks and the spread of serious insect pests, is not infrequently attributed entirely to fire. Where careful inquiry has been made into the question, it has often been found that the destruction of the timber by such insects as bark-boring beetles, preceded the fire, and again, that these and other timber-destroying beetles sometimes attack areas of timber over which fire has passed and which might, under normal conditions, have recuperated, but the beetles, taking advantage of the weakened vitality of the trees, completed the destruction. The question of insect attack is, in this way, closely connected with that of fires.

A study of European forestry literature and the excellent writings of Hopkins on American forestry give an idea of the enormous losses which a single insect is able to cause. In the latter part of the 18th century the attacks of the bark-boring pine beetle, *Tomicus typographus* L., resulted in the cutting down of over two and a half million trees and, in France, this insect, together with another species, brought about the loss of nearly two hundred thousand trees before it was controlled in 1872. In the United States, Hopkins estimates that the annual loss, direct and indirect, caused by insects to forest and forest products is about a hundred million dollars. The outbreak of the bark-boring beetle, *Dendroctonus frontalis* Zimm, in the western states in 1891-92 was estimated by Hopkins, who studied the insect, to cover an area of over 50,000 square miles. Although these figures are and can be estimates only, they serve to indicate in a graphic manner the enormous losses caused, and wide areas covered, by forest insects alone.

On account of the geographical position of Canada, our forests are composed chiefly of coniferous trees, and, in describing the most prevalent and injurious forest insects, only those attacking conifers will, with one exception, be considered. We are periodically troubled by a number of seriously injurious insects attacking ornamental and shade trees, such as, for example, the White-marked Tussock Moth (*Hemerocampa leucostigma* S. & A.), which is responsible for no little damage to shade trees in some of our cities. The Fall Webworm (*Hyphantria textor* Harr.) and Tent caterpillars (several species of *Malacosoma*) appear from time to time in considerable numbers and defoliate forest and other trees, but the results of their attacks are not so serious as those of certain of the forest insects attacking conifers.

The insects destructive to forests may be grouped into three main classes. First, those insects which defoliate the trees and by their continued prevalence from year to year cause the death of the trees. Included in this class we have, in Canada, such insects as the Larch Sawfly, the Spruce Bud-worm, the Brown-tail Moth, and the Pine Butterfly. In the second class are included the bark beetles and the borers. The former class of beetles are the cause of the greatest loss to coniferous trees by their attacks on the growing timber; many of them attack the healthy trees, others more weakly trees, and certain species cause the destruction of both classes. Thirdly, there are a large number of insects which affect the continued growth of the trees as a species by their attacks on the seeds, the seedlings and the young trees, but with this miscellaneous group of insects it is not proposed to deal, and the first and second groups alone will be considered.

At the present time the most widely spread forest insect in Canada is the Larch Sawfly or Larch Worm, *Nematus erichsonii*, whose injuries to the native larch or tamarack have proved very serious in the past and are to-day of great magnitude. In 1881–1886, this insect spread over the whole of eastern Canada, and, during that period, on account of repeated defoliation, practically all the mature larches over the whole of that area were destroyed. It again appeared in the east in the years 1894–8, but, in 1903, another large outbreak began, which has now assumed enormous dimensions and has spread over the whole of eastern Canada. In a recent tour out to the West, I found it on all the larches as far west as Winnipeg, and it appears as if the results would be as serious as those of the 1884–8 outbreak. Most of the larches which have grown up since that time and those which have recovered are being killed by frequent defoliation, which such a tree as the larch or tamarack is unable to stand. The seriousness of the result of this outbreak is increased by the fact that the larch grows especially in swampy and muskeg regions, where many other trees are unable to grow. In such an extensive outbreak in virgin forest, it is impossible to take any remedial measures against the insect and we are compelled to await its disappearance brought about by such factors as the destruction of its food supply and the increase of its parasites. I have not found this species attacking other conifers, even though these latter were growing among the larch, nor have I noted the sudden increase of its parasitic or other enemies.

The life history and habits of this insect have been studied in the United States, and more recently I was able to make a study of the species in England, where a serious outbreak has occurred during the past few years. The female sawflies lay their eggs in slits which they make by means of their saw-like egg-laying organs on the stems of the young terminal shoots of the larch, and as a result of this, these shoots subsequently die. The young green larvæ hatch out and begin to feed on the fresh green leaves, and, as they grow older, they feed in clusters, gradually stripping the whole tree of its foliage. By this repeated defoliation by the larvæ and the killing of the growing shoots by the female sawflies, the larches are killed. The larvæ are full-grown in a few weeks, being then of a greyish-green or bluish-green color. When full-grown they descend the trunks of the trees and spin a brown cocoon in the loose turf and dead leaves at the base of the tree, and the sawflies emerge from the cocoons in the following June. A number of parasites have been found, insect parasites which attack the larvæ when they are on the trees, and a fungal parasite which destroys the larvæ when it is in the cocoon. I also found that a large percentage of the larvæ were extracted from the cocoons and eaten by a species of field mouse or vole (*Microtus agrestis*). Most valuable assistance was rendered in England by several species of birds, and accordingly a system of bird protection and encouragement was instituted. As there were few insect-eating birds in the district where the outbreak occurred, nest boxes were distributed, and the first year's trial was so encouraging that additional nest boxes are being distributed each year. Too much stress cannot be laid on the importance of encouraging this important means of insect control. Bird encouragement and protection form an important part of many of the forestry systems in Europe, where it is the result of both State and private enterprise and where afforestation and forestry methods are carried on in a more scientific manner than in any other part of the world. Although Canada's forests are comparatively enormous, we must, in instituting conservancy methods, in adopting schemes of afforestation and, above all, in preserving the forests in our national parks, give careful attention to this important aspect of forest preservation. We are only at the beginning of these things and have every opportunity of adopting all those useful measures of forest protection which other and older countries have discovered by experience. It is our duty to undertake every measure possible to secure the ends that this Commission, as I understand its purposes, has in view.

Considerable damage has been inflicted on the balsam and spruce, especially in the eastern regions of Canada, and also on the Douglas fir in the West, by a small moth whose larvæ is known as the Spruce Bud-worm (*Tortrix fumiferana*, Clem.). During the summer of 1909, a serious outbreak of this insect in the upper Gatineau country was investigated by Mr. Arthur Gibson, of the Division of Entomology, to which a number of reports of the abundance of this insect had been sent, and it was found that the insect was spread over a very large area. I learnt, when visiting Vancouver in October, that it had been increasing in numbers on Vancouver Island, where it was attacking chiefly the Douglas fir. In some ornamental grounds on that island I found, by the presence of the empty pupal cases, that it was also able to feed upon the larch, silver fir, Norway spruce, deodar and African cedar.

The name of this insect is derived from the fact that the larvæ feed on the leaves of the young green shoots, which are consequently destroyed, and as the spruce is a slowly growing tree this results in serious injury to the tree. In fact, it has been described as one of the most destructive insects attacking the spruce. I believe, however, that, in its work of destruction, it is not infrequently assisted to no small extent by the bark-boring beetles. It bites off the leaves or needles and constructs for itself a shelter by binding them loosely together. The eggs are laid on the leaves and the young larvæ are pale green. The winter is passed in the larval stage, and, in the following year, they continue to feed and become mature about the end of June, when they are of a reddish brown colour. They change into pupæ in their loosely made shelters, and the small-brown moth, on emerging from the pupa or chrysalis, drags the latter partly out of the larval shelter, in which position the empty case remains suspended, These empty chrysalids were found in very large numbers. I was also informed, when in Victoria, B.C., that moths were carried by the wind into the city in enormous swarms, and this wind carriage contributes considerably to the spread of this insect and also, of the larch sawfly, as in the outbreaks of these insects that I have studied it was almost always found that the spread has been in the direction of the prevailing winds. The destruction of the foliage and the presence of the insect causes the trees attacked to have a reddish brown appearance, and, from a distance, they appear to have been swept by fire.

In Canada, we are, at present, threatened by a most serious defoliating insect. The Brown-tail Moth (*Euproctis chrysorrhœa* L.), which has, since its introduction into Massachusetts about 1890, spread far more rapidly in the eastern states than the Gypsy Moth, has established itself in Nova Scotia and New Brunswick. The first specimens of these introduced moths were discovered in New Brunswick in 1902, and in Nova Scotia in 1905, and the first winter nest was found in the latter Province and sent to my predecessor, the late Dr. James Fletcher, in February, 1907. Although a most vigorous campaign has been carried on, it appears now as if the insect had firmly established itself in the forest districts, though, as yet, the numbers are not large. In the eastern states hundreds of thousands of dollars have been spent in attempting to control these insects, which were allowed to become firmly established before any steps for eradication were taken. Such an experience has taught us the serious results which would follow the spread of the Brown-tail Moth in the provinces of Canada, and, in consequence, we shall take all measures possible to prevent its spread in the provinces where it now exists and its introduction into other parts of Canada. The first specimens were probably introduced into Massachusetts on imported nursery stock from Europe, where it is kept in control by such natural agencies as insect parasites. It is found that imported nursery stock is liable to be infested with the winter nests of the insect, in which stage it is admirably adapted for dissemination, as the insect is very common in many of the localities where this nursery stock is grown. To prevent its introduction, and as nests had been found on stock shipped into Ontario, the Division of Entomology carried on, with the co-operation of the provincial authorities, nurserymen and others, a careful inspection of imported nursery stock, and nearly two hundred nests were discovered and destroyed. As each of these winter nests may contain several hundred young larvæ, the value of this work is apparent. This inspection is being repeated this year, and I hope next year we shall have legislation which will render the shipment of nursery stock and other vegetation into this country without inspection for these serious pests, impossible.

This insect is especially adapted for wide and rapid dissemination, as the snow-white moths are able to fly well and the larvæ are liable to be carried in the winter nests. The eggs are laid in batches of about 200 to 300 arranged in a brown mass formed by the brown hairs from the end of the female's body. It is from this circumstance that it derives its name. They are usually deposited in July on the under-sides of the leaves, and, in August, the larvæ hatch out. At the end of the season, they are about a quarter grown, and, by drawing the leaves at the end of a branch together and binding them with silk, they make for themselves a nest or web in which they pass the winter, coming out in the spring to feed on the newly opened foliage. In this season they become full-grown and cause the greatest destruction. The larvæ are reddish brown and furry in appearance; the hairs with which they are covered, are minutely barbed and produce a most painful and, in in some cases, serious rash when they come in contact with the skin. The larvæ feed on the foliage of most of the fruit trees, such as the pear, apple, plum, cherry, and, in addition, they attack such forest trees as the oak, elm and maple, which may be entirely stripped of their leaves. The surest remedial measure is the destruction, during the winter and early spring, of the winter nests containing the hibernating larvæ. This procedure is being adopted in Nova Scotia, and several thousands of nests have been destroyed annually since active measures were instituted in 1907. It is a serious matter to control an insect such as this after it has established itself in the forests. In the eastern States it spreads so rapidly as to get beyond the ordinary methods of control, and now one of the most important experiments ever carried on in destructive insect control is being made under the direction of **Dr. L. O. Howard**, Entomologist to the United States Department of Agriculture. Collections of specimens are being regularly sent from different localities in Europe where the insect is native and where it is kept in check by certain species of parasitic insects and other insect enemies such as predaceous beetles. But these species are not present on this continent. The collections of the European Brown-tail caterpillars are parasitized; the parasites are carefully reared in large numbers and distributed at certain points in Massachusetts, where the infestation of the Brown-tail Moth is very serious. Several of the species of parasites appear to have established themselves already, as the species have been recaptured, and although it is naturally a matter of time, it is hoped that ultimately, by the introduction of the controlling parasitie insects, the Brown-tail Moth and also the Gypsy Moth will be controlled. If so, this will then be added to the already increasing list of instances where a thorough knowledge of an entomological problem has led to the control of a seriously injurious insect. The Division of Entomology is giving its most serious attention to this problem, and I hope that, with the co-operation of the provincial departments, we shall not experience the disastrous results which have followed its establishment in the New England states.

There are a number of other defoliating insects, such as the pine and spruce sawflies and the pine butterfly, (*Neophasia menapia*, Felder,) which occasionally defoliate considerable tracts, but I will now turn to what are perhaps the most serious of conifer-destroying insects, the Bark Beetles, belonging to the group *Scolytidæ*. The majority of them belong to the genus *Dendroctonus*, which means a "killer of trees," and Hopkins, the authority on these insects, states that, if the trees of the United States killed by these insects during the past 50 years were still living, the stumpage value of the timber would exceed $1,000,000,-000. The insects of this group are destructive by their boring through the bark, under which they excavate galleries in which their eggs are laid. There the small white larvæ or grubs continue the tunnelling. In this manner, not only is the vitality of the tree impaired, but the layer of growth tissue is very often destroyed by the ramifying borings of the larvæ, and the tree dies in consequence. Certain of these bark beetles attack the strong and vigorous trees and cause the death of the same. Others attack more weakly trees, sometimes previously weakened by a forest fire, and complete the destruction. Healthy trees, attacked by the first class, on becoming weakened, may be attacked by those beetles normally preferring unhealthy trees, and thus the result of their work is intensified in character.

The occurrence and distribution of these beetles have not yet been studied to any great extent in Canada, and, as I have reason to believe that they are much more prevalent than is generally considered, and as such information and also a knowledge of their life histories and habits under the prevailing conditions is very essential, I am hoping that it will be possible for the Division of Entomology to undertake a careful study of these insects. The practical importance of a more complete knowledge of these serious forest insects of Canada cannot be over-estimated.

In New Brunswick and other parts of the eastern region of Canada, great destruction has been caused to the red and white spruce and also the black spruce by the Eastern Spruce Beetle, (*Dendroctonus piceaperda* Hopk). It attacks the healthy mature trees and also those which have been weakened in any way. The evidence of its attack is the reddish dust on the bark of the trees caused by the larval borings, and also the reddish and dying appearance of the tops of the trees, which, I am afraid, has not infrequently been attributed to the attacks of the Spruce Bud-worm, whose attack is not so serious. The small reddish brown or black beetles, measuring one-fifth to one-quarter of an inch long, bore holes through the bark, thus forming a wound, and underneath this bark they excavate long galleries. Hopkins, who has studied the life history of this and many other species, finds that this takes place in the eastern States in June and July. The eggs are laid on the sides of these galleries and the larvæ on hatching begin to feed on the soft lower layer which, when the larvæ occur in numbers, causes the tree to begin to die. If the eggs are laid early in the season, most of the larvæ are full grown about August and are then transformed into pupæ and adult beetles. These beetles hibernate in the burrows underneath the bark and emerge from the trees about June, whilst those specimens which hibernate as larvæ, emerge later in the season.

The methods of control which a study of the life history of this insect suggests, are the barking of infested trees during the months in which the beetles hibernate, or the felling of as many of the badly infested trees as is possible during the same period. The barking and destruction of the bark, however, is preferable, as trees thus treated will remain sound for some time and may be felled later.

A number of species of this destructive group of bark beetles belonging to the genus *Dendroctonus* have been found in Canada in the coniferous regions of the Maritime Provinces, Quebec, Ontario and British Columbia, and a study of the seasonal histories of the different species which are dependent upon such factors as latitude, is urgently required. In addition to these bark-boring beetles, there are a large number of boring beetles whose larvæ penetrate deeper into the timber, both of living trees and of felled timber, and these are responsible for the destruction of a large amount of timber.

Not only are these timber-destroying beetles directly responsible for the destruction of trees and timber, but, by their borings, they provide means of ingress for timber-destroying fungi, which, in many cases, complete the destruction begun by the beetles. The two factors of forest destruction, therefore, are closely related in this respect. Not only do these boring beetles make way for subsequent fungal disease, but it is extremely probable that certain of the plant lice or aphides, such as the gall louse which infests the spruce and larch, by the punctures they make in the bark of healthy trees, provide entrance for the spores of such destructive fungi as the larch canker and others.

These examples of the workings of a few of the destructive forest insects which I have chosen, will serve to show you the importance of entomological enquiry in relation to the conservation of the forests and the maintenance of systems of afforestation in Canada. I trust that I have shown how exact entomological knowledge, such as can be gained only in the field and in the laboratory, must necessarily form the basis of all measures of insect control. A little knowledge is often a greater evil than ignorance, and nowhere is it so detrimental as in science and in the application of scientific knowledge. The Commission may be assured that the Division of Entomology will, to the best of its power, furnish, by the study of these insects, such information as will be of use in checking the inroads of such insects as are destructive to Canadian forests.

The meeting then adjourned.

THURSDAY MORNING

The Commission of Conservation met at the Carnegie Library on the morning of Thursday, January 20th, at 10 o'clock. The Chairman called upon Mr. Charles R. Coutlee, C.E., Engineer-in-charge of the Ottawa Storage Survey, to give an address on

THE WATER WEALTH OF CANADA: WITH SPECIAL REFERENCE TO THE OTTAWA RIVER BASIN

Mr. Coutlee said:

The only source of water, no matter where we find it, whether coursing down in rivers or rising from the soil in springs, is the rainfall. This rain, flowing in rivulets on the surface or seeping through the ground, eventually reaches a creek, a swamp, or a lake, thus collecting to form a flowing river.

There are four uses of water to mankind. First and foremost, drinking water is an absolute essential to life, and this constitutes a first call upon all our sources of supply. Secondly, if the rainfall is not sufficient, plant life is possible only by means of irrigation. Irrigation, however, not only furnishes moisture, but the water conducted to the soil contains silt and mineral salts which renew the land. This is well shown in the Nile valley, where the overflow, covering the ground with silt and mineral salts, has made it possible to raise unrotated crops for thousands of years. This phase of irrigation is often forgotten, but, when more intensive methods of cultivation are adopted, many streams in the well-watered provinces of the east may yet be turned on to the land for the sole purpose of fertilizing it. In the third place, transportation necessitates an assured depth of water in our streams, and, to this end, it is necessary to conserve the rainfall in swamps, lakes or artificial reservoirs, so that low water in the autumn will not prevent a continuous service. The use of water for power purposes is the last charge upon the supply. It is a remunerative business, and so the production of energy adjacent to centres of population has been seized upon by capital which, if not controlled, would demand the whole flow for this purpose alone.

Under these four heads of usefulness each of the five river basins of Canada will be discussed, that is, under a geographical arrangement, we will consider the principal rivers in their relationship to the population. This practically means the relationship of water to each city in a particular district.

Pacific Coast—Beginning on the Pacific, the rugged coast-strip which extends 50 to 100 miles inland from the ocean and rises in that short distance to a general elevation of 8,000 feet, serves to condense the moisture-laden wind of the Pacific, the result being that the rainfall attains the extraordinary amount of 100 to 150 inches per year. The high peaks condense the moisture directly into snow, which, constantly gathering, creates a pressure sufficient in the presence of a very moist atmosphere to harden into ice which gradually moves down the mountain valleys as glaciers. These glaciers as they reach lower elevations melt into water, so that the frozen masses represent reservoirs from which the streams are fed until late in the autumn. Although the lake-basins, or natural reservoirs, are small, still these glaciers and the heavy rainfall give a fairly constant supply for domestic and other purposes.

DOMESTIC SUPPLY OF VANCOUVER—The site of the present city was a forest in 1885. Since it was surrounded by salt water, a source of supply was selected on Capilano creek, where a pond was created by a wooden dam. The water is led down through steel pipes and carried by a submerged conduit beneath the inlet and into the Stanley Park reservoir, from which it is distributed by gravity.

DOMESTIC SUPPLY OF NEW WESTMINSTER—This city is situated on the lower reaches of the Fraser river. As the tide extends up this river, the water is brackish and unfit for domestic use. It was therefore necessary to obtain a supply inland, and a gravity system was installed.

This indicates that, even in the newer districts, the large Canadian centres of population are well supplied with water for drinking and for fire protection. The increasing and, in many cases, unrestrained contamination of streams under the conditions of rapid growth in our population indicates a necessity for central supervision of at least those rivers whose waters wash alternately the shores of different provinces. By authoritative investigation of matters relating to river pollution, the public will be led to understand that our magnificent Canadian streams should not be polluted by allowing sewage or factory wastes to enter without adequate purification.

The relation between pure and ample water supply at all seasons, and the public health, is a question of paramount importance. The ignorance of the public regarding sanitary matters and the laws governing the right to consume water from lakes, streams or springs, and the right to dispose of drainage into the same, prevents effective protest against pollution. Central control founded on technical examination, instead of adjustment through the courts, will give assurance to municipalities as to the future conditions of our streams, and, even with growth of population, the dangers will diminish rather than increase. Life will be protected, litigation will be avoided, and the municipalities will stand on firm ground respecting their rights with regard to water supplies and drainage.

Under central auspices, extended inquiry and experiment into problems of water supply, sewage and sewage disposal, would secure a fund of valuable data from which local authorities would derive benefit, and the public would understand and demand the blessings of modern sanitary research. A correct moulding of the popular mind, founded on a study of local conditions, is much to be preferred to the intermittent and unintelligent enforcement of general legislation. Annual reports, or, preferably, occasional bulletins describing the conditions of water supplies, sewers and disposal systems and projects would build up a sentiment to have and to hold our heritage of water, pure.

The studies required would be systematic examinations of the drainage areas of our principal rivers as to existing or probable pollution from towns, summer residences or manufactories. Physical, chemical and biological tests at regular intervals would determine the relative purity at different points. The determination of discharge quantities for various river basins would be of service in studying the economic possibilities of streams for future power development. It would also serve to prevent the encroachments of private dams, bridge piers, etc., upon the natural flow area—a fruitful cause of floods.

The disposal of sewage and trade wastes is now demanding a great deal of attention from scientists. The capability of a river to purify itself and the necessity of demanding a more or less perfect degree of purity in drainage entering the streams, are subjects that will engage the best scientific thought of the immediate future.

IRRIGATION—Although the rainfall is very plentiful on Vancouver Island, yet there are portions of the island which require irrigation because the moisture-laden clouds drift over to condense against the Coast range. The irrigation systems, however, are small and generally consist of creeks led on to individual ranches.

Along the coast of the mainland very little irrigation is practised, although the months of July and August are sometimes very dry, and the gravelly soil does not long retain the moisture of the wet months. The islands in the Fraser delta and lower Fraser are protected from the sea by dikes. When the dikes are overtopped by the high water, the result, of course, is a refertilization which is a most important feature of all irrigation.

INLAND NAVIGATION—The rivers fall down steep mountain slopes and are generally too rapid for any kind of navigation, but the deep inlets along the coast afford access by boat to many points quite inland. It is possible to navigate the Fraser up to New Westminster with sea-going vessels, and above that there are a few stern-wheel steamboats. The Skeena is a large river with many rapids, but has been navigated for 150 miles to Hazelton.

POWER—There is plenty of coal on Vancouver island and on the mainland also, but, owing to the high price of this fuel, water-power was early sought after. About 1903, the Vancouver Power Company developed a site on the shore of Burrard inlet, 18 miles north of Vancouver. Coquitlam lake is joined by a two-and-a-half-mile tunnel to Buntzen lake, thence through wood-stave pipe, to the plant, 400 feet below. Although the drainage area is only about 200 square miles, yet the excessive rainfall is sufficient to maintain 22,000 H.P. This is transmitted to Vancouver, New Westminster and the Delta, supplying over 100,000 people with light, operating electric roads, etc. The transmission line crosses Burrard inlet by a single span over half a mile in length.

Another station will soon be completed at Stave lake, 35 miles from Vancouver. The drainage area is only 360 square miles, but the rainfall of over 100 inches per year ensures 25,000 H.P., the head being 90 feet. The great rainfall and high heads are, of course, most remarkable conditions.

Central British Columbia—In this area the mountains are separated by four parallel north-and-south valleys, viz., the Fraser, 400 miles long, fairly straight and almost north and south; the Okanagan valley, with Okanagan lake nearly 80 miles long; Columbia river and its lake-expansions, the Arrow lakes, extending 200 miles north and south; and the Kootenay valley parallel to, and a few miles west of, the Rockies.

The Coast range intercepts a large part of the moisture from the Pacific, so that the Fraser and Okanagan valleys are semi-arid, but the Columbia and Kootenay valleys have an ample rainfall and snowfall.

Applying our division of uses to the Fraser river, we find that it furnishes, so far, no domestic water supply. The banks are usually steep and rocky, or else high gravel slopes, which are without arable areas or towns of importance. Owing to the salmon pack, it is a question if the river can ever furnish potable water. The fluctuation of the surface is 50 feet, and the great floods carry quantities of silt which also militates against its use for household purposes. The lower reach of the Fraser, however, from Yale to the coast, is alluvial, but is exposed to extensive floods. Irrigation is practised only at a few points, so far.

POWER—There are great falls along the Fraser, with rocky cañon sides, where power might be developed by the use of rock-fill dams if the river could ever be regulated to obviate the extreme conditions of high and low water. The Thompson river, however, which enters the Fraser at Lytton, furnishes a domestic supply for the town of Kamloops, which is pumped by a vertical engine set over a well. Its tributary, the Bonaparte river, supplies irrigation systems near Ashcroft. Two large reservoirs, Adams and Shuswap lakes, modify the flow of the Thompson somewhat and offer sites for power development.

OKANAGAN VALLEY—Irrigation is practised throughout the valley, where fruits of all kinds have been cultivated with great success. Navigation by stern-wheel steamboat is, so far, the means of communication in the valley, which is reached by railway only at its north end. Power has not been developed to any great extent and no large developments are to be expected, but the fertility of the valley and its fine climate will attract a class of people who will become great users of power.

COLUMBIA AND KOOTENAY VALLEYS—There are four towns in this basin. Revelstoke, on the Columbia, obtains a water supply, not from the river itself, but from the Illecillewaet, which joins the main river at that point. Irrigation is not practised in the Columbia valley to any great extent.

Navigation on the Columbia is, so far as Canada is concerned, confined to the stern-wheel steamers on the Arrow lakes and on the river above Golden. Navigation on the Kootenay river is broken between Nelson and its confluence with the Columbia at West Robson, but is resumed between Nelson and Kootenay Landing.

On the Kootenay river, power has been developed by a very modern plant at Bonnington Falls near Nelson. The head varies from 55 to 65 feet, for, during high water, the flow becomes obstructed by the narrows below the falls. The flow is 6,000 c.f.s. from a drainage area of 10,000 square miles that possesses several glaciers. Eventually 25,000 H.P. will be developed, but only one half is being developed and sold, at present, to Phœnix, Grand Forks, Greenwood, Rossland and Trail, for mine haulage and hoisting, pumping, air compression, and for lighting and municipal purposes. The city of Nelson operates a municipal plant on the opposite side of the river.

Mackenzie Basin—The drainage area of this basin is nearly 700,-000 square miles. The Athabaska and Peace rivers unite to form the great Mackenzie, which presents a few power possibilities, although it flows to the Arctic in an almost even grade. They, however, admit of navigation, with interruptions at Grand rapids and at Fort Smith rapids, from Athabaska Landing to the Arctic, a distance equivalent to that from Winnipeg to Halifax. An idea of the coming development of this great basin may be had from the fact that a flour mill has, for years, been operated on the Peace.

The prairie rivers of Manitoba, Saskatchewan and Alberta drain nearly a million miles of territory—that is, twice the drainage area of the St. Lawrence—through two outlets, the Nelson and the Mackenzie rivers. It is rather a fortunate circumstance that the precipitation is not as great as that in the east, and that the area is not covered with a dense timber, because it would prevent a gradual melting of the snow by the sun during March and early April, and would cause the whole flood of melted snow and spring rains to pour down together during the latter days of April.

Lake Winnipeg Basin—It is not generally appreciated that lake Winnipeg is the size of lake Erie, that is, nearly 10,000 square miles in area. The basin that drains into this lake is 350,000 square miles in extent, or nearly the size of France and Spain, which two countries support a population of 58,000,000. The Saskatchewan river, which drains 158,800 square miles of this area, extends west to the mountains and from Edmonton to the 49th parallel. The mountain streams constituting the sources of this great river are very numerous. Many of them are fed by glaciers and offer a continuity of flow that promises well for water-power when an increasing population provides the demand.

The next great tributary of lake Winnipeg is the Red river, rising in Minnesota and flowing north to Winnipeg, where it is joined by the

Assiniboine. From there it continues through the St. Andrews rapid to the lake. Both the Red and the Assiniboine, like the Saskatchewan, are alluvial rivers worn deep down in the prairie soil to an almost even grade, and are, in general, without the valuable falls over rocky ledges that so easily lend themselves to power development. Their swift running floods and ever changing shoals are a great detriment to navigation, especially on up-stream trips. As there are no lakes along these rivers, the spring thaws and early rains sweep down unrestrained by swamps and ungathered by reservoirs, so that their beneficial uses are largely lost to the communities along the river banks.

The prairie river generally occupies the bottom of a great depression a mile or more in width, with steep sides 100 to 200 feet in height, which are deeply furrowed by gulches of accessory streams, creeks and rivulets that are generally dry in summer. The main stream meanders through the bottom land, and during great floods, the minor banks are overtopped and the bottom of the valley flooded.

The prairie lakes are often of considerable area, 40 square miles or more, but are generally shallow. The sloughs are filled with a fair depth of water during wet years. They have no outlet streams, but in midsummer they shrink to insignificant ponds. This decrease in volume renders them very alkaline. These peculiar conditions of the prairie water supply can be understood by giving examples of the methods employed or projected to make the most of them.

DOMESTIC USE—Edmonton, the capital of Alberta, derives a water supply from the Saskatchewan. Calgary has a water supply owned by a private company and drawn from the Bow river. A pile dam has been made across the entire river, and a wooden flume along one shore leads the water about half a mile to the wheels. The population is now over 20,000, principally located upon a flat about forty feet above the river. Residences are now being built upon the surrounding plateau, 200 feet higher, so power for pumping must soon be increased. The coal mines at Canmore and Banff are only 80 miles distant by rail. Medicine Hat pumps its supply from the South Saskatchewan. The power used is natural gas, of which the locality has a plentiful supply. Increase of population at Calgary, Macleod and Lethbridge will bring up the question of sewage contamination at Medicine Hat, which is down stream from all these places. The same difficulty, too, will arise, later, at Saskatoon and Prince Albert. Regina is at present supplied from Wascana creek.

Later, it may be necessary to utilize Last Mountain lake. Brandon takes its supply from the Assiniboine, which also furnishes the power for pumping. Winnipeg, the third largest city in Canada, obtains water from a system of artesian wells. The pumping was formerly done by steam, but the high price of coal has led to the adoption of electric power generated on the Winnipeg river.

IRRIGATION—Two extensive irrigation schemes are now in operation. One near Lethbridge, takes water from the St. Mary river, the main canal being led along side hills and into sloughs which act as reservoirs. The system was begun in 1897, and very good results have been obtained from land that, without water, would have yielded very uncertain crops, although, during wet years, there is sufficient rainfall for general farming. Calgary has become the centre of a large system built and operated by the Canadian Pacific railway. This Company received the final allotment of its land grant in one block near Calgary. In 1903, a main canal 100 feet wide, was begun, and now carries water from the Bow river by branch ditches, to serve 1,000,000 acres. Further extensions are proposed for the near future.

Because the prairie rivers have cut so deeply into the soil, they do not lend themselves easily to the irrigation of the general prairie level. Their swift current, however, points to a method of pumping up the water, and as the amount required is very moderate, only 1 c.f.s. being necessary for 100 acres of land, the systems of pumping need not be elaborate. In Washington state, the current of Snake river is utilized in the following manner. A long, narrow raft is anchored in the stream; each end is furnished with rollers and an endless belt with wooden vanes or paddles is revolved over these rollers by the current into which the paddles dip on the under side of the raft, the upper paddles returning in air. The power thus generated runs a Jacobs-ladder pump that lifts the water up to a trough, through which it is led to the land. Another method of obtaining power from a river current is by a series of screw propeller wheels mounted on a shaft which is held beneath a float in the direction of the current. Windmills are also frequently used, and the winds are generally fairly constant over the area in question.

NAVIGATION—A boat, launched in the Red river, sailed down to lake Winnipeg and through it to the mouth of the Saskatchewan, thence it was hauled and poled up the Grand rapids to Cedar lake, whence it proceeded to Edmonton. This boat was used during the rebellion of '85, and finally went to pieces against the piers of the Edmonton bridge. This gives some idea of the immense stretch of navigable waters through our prairies, but, owing to the swift current, the economy of such transportation is not quite assured. If a large quantity of heavy raw material like coal or iron ore were offered for through transportation, then a system of cheap barges pushed in front of a stern-wheel steamer might be used. Such barge rafts carry coal down the Ohio and Mississippi to New Orleans, where the barges are broken up and sold as lumber.

On lake Winnipeg there is considerable navigation, largely connected with the fish industries. The new lock at St. Andrews rapid, when completed, will extend navigation to Winnipeg and above.

Although the Saskatchewan is subject to extreme freshets, yet piers for bridges have been built in the river at many places and have withstood for years the force of its floods. It is, therefore, reasonable to expect that a dam consisting of high piers upon a heavy floor of concrete extending across the bottom of the river, could be economically built. Between these piers, steel curtains, forming the actual dam, could be raised vertically during freshets, permitting the flood water to pass unimpeded. As the flood decreases the curtain would be gradually lowered into the water so as to keep the upper level at a fixed height, while the natural flow of the river passed between the lower edge of the curtains and the concrete floor. Such constructions would regulate the river into convenient steps, or reaches, each of which would form a conservation reservoir that would save for summer use the valuable water supply of the prairies that is now dissipated in spring floods. Water held at a high and constant level is always a most valuable asset to any community.

POWER—At present the prairie rivers furnish very little power, although their tributaries in the mountains are already being exploited for use at Calgary and other points. Coal is cheap and abundant in the western section, but further east, with increasing population, cheap power will be in demand, and the moveable dams above described may yet be tried. Lake Winnipeg is an enormous reservoir 700 feet above Hudson bay. It flows out through the Nelson river, which tumbles over many rocky ridges, giving exceptional opportunities for water-power.

A great rock outcrop along the west side of lake Winnipeg separates it from lake Winnipegosis and Dauphin lake, which are 100 feet higher. This outcrop also crosses the mouth of the Saskatchewan, creating the Grand rapids, with a fall of 71 feet, 250 miles north of Winnipeg.

There is, however, a third great tributary of lake Winnipeg, the Winnipeg river, which has a drainage area the same size as the Ottawa,

55,000 square miles, or the size of England and Wales. It also runs through a similar gneissic rock territory. Its upward extension is Rainy river, forming the boundary between Canada and the United States, and emptying into the lake of the Woods. The Winnipeg river flows out of this lake over two falls, giving exceptional opportunities for power. Near Kenora 5,000 H.P. is generated and used for flour milling and for municipal purposes. The head is 18 feet, and a remarkable dam of loose rock thrown into the bed of the river maintains the elevation of the lake; the river flow, 15,000 c.f.s., is passed through stoplog sluices. Farther down the river, and 75 miles from Winnipeg, is Pointe des Bois, where the city of Winnipeg is building a municipal power station with 46 ft. head. Here, another rock-fill dam has been built.

Farther down, the river branches into two channels, and upon the Pinawa channel a power with 35 to 40 feet head is operated by the Winnipeg Street Railway Company for street railway and other purposes.

St. Lawrence Basin—The watershed area is 550,000 miles, one-sixth of which is the water system of the Great lakes, which constitutes the most remarkable reservoir system in the world. The north coast of lake Superior is rocky and sparsely peopled; consequently, apart from the demands made upon it by Fort William, Port Arthur, and Sault Ste. Marie, lake Superior is but little drawn upon for domestic supplies. The drainage of Fort William and Port Arthur discharges into the lake.

The western portion of Ontario contains numerous flourishing towns. The two chief rivers are: the Thames, flowing through London and Chatham, the latter of which derives its supply from its waters, and the Grand, which furnishes the supply for Brantford. Toronto pumps its supply from lake Ontario, the water being carried beneath the harbour through a tunnel. The drainage has been deposited without treatment in the lake, but plans are now under way to instal a large filtration plant. This cannot be too highly praised, for, although lake Ontario is too large, and the flow is too great, to admit of gross contamination, still wind storms constantly tend to drive pollution ashore, whence it is liable to be carried by flies and other agencies to the inhabitants of the city, or, what is the same thing, to the farms whence their milk supply is derived. Port Hope, Cobourg, and Kingston derive domestic supplies from the lake also, and, unfortunately, drain into it.

Montreal has, for 50 years, obtained water from above the Lachine rapids. It was conducted through an open canal to the pumping station, whence it was raised to the reservoirs upon the mountain. Lately, however, closed concrete conduits have taken the place of the open canal. Much has been said regarding the use of this raw water, and there are chances of dangerous pollution from a dense population, but, a much more pressing question is whether this great city should be allowed to pour its drainage into the river. We are inclined to expend enormous sums to get good water, but it is far more important to be certain that this water supply is returned to the river in an unpoisoned condition. People have been accustomed to make money by supplying water; therefore, they seem to see no gain in proper drainage, simply because it gives no direct money returns.

The great tributary of the St. Lawrence, the Ottawa river, furnishes domestic supplies to various towns from New Liskeard to Montreal, a distance of 400 miles. Haileybury and New Liskeard pump by steam from lake Timiskaming; Pembroke pumps by steam from Allumette lake; Ottawa has its supply led through two miles of steel pipes laid in the bottom of the river and pumped direct throughout the city by water-power.

IRRIGATION—Notwithstanding the fact that the farm districts of Ontario and Quebec suffer annually, from drought during the summer, yet no attempt is made to irrigate, although many suitable creeks are to be found. This is remarkable because the whole population is accustomed to building small dams for lumbering and milling purposes and also to digging ditches for drainage purposes. It is a natural step to conduct water in ditches from a dam above, for use as a fertilizer, as well as for a source of moisture.

DRAINAGE—If the people of central Canada do not resort to irrigation, they undertake extensive drainage schemes. Kent and Essex counties in Ontario are remarkable in this regard, and other districts are constantly extending the area of tillable land. This is beginning to have an effect upon the rivers. Swamps are reservoirs, just as lakes are reservoirs, in which the upland drainage is collected to seep slowly through the muck and earth toward streams and rivers. When the drainage is led past these valuable reservoirs by free flow in ditches, it sweeps forward without restraint, and the rivers receive a great bulk of water in a short time, causing the annual floods that scourge many districts. Again, of the water that falls from the clouds, 50% is "fly-off," or evaporation, 33% is "run-off," or stream flow, and the remainder, 17%, is "cut-off," or stored in the ground. This ground storage serves to keep the land moist and also to maintain the stream flow during the late summer until the autumn rains restore the supply. It will be seen, therefore, what an important part the swamps play in the regulation of our streams, and I submit that they should be jealously guarded as reservoirs and as forest reserves throughout the whole Dominion.

NAVIGATION—The Great lakes and the St. Lawrence afford the greatest inland navigation route in the world. Jacques Cartier and Champlain could reach Montreal only in row boats, but, since 1850, an immense amount of dredging has been done in the St. Lawrence, so that, to-day, ocean liners of 30 feet draft freely ascend to Montreal. West of Montreal, a great system of canals has been constructed at a cost of $80,000,000, so that a 2,200 ton boat can sail from the Atlantic 2,200 miles into the heart of our Continent. This great enlargement of the actual river has, of course, improved the freedom of its flow and therefore tends to somewhat lower the general water surface from Superior to Quebec. With the increasing size and draught of boats upon the Great lakes, this lowering of the surface is making itself felt, especially in lake Erie. To maintain a navigable depth it is proposed to build a dam across the Niagara river above the Black Rock bridge. The proposition is fraught with difficulties. Storms from the south-west "pile" the water of lake Erie toward the Niagara outlet, and this "pile" upon the already raised surface will flood valuable property. Again, as part of the natural flow is arrested and held upon lake Erie, lake Ontario does not receive as great a supply, and its surface would tend to fall, unless, in turn, its outlet were also dammed; and so on down the river through lake St. Francis to the head of Montreal harbour, where the loss of every inch in height necessitates expensive dredging to ensure, in the autumn, sufficient depth for ocean-going vessels. It is hoped, however, that a general system of raised levels throughout the St. Lawrence will yet be secured.

POWER—The St. Lawrence system, having the most densely settled communities along its banks, has been called upon to furnish power for manufacturing and municipal needs. Fort William and Port Arthur on lake Superior derive power from the Kaministikwia river at the Kakabeka falls, 19 miles distant, where a head of 175 feet generates 7,000 H.P. Sault Ste. Marie depends upon water-power for its existence. The head is only 18 feet, but the discharge is 60,000 c.f.s. and very constant. Pulp mills, a steel plant and municipal utilities are the chief users of the power. Nipigon river just below Fort William, offers great power, which will be developed when a market presents itself. Sudbury is the centre of a mining district which has received power from the Spanish river at Turbine since 1904. The head is 85 feet. Vermilion river is now furnishing power to other mines in this district. The French river has not been developed, but, as the western link of the Ottawa navigation, it may yet furnish considerable power at the proposed dam sites.

The Severn and other rivers in western Ontario have small local powers, but the great Niagara developments completely overshadow anything else in the district. Unfortunately, only half the descent between lakes Erie and Ontario has, so far, been utilized, except in the case of the Cataract Power Company, where the head is 270 feet. The Trent river, flowing diagonally through Ontario to the bay of Quinte, has several powers developed, and the dressing up of the river for navigation purposes may lead to further installations. Below Prescott, the St. Lawrence river plunges through a series of rapids, falling 100 feet in 30 miles. The sloping surface does not lend itself as readily to power purposes as an abrupt fall, and the rapid water creates ice difficulties. Consequently, nothing has been done so far, but a company is now seeking permission to build a dam and power house in the vicinity of Cornwall.

From Coteau, at the foot of lake St. Francis, to the head of lake St. Louis, 20 miles above Montreal, the St. Lawrence falls over 80 feet in 15 miles, but the same difficulties present themselves as at Cornwall. Lately, however, a power has been obtained from the Soulanges canal, and another development is proposed at Cedars; while the old Beauharnois canal has been transferred to a company that is constructing a power at St. Timothée. No attempt, however, is being made to completely dam the river, although the numerous islands indicate this to be possible, and a river arranged in successive steps is a most valuable power stream.

Montreal has had a hydraulic pumping system since 1854, but not until 1897 was an attempt made to procure power from the great Lachine rapids. Only 14 feet head was secured, and great trouble was experienced from ice. It is an example of the waste incurred by partial development. The rapid water above Montreal prohibits surface ice from Dorval down to Lachine, and large quantities of anchor ice form in this open stretch. This drifts down through the rapids and blocks the whole river in the vicinity of Montreal, so that the water rises and floods the wharves and shores in its endeavour to pass through its ice-gorged channel. If a large rock-fill dam, similar to those used on the Winnipeg river, were constructed across the Lachine rapids, then the surface of lake St. Francis would be produced to Heron island, where sluices and a power house could be constructed, making the whole flow available through a fall of 25 feet. Another dam at St. Helen island would pen up the Laprairie basin 25 feet higher than the harbour, creating another great water-power. As the surface of these ponds would be level and quiet, they would freeze over early in the season, thus preventing the formation of the ice that now causes such havoc in the port of Montreal, and boats would pass up from the harbour through only two locks with great basins between them, instead of through the many locks and narrow channel of the Lachine canal.

Montreal also obtains power from the Shawinigan falls, on the St. Maurice, 85 miles distant, and from the Chambly plant on the Richelieu river, 20 miles distant,

Quebec has three power stations, one each on the Jacques Cartier, the Montmorency and the Chaudière. The tributaries of the St. Lawrence below Quebec present remarkable power possibilities, as they flow in rock basins with many abrupt falls.

New Brunswick—An abundant rainfall, and a snowfall which does not melt until April, fills the lakes and swamps with a store of water that keeps the rivers replenished until the autumn, when the rains augment the flow to some extent and maintain it beneath the snow. The spring melting furnishes a great body of water, most of which, unfortunately, runs away. There are several rivers with exceptional power possibilities, but, so far, only the St. John river has been exploited. The Grand Falls Power Company is building a plant at that place to develop 80,000 H.P. eventually, under a head of 130 feet. This will be used for the manufacture of pulp and for the municipal supplies of Woodstock, Fredericton and St. John, the latter 165 miles distant.

Nova Scotia—The Province is 300 miles long, but only 75 miles wide. It is not to be expected, therefore, that large rivers offering great power would exist. Numerous power plants are furnishing light, but steam plants will probably form the chief source of power in a province whose coal supply is so great and so well distributed.

DOMESTIC SUPPLIES—These are generally taken from the local streams, which are small, but which are maintained in many places by large swamps or mosses. Pumping is generally done by steam power.

IRRIGATION AND NAVIGATION—No irrigation is practised.

Although the coast is navigated from end to end, and many of the rivers' mouths are entered by large tramp steamers, yet the upper reaches are too shallow or too rapid for the use of steamboats.

POWER—There are several small power plants for pulp grinding, etc., but electric energy will likely be developed through steam, there being such a plentiful supply of coal.

Ottawa Basin—It has previously been mentioned that the Ottawa river would be treated last. This was because an investigation of its watershed has been made in connection with the navigation scheme, and the knowledge gained has resulted in storage works being commenced. The Ottawa watershed is very similar to those of the north slope of the St. Lawrence basin, and a detailed description is of interest because the Ottawa is typical of this class of river.

The Ottawa basin is 56,000 square miles in area. Ten thousand of this lies south of the river, and is drained by the Petawawa, Bonnechere, Madawaska, Mississippi, Rideau and South Nation rivers. Five thousand square miles drain into the main stream through insignificant tributaries. Forty thousand square miles lie north of the river. The Dumoine, Black, Coulonge, Gatineau, Lievre and Rouge rivers drain 20,000 square miles of this, and the other 20,000 square miles, which includes the drainage area above Mattawa, forms the upper basin.

This upper Ottawa basin contains Grand lake Victoria, with an area of 40 square miles, and Quinze-Expanse, having an area of 100 square miles. The area draining into Grand lake Victoria, 4,500 square miles, contains twenty lakes aggregating 300 square miles of surface and several large rivers, the Kamshigama, Kapitachuan and Shoshokwan. At the outlet of Quinze-Expanse lake the watershed area has increased to 10,000 square miles, and the Kinojevis and Opasatika systems of lakes and rivers have increased the high-water flow from 25,000 c.f.s. to 80,000 c.f.s.

This stream now enters the north end of lake Timiskaming, having, in the intervening stretch of 15 miles, descended 300 feet over rocky barriers that present wonderful visions of water-power. All this power has, virtually, been disposed of by lease, for the remainder of this century. Lake Timiskaming extends 60 miles south from New Liskeard to Timiskaming wharf. Between Timiskaming wharf and Mattawa the river is broken by the Long Sault and Mattawa rapids with a fall of 40 feet each. To the west of lake Timiskaming is lake Timagami, part of which flows in *via* the Montreal river, and to the east of Timiskaming is lake Kipawa, draining a territory of 2,300 square miles. The latter has a surface of 100 square miles and is nearly 300 feet higher than Timiskaming. The whole basin is 20,000 sq. miles in area, and the run-off at Mattawa is 110,000 c.f.s. during floods, but dwindles down, to about 10,000 c.f.s. or less during the low-water period.

The regimen of a river, that is, the discharge at high water, at low water, and at intermediate stages, is studied by keeping a daily record of its surface at several points—lake expansions if possible—and then metering the flow at high water, medium water and low water. As the lake rises, the discharge increases in a regular ratio, and, as it falls, the discharge diminishes at a similar rate.

The lockmasters on the Canadian canal systems measure the depth of water on the lock-sills every day in the year. This has been done at Ottawa since 1844, and, owing to this most fortunate circumstance, we can deduce the discharge on each day of the twenty odd thousand days since. I cannot too strongly urge upon all who desire to conserve our water supplies this simple matter of keeping daily gauge readings, winter and summer, for, whenever information is required to develop water-power, to build locks, or to construct reservoir dams, this record is a fundamental requirement.

The record of the Ottawa river has been charted, and, from it, the following general facts have been obtained. The average flow during sixty years has been 55,000 c.f.s., or about 1 c.f.s. for each square mile of watershed. That is, if the main river and all its tributaries had the spring flood conserved in reservoirs, the flow at Besserer Grove would then average 55,000 c.f.s., instead of rising to 250,000 c.f.s. in May, 1876, and shrinking to 10,000 during the winter months of other years.

Diagrams made by the Georgian Bay Canal Survey branch of the Public Works Department show how the flow accumulates *en route* from Mattawa to Montreal during some typical years in the history of the river. The peak of the flood is always reached during the month of May, generally between the 10th and 30th. The flow begins to increase about the 1st of April and falls to normal during July, whence it falls steadily till the succeeding month of April, except for the rise due to the autumn rains during October and November. September shows the lowest water, and January, February and March are always near the danger point for power developments, thus immensely diminishing the value of the river. In fact, during the winter of 1908, it was difficult to get from this great river power enough to carry on the public utilities at Ottawa. This brought affairs to a crisis, and the local power holders came to an agreement to construct a series of stop-log sluices across the Chaudière falls, thereby saving the water that formerly ran to waste, and also creating a head-basin to lessen the ice difficulties. The basin formed, however, is only three square miles in extent, and a draught of 10,000 c.f.s. would lower its surface 10 feet in a day. It was therefore necessary to examine the lake reservoirs along the route with a view to storage. Above Ottawa is Deschenes lake, 45 square miles in area, lac des Chats, 40 square miles in area, Coulonge lake, 25 square miles in area and Pembroke lake, 60 square miles in area, and, above Mattawa, is lake Timiskaming, 115 square miles in area, with Kipawa, 110 square miles in area, and the Quinze-Expanse, 100 square miles in area. Timiskaming, Kipawa, and Quinze-Expanse form a system of reservoirs that can be cheaply controlled. It is greater in extent than all the other lakes in the Ottawa basin put together, and capable, owing to the character of the country, of being raised, not 4 or 5 feet, but 15 or 20 feet.

A stream 100 feet wide and 3 feet deep, running 1 foot per second, or two-thirds of a mile an hour, would fill 1 square mile a foot deep in 24 hours; in other words, 322 c.f.s. will fill or empty a square mile in one day. Now, if a reservoir is 100 square miles in extent and a layer 20 feet in depth is stored on it, there would be 2,000 square mile-feet of storage. This is just about the capacity of each of the three lakes, Timiskaming, Kipawa and Quinze-Expanse, so that, altogether, their storage would amount to 6,000 square miles 1 foot deep. It would take a flow of 18,000 c.f.s. to empty the three reservoirs in 100 days, or a flow of 12,000 c.f.s. to empty them in 150 days—the average low-water period of the river. If we encroach upon the spring flood and allow only a normal flow to pass, these three great reservoirs would be filled up with a reserve supply to be fed out during November, December, January, February and March, and would, thereby, double the present insufficient low-water flow.

This conservation is necessary, not only to augment the winter flow, but also to restrain the flood and prevent unduly strong currents in the navigation scheme. The scheme is, briefly, to dress the river up in convenient reaches by large rock-fill dams provided with sluice openings to pass the flow. from basin to basin, locks being provided at each dam. It would be possible to build the dams required at any point as soon as the reservoirs are completed, and offer, in advance of a navigation project, sites for power development with a guaranteed steadiness of flow, and a constant head without ice difficulties.

The river being thus arranged by dams, power would be developed on a general scheme, which could be enlarged to utilize the whole flow at each point in years to come, when transmission may convey to unheard-of distances, and when large blocks of power will be required for heating, for nitrogen fixation, for smelting and for other electro-chemical processes. .

The key note of conservation is not only to prevent waste, but also to encourage useful development. Our winters furnish snow.

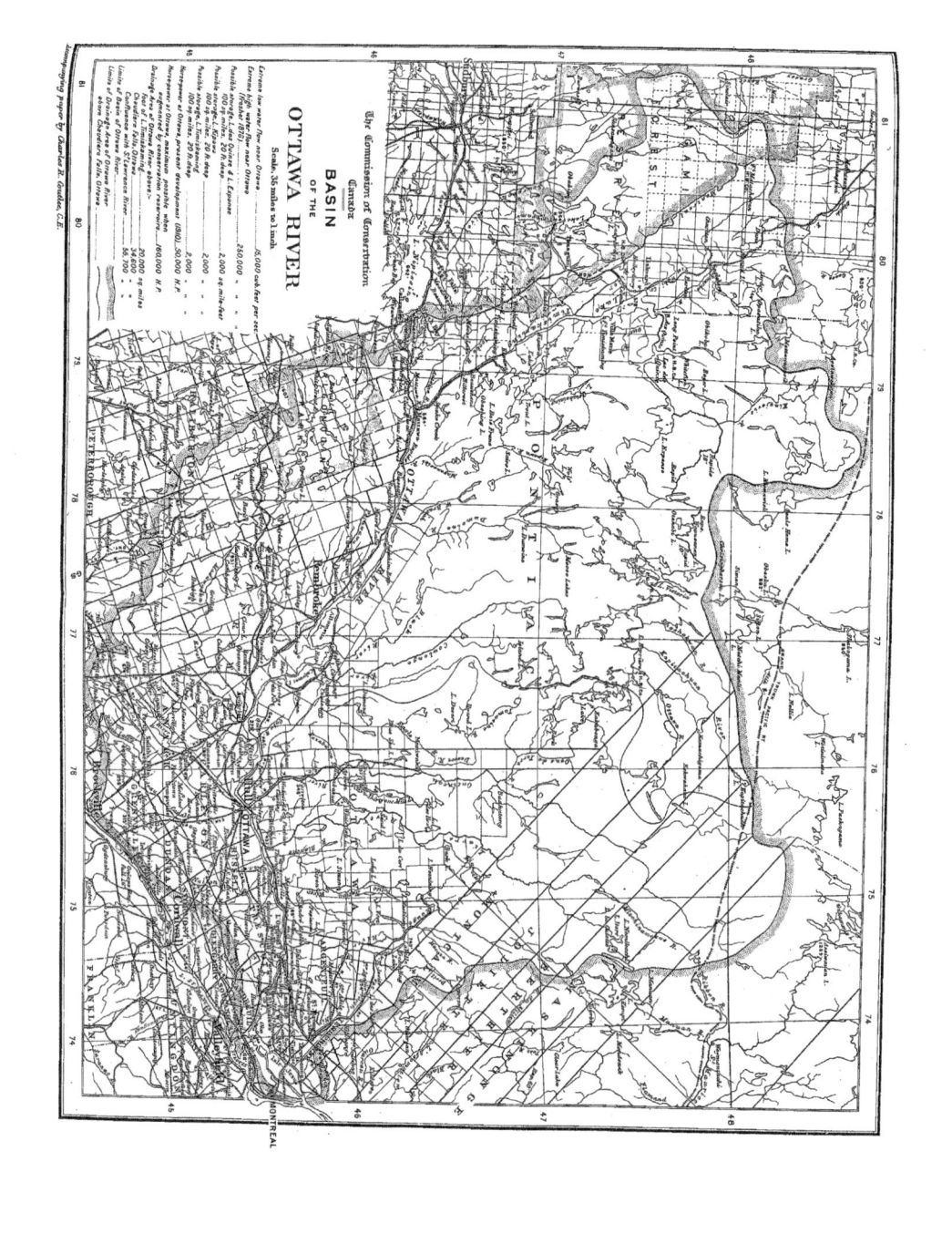

The Commission of Conservation, Canada
BASIN OF THE OTTAWA RIVER
Scale, 36 miles to 1 inch

Lowest low water flow near Ottawa .... 6,000 cub. feet per sec.
Lowest high water flow near Ottawa (flood of 1876) ... 240,000 " " " "
Passable strength, Lake Quinze & L. Expanse
  2,000 sq. miles, 20 ft. deep .... 2,000 " " " "
Passable strength, Lake Kippewa
  100 sq. miles, 20 ft. deep .... 2,000 " " " "
Horsepower at Ottawa, present development (1910) .... 50,000 H.P.
Horsepower at Ottawa, maximum possible when
  augmented by conservation reservoirs .... 160,000 H.P.
Drainage Area of Ottawa River above
  foot of L. Timiskaming .... 20,000 sq. miles
Confluence with St. Lawrence River .... 54,800 " "
Limits of Basin of Ottawa River
  above Chaudière Falls, Ottawa .... 56,700 " "

Lithographing prepared by Charles E. Goulden, C.E.

that is, water in the best form for storage, and it is following the trend of nature to create reservoirs for its conservation. The ultimate result will be that the territory from Labrador to Fort William must become a great power centre, and, by improved transmission, distribute power to great distances. Indeed, by the end of the twentieth century, the Ottawa valley may be the power heart of the world and the centre of a delightful district unsullied by coal smoke and beautified by reservoirs of unrivalled natural beauty.

DISCUSSION ON ORGANIZATION

Hon. CLIFFORD SIFTON: We have concluded that portion of our programme which consists in getting information from our friends who are specialists in the various subjects they have discussed. We have now arrived at the point at which we must organize for business and determine the lines upon which we shall proceed. In connection with the organization, one difficulty has presented itself to my mind, and it is a somewhat serious difficulty, but one which, I think, we can overcome. This Commission, of necessity, embraces representatives from all over the country. The statute provides for one regular annual meeting, and it provides also, for other meetings being held upon emergency for particular purposes. It must be obvious that the natural tendency of such a Commission as this would be to make the annual meeting one for the purpose merely of ratifying what the officials had done during the year. Unless that tendency is checked at the outset, that is what it would naturally develop into, and obviously that would be very objectionable. I do not want this movement to be driven by the power of the man who happens to be chairman for the time being: What we want is the moral support of every member of the Commission and of his friends in every section of the country. How can that best be achieved? It would be absurd to think that a commission consisting of twenty-six or twenty-seven men could themselves conduct investigations into all the special subjects entrusted to us. Ordinarily speaking, a commission is efficient in proportion as it is small, but our work must necessarily consist in obtaining as widespread support as possible of the objects we advocate. I make this suggestion for your consideration. It seems to me that the best method of accomplishing our work would be to organize into a number of Committees, dividing the Commission up into committees upon various important branches of natural resources, and appointing one man as chairman of each committee. The result of that would be that the Chairmen of the committees, with myself as Chairman of the general organization, would be a working executive of the Commission, and we would have a much more effective influence brought to bear in favour of the matters we advocate in that way than in any other. There are various departments, lands, minerals, waters, water-powers, forests, fisheries, public health, and, besides these, we should have a committee to preserve friendly relations with the press and other organizations which may be engaged in doing work of the same kind. For instance, Mr. Kelly Evans is at the head of an organization for the preservation of fish and game in the province of Ontario; while the Canadian Forestry Association has done useful work in furtherance of their objects. These and other organizations we must keep in touch with, and, at the same time, give them to understand that we are not interfering with them, but that we desire to help them in every possible way. We ought to have a committee to ascertain what organizations of that kind there are and in what way they can help us and we can help them. I should like to have your views on this suggestion, and, if there is any other suggestion of a different character, I should like to hear it.

Hon. Mr. Cochrane: Do you mean that the sub-committees would investigate and report to a general meeting so that there might be a discussion before any conclusion is reached?

The Chairman: That is my idea. We can appoint sub-committees now and, in that way, we will make a beginning and, to some extent, determine on the lines of work. I presume that, with regard to most of the subjects, it would take a committee the best part of a year to ascertain the general development of the subject and determine what could best be done. The sub-committees might be appointed to-day, hold their meetings and take stock of the conditions.

Hon. Mr. Cochrane: My idea was to form committees and let them go on with their investigations and have a meeting six months or a year hence, but, if there is any better suggestion, I would be glad to agree to it.

Hon. Mr. Fisher: If the Committees are formed at once, it would be well for those committees to have a little informal discussion before this meeting of the Commission be concluded; otherwise there would be a danger that no definite action would be decided on during the coming year. We cannot attack everything at once, but there are some things, perhaps, upon which it would be necessary for the committees to have a little preliminary discussion as to what they would take up and ask for immediately, and what they would ask for a little later on. If you appoint the committees this morning, some of them will meet this afternoon and to-morrow morning, and, probably, we might have reports from them for consideration to-morrow afternoon.

The Chairman: Is that the wish of the Commission?

Mr. HENDRY: The Hon. Mr. Fisher has expressed my views on the matter.

SENATOR EDWARDS: Is it the intention that the central authorities do everything, or will the provinces by themselves take up these matters?

THE CHAIRMAN: We hope that everybody will assist in the work of the Commission. The statute is extremely wide; it gives us power to deal with any question that we may consider to be a question of conservation of natural resources, but, of course, our power is purely advisory. However, inasmuch as Parliament has unanimously constituted this body, we have a right to expect that Parliament will do a good deal towards carrying out our recommendations. If Parliament was serious in constituting such a body as this, then Parliament should be prepared to go a considerable distance to carry out such recommendations as may be made. I think we have every reason to hope, judging by the cordial way in which the matter has been taken up by our friends of the Provincial Governments, that they also, will look with a friendly eye upon such recommendations as may be brought to their attention. Of course, the value of the recommendations will depend upon the care with which the subject is investigated by us. It is our object to co-operate with every government and every body and every association that is engaged in work similar to the work we have in view. There are many branches in which voluntary associations are doing valuable work, and they can assist us and we can assist them. Is the view expressed by Mr. Fisher the view of the meeting?

The meeting expressed assent.

THE CHAIRMAN: I would suggest that we appoint, as we do in the House of Commons, a committee to strike the Committees, and which will report this afternoon at three o'clock. I would suggest that the ex-officio members of the Commission who are here, those who are members of the Federal and local Governments, should act as a committee to strike the Committees.

It was moved by Mr. J. F. Mackay, Toronto, seconded by Hon. Mr. Grimmer, and adopted: "That the members of the Dominion and Provincial Governments present, together with Senator Edwards, be a committee to strike Committees on the different subjects."

SENATOR EDWARDS: We have spoken about the conservation of a great many things, but no one has referred to a very important matter —the conservation of property that has been already constructed. Millions and millions of dollars are lost annually, which might be saved if fire-proof buildings were erected. It may be said that the insurance companies make good this loss to individuals, but, after all, it is a waste. I think that industrial establishments, as well as dwellings, should be constructed to-day so as to minimize the enormous loss by fire. To give an illustration, the company of which I am president, had a property which was burnt down, and, before it burnt, it cost $19,000 a year to insure it; but, to-day, we have a new fire-proof building, and we can get the same amount of insurance for $600 a year. There is a saving effected in that way, and besides, there is the additional guarantee that it will not burn down again. That property is within a mile of where we are meeting, and if, before we separate, the Commissioners desire to see it, I should be glad to have them come.

Not only is it fire-proof, but it is a property constructed to conserve power. Before we bought that property, the person who owned it was going to put in a steam engine to run the mills. That same property is run to-day by hydraulic machinery, and, after supplying ourselves, we will have 6,000 H.P. to sell. It is a very interesting property, not only to lumbermen, but to all those engaged in industrial pursuits.

THE CHAIRMAN thanked Senator Edwards for the invitation to visit the property.

MR. SNOWBALL: In the different provinces we have natural resources that we do not, to-day, know the value or the extent of. I would suggest that there should also be formed a committee representing the provinces, each with a Chairman, which would hold regular meetings during the year, so that a provincial report, covering the natural resources of each province and the possible means of developing them, may be submitted to the regular meetings of the Commission. For instance, the lumbermen of the whole Dominion, scattered as they are from British Columbia to New Brunswick, might bring in a forestry report dealing generally with the question, but there might be other forestry interests in New Brunswick, for example, that would not be touched upon. I think it would aid us very largely in our annual meetings if we had from the representatives of each province suggestions as to the conservation of the natural resources within that province.

DR. FERNOW: I believe that suggestion to be a good one because, by it, we would be enabled to consider the problems peculiar to each section of the country.

THE CHAIRMAN: We have not decided anything as yet as to what we shall do. I think the suggestion made by Mr. Snowball and by Dr. Fernow is an excellent one, and I do not see how we can successfully hope to do our work unless it is carried out. We must organize a centre for the propaganda of the objects of this Commission in the capital of every province, and it will be a splendid thing if we can get a strong commission in every province to co-operate with us. If that is done, we shall have some hope of doing our work successfully. We must secure the good-will of as many co-operating organizations as we can, and the first part of our duty will be to appoint just such committees.

Hon. Mr. Fisher: The two main things before us at the present moment are: an inventory of the natural resources of the country, and a spread of our propaganda through the country so as to arouse public opinion along the lines in which we are interested. These are the pressing needs of our work at the moment, and I would like each committee to bear these two things in mind.

The Chairman: I would suggest that the Commission adjourn now and that the committees meet and prepare their reports.

The meeting then adjourned.

THURSDAY AFTERNOON—THE COMMITTEES

The Commission met at half-past two o'clock. There was a general and informal discussion as to the best method of organization, and the following committees were formed, after which the meeting adjourned until Friday morning.

FISHERIES.—Hon. F. L. Haszard (Chairman), Hon. Hugh Armstrong, Hon. Frank Cochrane, Hon. Price Ellison, Hon. W. C. H. Grimmer, Hon. A. K. Maclean, Dr. Howard Murray.

FORESTS.—Senator W. C. Edwards (Chairman), Mr. Frank Davison, Dr. B. E. Fernow, Mr. John Hendry, Mgr. J. C. K. Laflamme, Hon. Frank Oliver, Mr. W. B. Snowball, and the ex-officio members of the Commission who represent the various provinces.

LANDS.—Dr. J. W. Robertson (Chairman), Dr. Geo. Bryce, Hon. Sydney Fisher, Hon. Benj. Rogers, Dr. W. J. Rutherford, and the ex-officio members of the Commission who represent the various provinces.

MINERALS.—Dr. H. S. Béland (Chairman), Mr. John Hendry, Dr. Howard Murray, Hon. W. Templeman, and the ex-officio members of the Commission who represent the various provinces.

PRESS AND CO-OPERATING ORGANIZATIONS.—Mr. J. F. MacKay (Chairman), Hon. Jules Allard, Dr. Geo. Bryce, Dr. Howard Murray, Dr. H. M. Tory.

PUBLIC HEALTH.—Mr. E. B. OSLER (Chairman), Dr. H. S. Béland, Hon. J. A. Calder, Hon. Sydney Fisher, Sir Sandford Fleming, Dr. Cecil C. Jones.

WATERS AND WATER-POWERS.—Mr. F. D. Monk (Chairman), Hon. Jules Allard, Hon. Frank Cochrane, Hon. Price Ellison, Hon. W. C. H. Grimmer, Mr. C. A. McCool.

Moved by Mr. John Hendry, seconded by Mr. C. A. McCool, that the designation of the Committee on Fisheries be changed to read "Committee on Fisheries, Game and Fur-bearing Animals."—Carried.

That the report of the Committee on Resolutions, as read by the Secretary, be adopted.—Carried.

Moved by Senator Edwards, seconded by Mr. Hendry: That the Committee do now adjourn to meet again to-morrow (Friday, Jan. 21st) at 11 o'clock, and that, in the meantime, the Committees meet to consider their recommendations.—Carried.

The Commission then adjourned.

FRIDAY MORNING—REPORTS OF COMMITTEES

The minutes of the last meeting were read and confirmed.

THE CHAIRMAN: I shall now call on the Chairman of the Committee on Forests to present the report of that Committee.

SENATOR EDWARDS presented the report of the Committee on Forests.

COMMITTEE ON FORESTS

Your Committee on Forests begs to report as follows:—

That, through fires originating from various causes, and through reckless cutting by many engaged in lumbering, the forests of Canada have been unduly diminished. That, in view of the general approaching scarcity in the world's supply of lumber, and in view of the rapidly growing needs of Canada for timber for use in the future within our own borders, as well also, as the fact that the maintenance of the forests means the preservation of our water supply, so necessary for domestic use, for navigation, for irrigation and, last, but not least, for motive power, which, through electrical development, is to play so important a part in future industrial and manufacturing operations of all kinds, it is expedient that a policy of forest conservation be entered upon at once. Next to our great agricultural development and conservation, and the conservation of public health, there is no more important matter for the Canadian people than the conservation and perpetuation of our forests. In fact, such is vital to the future well-being of our country.

The question then arises—Can our forests be conserved and perpetuated, and can waste lands denuded of forest growth and unsuited for agricultural purposes be reforested and made a source of value to the State? The answer is—Yes; your Committee believes that such can be accomplished. Other countries, notably France and Germany, have accomplished it, and why not Canada? But the accomplishment of this highly desirable result can be brought about only through the co-operation of the Dominion Government (in whom is vested the ownership of the timber on the public domain of the provinces of Manitoba, Saskatchewan and Alberta, and the unorganized territory) with the various other Provinces of the Dominion and the people of Canada generally.

The three great requisites are: the prevention, in so far as such can be accomplished, of forest fires; systematic cutting on the part of lumbermen, under well-devised and strictly enforced regulations and reforestation of the burned-over areas unsuited for agricultural purposes.

With the object of bringing about the much desired results, your Committee begs to suggest that the first steps to be taken are to ascertain as nearly as such can be done, the quantity of each kind of standing timber in the provinces and unorganized territory, in order to get a reasonable estimate of the annual growth of each and the amount annually cut for domestic use and exportation; and, with the view of endeavouring to bring about uniformity of operation, in so far as conditions will permit, to procure all available statutes and regulations governing the cutting of timber and the prevention of forest fires in the various provinces and unorganized territory. Also we would suggest that the best means possible be taken to ascertain the systems adopted in France, Germany and other countries for the preservation and perpetuation of their forests and for reforesting areas denuded of forest, in order that your Committee may be placed in the best possible position to recommend the most desirable means of conserving for Canada and its future use one of its most valuable assets.

If the suggestions given in this short report are approved, your Committee will be glad to receive such instructions as will enable it to carry out, in so far as it can be done, what is herein suggested.

All of which is respectfully submitted.

(Sgd.) WM. C. EDWARDS, Chairman

DISCUSSION ON REPORT OF COMMITTEE ON FORESTS

DR. BRYCE: Mr. Chairman, I think the report is very comprehensive, but it leaves out the very important questation of afforestation. The third part of the report speaks of regions being burned over, but we have in the West millions of acres that never were in forest. It is all looked at in the report from the standpoint of land that has been under forest. I am not objecting to the report, but it would seem that there was an omission there.

SENATOR EDWARDS: We could amend the report by simply adding a sentence regarding afforestation in such prairie sections.

HON. MR. FISHER: The immediate actual suggestion is to ensure an inventory of practically all our present forest wealth. I think that it is one of the most important works that we can undertake. I did not understand, however, that the Committee made any suggestion as to how that can be done. It is a pretty difficult undertaking and I do not know at present how it can be done unless we simply take the reports of the different forestry departments. That is not sufficient. Somebody will have to do more than that in the near future and I would ask for a little discussion as to how steps may be taken to obtain a more accurate inventory of our forest wealth.

SENATOR EDWARDS: The same idea occurred to the Committee, but we thought that perhaps it would be going a little too far; that that question was one which involved ways and means and that we could not very well suggest how it should be done. The Committee also were of the opinion that working out anything of that kind would take some little time. I agree with the Minister of Agriculture that the present information is not at all sufficient, and, if the various provinces and the Dominion on its part, having regard to the lands over which it has jurisdiction, would take up that question of getting accurate information, it would be a great advantage. But again, I say, it involves ways and means and, to do it accurately would involve a great deal of work. I think it could be done without involving very great expense. For instance, take Ontario; they think that they have a pretty good idea to-day of what timber they have, but, I think, in New Brunswick, the information is not at all complete. In Quebec, too, there are cursory surveys and estimates, but they are not at all sufficient. As to the other provinces, I cannot speak. I do think, and agree most thoroughly with the Minister of Agriuclture, that there is nothing more important than that one thing of finding out just what we have got and where we stand, but, as I have said, it involves ways and means.

MR. HENDRY: So far as British Columbia is concerned, we have a large territory, but we have a certain amount of information regarding our forest resources. A Commission was appointed a year ago by the Provincial Government, of which Mr. Goodeve, who is here, is a member, and Mr. Goodeve will be able to give a great deal of information. Of course, there is a great extent of country that has not yet been gone over. That will take some time. There is no doubt that, as far as we have gone, we will be able to give in reference to the country that has been explored, a great deal of the information which we are now looking for. The Dominion Government owns a considerable part of the lands in British Columbia, having obtained them for railway purposes. Besides, they have some three and a half million acres in the Peace River country, which, of course, they will administer. They

Dense cluster of cones on upper branches of Lodgepole Pine.

have already been administering the fire protection, jointly with the Province; that is, so far as anything has been done in that direction. I think we will be able to get a great deal of information from the Provincial Government which will be of assistance. Mr. Goodeve can explain better than I can, as he is a member of the local Commission on Forestry in British Columbia.

MR. SNOWBALL: I am very much pleased to hear the Minister of Agriculture bring up this matter of tabulating natural resources, especially when we consider that it will involve a considerable expense for the Dominion to secure such an inventory. I rather inferred from what I read in the newspapers that his Department will be the one responsible for the raising of the finances necessary to carry on this work. I see he has at once grasped what is needed of the Commissioners and, having grasped it, I am more confident in the hope that we shall be able to get the funds necessary to find out what the natural resources of our country are.

In New Brunswick the Provincial Government has, I think I can say, a fairly accurate, if not absolutely definite, knowledge of what timber exists on their Crown lands. They have never had a full report on the lands in the Province and have to depend very largely on the holders of leases for the information they get respecting the timber on the lands under lease. A large amount of land in that Province was given away years ago to railway companies, and we would have to depend on information supplied by these corporations unless we are prepared to spend a large amount of money to make a full survey of the province of New Brunswick. However, I think a cursory survey, one that is not so very full, can be made for that Province; and, if the Commission should recommend that some assistance should be given to the several Provinces towards a survey to find out what the natural resources are, not only those they know of, but others that may exist of which they are unaware, it would be a very good thing and an expenditure well made on the part of the Dominion.

It may be contended that it is the provinces who will benefit. That is true to a very large extent, but any assets discovered within any province of the Dominion benefit the whole Dominion and are assets of the whole Dominion as much as of any province. I have had doubts, and I brought the matter up in the Committee in order to find out how great an expenditure we, as a Committee of this Commission, should suggest that the Government make for a forest survey. Other Committees, no doubt, will make suggestions along similar lines and, if the Government saw fit, a general suggestion could be made of the same kind that the provinces should investigate the forests, mines and other resources at the same time, and thus bring in at a very early date, their reports of what the real resources are.

Referring to fires, that is something we should deal with before the Commission meets again. In New Brunswick the Intercolonial, a Government railway, passes right through the Province from north to south, coming in at Campbellton and going out at the southern border into Nova Scotia. Then it runs from St. John through to Shediac and from Miramichi through to Fredericton. Those who are familiar with the Province will at once see that the Intercolonial passes through great timber areas that are of great value to the Province and to the Dominion. That Government railway is the only work that does not come under the general laws of the Province as far as fire guardianship is concerned, and the great devastating fires that we have had in the province of New Brunswick have been along the line of the Intercolonial. What should be done by the Chairman and this Commission is to exert their influence on the Government in order to secure immediate legislation whereby the Intercolonial railway will have to conform with the laws of the several Provinces, so far as fire guardianship is concerned. That is an important subject in the province of New Brunswick, one on which I think this Commission will feel it its duty to see that some action is taken at this session of Parliament, or some promise given by the Intercolonial Commission that they will co-operate with the Crown Lands Department of New Brunswick to assist in watching their road, as far as possible, cleaning up the right-of-way and having fire wardens on duty in the dry season, so that fire will not devastate the area through which the road passes.

THE CHAIRMAN: That does not apply to the Intercolonial railway alone. There does not appear to be any excuse for this exemption of the railways. They are practically free from any control in regard to fire.

HON. MR. GRIMMER: The Commissioners last year, in correspondence with me, finally stated that they would conduct the Intercolonial railway under the Railway Act of Canada.

In connection with the suggestion for the electrification of the National Transcontinental railway through Quebec and New Brunswick, the preservation of standing timber is an important consideration. The line runs through 800 miles of the province of Quebec and 259 miles of the province of New Brunswick. Eighty-nine miles of that 259 is Crown land, where, in many cases, the axe has never yet been put to a tree. The virgin growth of forest is there, magnificent timber, lumber of the best kind and highest class. Another portion of it runs through lands owned by the New Brunswick Railway Co., which were given away, as Mr. Snowball said, years ago by the Province. These are magnificent timber lands, lumber of untold wealth is there; and, unless the road can be electrified, or some stringent measures are laid down whereby fire will be prevented, that whole country will burn up. If I had a map of the Province here and could show you just how that railway runs through the counties of Restigouche and Northumberland, you would at once see how fires starting out from the right-of-way of the National Transcontinental railway would destroy all that is left of the valuable timber lands of New Brunswick. I wish to say in this connection that the Commissioners of the National Transcontinental railway and the Dominion Government have assisted and are doing very well in the prevention of fires during the construction of the road. We suffered to some extent this year by a fire which started on the right-of-way. Last year we had practically no fires at all. The Dominion Government appointed 45 or 46 fire wardens. The only complaint I have to make in connection with that is, in some cases, with regard to the selections of men that were made. However, they appointed the men and the Provincial Government clothed them with all the authority of fire wardens under our Provincial Act and we swore them in as fire wardens so that they had full power to arrest without warrant, any person found violating the fire law. Last year, this arrangement worked satisfactorily and there was no fire to amount to anything along the right-of-way, but this year, a fire did get away and ran about twenty miles by seven in the Province through Crown lands, fortunately not through a valuable tract. It was quite a serious fire, but it was coped with, and we have reason to congratulate ourselves on the result so far. Last spring, from May until July, we had absolutely dry weather down there, no rain at all. The year before the fires occurred in the fall of the year. The spring fires are not, as a rule, so dangerous to the forests, as they are what we call leaf fires, while the fall fires are soil fires. The leaf fire will run through the woods and, while it destroys a lot of timber, it does not have the same effect as a fire in the fall because that not only takes the leaves and wood, but it takes the soil as well and burns down five feet, so that for a thousand years nothing will grow on that land. Look at the line of the Intercolonial railway from Chatham to Fredericton. For miles and miles after you leave Chatham junction you can see the splendid timber of our Province cross-piled and burned where it has been ruined by fire, the soil burnt out, the timber being blown over by the first strong wind that blows. The next wood that comes on, if there is any soil left, is the white and grey birch, which is useful for firewood, but for nothing else, although you can make spools of the white birch. Those valuable lands have been entirely denuded. Whatever may be said as to the National Transcontinental railway, I do feel that we in New Brunswick have a grievance so far as the Intercolonial railway is concerned. The Intercolonial railway line from Fredericton to Chatham is a hard road, the grades are heavy, and the result is that the engineers could not make time with their trains if they had the proper hoods on their smokestacks. The result is that the hoods are taken off.

In May last, Honourable Mr. Birchall, a member of the Legislature of New Brunswick, telephoned me that there were three fires on the line between Fredericton and Chatham junction in one afternoon. If we had not had fire wardens there and taken immediate steps to check the fires, there would have been a great conflagration. When I asked the Intercolonial Railway Commission to give me transportation for some of our fire wardens, the chief men whose duty it is to fight the fires, they absolutely refused to give transportation for two men over the Intercolonial railway. Mr. Butler said, in replying to me, that he would not do it because they were being asked every day for transportation for Provincial officials. No Provincial official, no head of a department, asked for transportation, except for the two men for whom I applied, and they did not get it. Yet these wardens had to go. The telephones are used everywhere, and, when a fire starts in a certain district, a warden is notified and he gets there as quickly as possible and fights the fire. We feel that we need some protection, and when we go to the Intercolonial Railway management in an effort to improve the conditions, they say they will manage the railway under the Railway Act of Canada. We cannot put ourselves up in conflict with the Dominion authorities in respect to the Intercolonial railway, but we feel there is so much involved in this matter of forest fires that there should be no question, as far as railways are concerned. If they do not wish to do anything else, they should at least clean up the right-of-way. If the right-of-way is not broad enough, we will consent to its being widened. Then let them clean out all stumps and stones and plough it up next to the forest land, so that sparks cannot do damage. But that right-of-way is not cleaned up and no attempt is made to clean it as other railways do. I called upon the Canadian Pacific railway, the Grand Southern and other railways, and they all sent crews out and burned off their rights of way. Sometimes a fire of that kind gets away from the men, but then the railway company is responsible for the damage. They make an effort to comply with the law. I am not sure about the appliances on their engines, but they clean out the right-of-way.

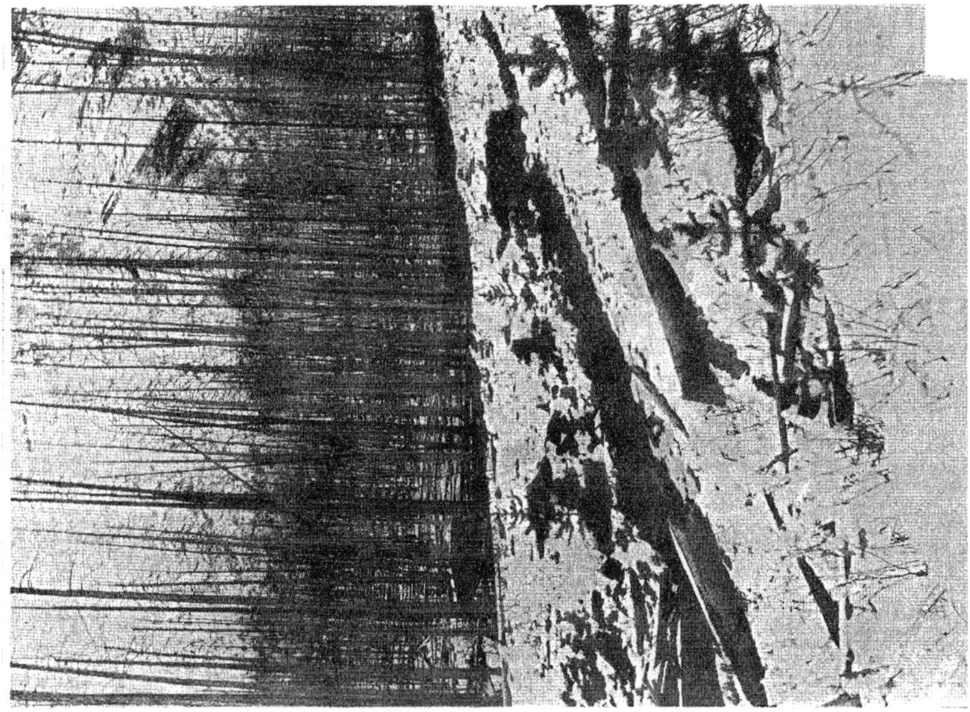

In addition, we want to cultivate and educate sentiment in respect to sportsmen, fishermen and others going into the woods, particularly in the spring. This applies to all parts of the Dominion. There is no other source so prolific of forest fires as this. We had sixty-six reported in New Brunswick this year, and of these, ten or fifteen were started by fishermen. It is a pretty hard thing to say that men shall not go in to fish in your streams, especially when you have good sport to offer them, but the majority of these men are absolutely careless, having nothing in view but the day's sport, what they are going to bring back and the size of the fish they will be able to tell about in the newspapers. They will boil a kettle against an old stump. There is nothing more fatal than that. They build a fire against an old pine stump because they find it sends back a splendid heat, but in many cases they do not take the pains to carry water and put the fire out.

Mr. Maclean: Do you issue a license?

Hon. Mr. Grimmer: We do not yet. If the provinces all joined together in doing this, it would be a benefit to the whole of Canada.

What I want particularly to impress upon the Commission is the absolute necessity of doing something to control this railway situation and make the railways, particularly the Intercolonial railway, feel that they must recognize the Provincial laws so far as fire protection is concerned; because there is nothing but a waste all along the line of the Intercolonial railway in the province of New Brunswick. I do not care what part of the road you are on, you ride through a barren waste, and, for generations to come, there will be no more timber on these lands unless they are reforested.

Dr. Fernow: I would like to accentuate the position taken by Mr. Grimmer. Here is a subject that can be taken in hand by the Commission without further planning. The rest of the recommendations, I feel, with the Minister of Agriculture, are rather in the air, are rather indefinite. Methods of procedure have not been proposed. We could probably have all the information that is in existence collated by some clerks in the office, but it is quite correct that this information is not sufficient. The task of taking stock of our natural resources in timber alone is an enormous one, a greater task than is, perhaps, realized, even if we only wish to have approximations; and, as for exactness, you might just as well strike that word out of your dictionary in so far as it applies to resources.

Some things the Committee asked are absolutely impossible to secure. The rate of growth is something which every forester would like to see answered, but it is almost impossible to ascertain it. It can only be guessed at.

There are propositions here that would take a lifetime to ascertain, and so I would suggest that the Committee be at once instructed to furnish an extensive report on the methods of fighting forest fires. As we have seen, various conditions require different methods; the provinces present conditions more or less unlike, and the methods must be varied. I think we too often generalize from short experience. We could, however, have a thorough investigation of the methods in existence and form a judgment as to where their application would be desirable. That could be done in a very short time, while the taking of stock, generally, of the standing timber would last a lifetime and involve a great expense. I have some opinions as to the methods to be pursued in reference to that, which include a personal canvass from province to province, and that brings me back to the original proposition to have the Commission further organized so as to have Provincial Committees, all meeting in the separate provinces and arranging a comprehensive plan so that some subjects can be attacked at once, like this question of forest fire protection.

MR. GOODEVE: I would like to say a word endorsing what has been said regarding destruction by forest fires. Our Commission in British Columbia has spent several months taking evidence and collecting data in regard to the various features of our timber resources. The matter mentioned by Mr. Grimmer in regard to the starting of fires by sportsmen, we have found little difficulty in controlling. We have amended our laws in this particular and have issued a large number of extracts from the law, printed on linen. The fire wardens take these and place them on the various trails and the places of ingress to the different districts, and the sportsmen are all warned. Furthermore, no settler is allowed to set out a fire in a timber district without first getting a permit from the fire warden. Timber men and others are now asking that no permit be granted for the three months of summer—June, July and August—under any conditions, and the Commissioner of Lands has that under his consideration. We find that this has greatly increased the protection, and public opinion has kept the number of fires due to sportsmen almost at a minimum.

Coming to railways, the evidence before the Commission bears out what the previous speakers have said. A very large proportion of the fires are caused by railways. It is important to bear in mind that there are conditions, in that connection, even with the railways. In my Province the grades in some districts, particularly the

A skidway left in the woods after logging.

timber districts, are heavy. I have been on trains that were stalled going up these grades and that had to wait to get up steam. The result of that is that, while the Railway Commission has laid down certain rules and regulations regarding fire appliances on engines and fire-boxes, there is a great temptation for the engineer and his fireman, when they find it nearly impossible to carry the train, to keep steam up in some way; on many occasions either to remove the fire screen altogether or, as shown in some evidence, to break through it, run a bar through it in order to get a draught. That, in some cases, becomes a great temptation. It is difficult to say just how far the Commission can go in making these mechanical restrictions. Moreover, they would have to be carefully worded. The very suggestion that was made by the Chairman has been made to the railroads, viz., that they should have an electric or gasoline track motor equipped with a hose and carrying a supply of water, with which they could follow up at regular intervals, trains going through valuable timber or have a telephone line along the telegraph line, so that a warden could telephone to a fire station and have this truck go to the scene of the fire. Of course, they demurred at the expense; but we must consider that, while nothing unfair should be done, they—the railroads—must be made to feel their responsibility.

The clearing of the right-of-way has been largely successful. The débris is left in many places; it dries in the hot summer and simply forms tinder for a large percentage of fires that come from the railways. Two of the most practical suggestions that have been put forward are, that the rights-of-way should be cleared and that the railways should be held directly responsible for fires caused by them, thus not placing on the average man the whole onus of fighting a great railway corporation. It is nearly impossible to do this. We did carry one case against the Great Northern to the Privy Council and got a verdict of $22,000 and all costs. It was a long, hard fight; but they had taken the number of the engine, knew when the fire occurred, how it occurred, and where it went to.

THE CHAIRMAN: The destruction of forests by fire is a large question affecting every province, not only as regards its interests, but as regards the interests of the whole country. We ought to have a distinct, clear and definite resolution on the subject which would authorize the Chairmen of the Committees, along with myself, to make the strongest representations on the subject to the Government. I have had to do with railway companies for twenty-five years and there is one thing you can be pretty sure of: just as soon as the law makes them responsible for anything, they will attend to it. So long as the law does not make them responsible they will not pay any attention to it. I have never been able to work out the principle on which we permit railways to go through the country spreading destruction. We do not allow anyone else to do that, and why we should permit the railways to do so, I cannot understand. For my part, I would be prepared to support the strongest possible resolution urging the Government to make the laws such that the railways will be primarily responsible. As to the Intercolonial railway, my own opinion is that it should be in the same position as any private corporation.

MR. DAVISON: As far as conservation is concerned, it is burlesque to put in our time talking about it while the railways are allowed to burn the country from Nova Scotia to British Columbia. If the destruction caused by them is not stopped, it is nonsense to attempt to conserve what we have.

Mr. Snowball suggested a resolution dealing with fires along Dominion railways.

THE CHAIRMAN: The words "Dominion railways" are subject to two interpretations. They mean either railways owned or operated by the Dominion Government, or railways operated under a Dominion charter.

HON. MR. FISHER: I think we ought first to recommend an amendment to the Railway Act which will make the railways responsible for the damages resulting from fires caused by them. Then, the question of the Intercolonial railway is a separate one.

MR. SNOWBALL: I shall redraft my resolution, if I may, and present it later in the proceedings.

DR. FERNOW: I would like to introduce another resolution as follows:

That the Committee on Forests be instructed to prepare, as soon as practicable, a comprehensive report on the methods of fighting forest fires, in existence in this country and elsewhere.—Carried.

THE CHAIRMAN: I suggest that this resolution should be brought in with Mr. Snowball's at the close of the discussion.

HON. MR. FISHER: These are two totally different subjects.

SENATOR EDWARDS: My judgment is that the suggestion in the report is the best. What this Commission is trying to arrive at, is to try and devise the best suggestion that can be recommended to the whole Dominion for the prevention of these fires, and what we have asked for is to obtain from the various provinces their existing laws and regulations in that respect in order that we may arrive at some conclusion to suggest to them all the best means to adopt. To proceed at once, I think, would be going too fast. I think it is all right to amend the Act so far as railways are concerned. I think the best suggestion came from Mr. Maclean yesterday. What is the use of our suggesting something to-day when the various provinces have existing regulations and laws? Let us get them together and, out of the whole, construct a scheme that we think is the best, and ask them to apply the suggestions we make. I think the provinces may say, if we offer suggestions to them, that we are going too fast.

DR. FERNOW: This resolution does not suggest anything to anyone; it simply proposes to bring together the information we possess, so that anyone who wishes can choose what, in his particular locality, is applicable. I believe it is within the scope of the duties of the Committee to make reports, but I propose, instead of waiting for reports on on all the subjects, to take up this important subject immediately and to secure the information that we can secure with no great difficulty.

HON. MR. HASZARD: It appears to me that, if we undertake too much just at this moment, we may lose the whole. I believe, if we could adhere to the first recommendation, that is, not only to impress but to insist, as far as possible, upon the Government so amending the Railway Act as to bring the Government-owned railways under the provisions of the various laws of the provinces which necessitate their protecting their own lines and protecting the public lands as well, it is about all we should undertake at this moment. There is no doubt that there is a great deal to be done along the other line suggested, but I think that, if we limit the resolution at present, to asking for the one practical amendment so as to bring the Government-owned railways within the provisions of the law, it would be about all we should undertake now.

THE CHAIRMAN: The principle applies to railways chartered by the Dominion as well as to the Intercolonial railway.

DR. MURRAY: I cannot see the objection to the resolution of Dr. Fernow. It seems to me to provide simply for collecting information from the different provinces and the formulation of a scheme.

SENATOR EDWARDS: That is what the report is.

DR. MURRAY: To my mind, the wording of the resolution makes it clear that all that is suggested is the collecting of the plans of the different provinces. I have much pleasure in supporting the resolution.

DR. FERNOW: It deals with but the one subject which is also dealt with by the report. It will be the first duty of the Committee to report on this subject, and the information can be secured without difficulty.

The resolution was adopted.

On the motion of Hon. A. K. Maclean the report was adopted.

COMMITTEE ON FISHERIES, GAME AND FUR-BEARING ANIMALS

THE CHAIRMAN: I shall now call upon the Chairman of the Fisheries Committee to present his report.

HON. MR. HASZARD: Owing to the fact that members of our Committee are on several other committees, we have found it impossible to discuss anything in connection with fisheries. The question being such a large one, and so many diversified interests being involved, we came to the conclusion that it was really impossible to consider it, and I agreed to tender a formal report saying we were not able to deal with the matter. Since this report was made, a communication has been handed to me from British Columbia regarding the salmon fisheries there and asking very urgently that steps be taken for the protection of those fisheries and declaring that, unless something is done immediately, the extinction of that very valuable fishery will take place within a short time. So far as I can see from the letters we have received, there is quite an international question involved that must come up if we are to deal with this matter. It is in regard to the run of the fish. They say that in Puget sound, where the fish have to pass up the Fraser river to the spawning ground, they are being taken in immense quantities on the American side. Of course, it would be difficult to know what any Commission could do in such a matter.

THE CHAIRMAN: We have heard that matter discussed for many years.

HON. MR. HASZARD: Yes, I mentioned it to show that this question will require a great deal of consideration and time. In the Maritime Provinces the lobster and oyster fisheries are the two very essential fisheries that require the attention of this Commission, but these are subjects that will take a great deal of time.

I beg to submit the formal report of the Fisheries Committee:—

Your Committee beg to report that, within the short time at their disposal, it was impossible to obtain any information on the subject of this enquiry which would be of practical use, and that it will take much time and involve much enquiry, as well as a considerable expenditure of money, before a report can be made.

(Sgd.) F. L. Haszard, Chairman

On the motion of Hon. Mr. Grimmer, seconded by Hon. Senator Edwards, this report was adopted.

COMMITTEE ON MINERALS

THE CHAIRMAN: I shall now call upon the Chairman of the Committee on Minerals.

DR. BÉLAND: Mr. Chairman, as in the case of the Committee on Fisheries, we have found it almost impossible to submit to the Commission any important recommendation, for the same reason, viz., that an enormous amount of technical information was necessary but was not readily available to the members of the Committee. Our report leaves almost entirely in the hands of the Commission what is to be done. When the Committee sat yesterday, I took upon myself to call upon Dr. Haanel, of the Mines Branch, to give us some advice.

The doctor was kind enough to come over, but he was not ready to advise the members on such short notice. This morning, however, he submitted to us some recommendations which the Committee did not care to adopt, but decided to submit to you for consideration. I beg to submit the report of the Committee and also the recommendations of Dr. Haanel:—

Your Committee begs to report that it is deemed desirable to obtain at once, a compilation of statistics relative to the known mineral resources of Canada, the annual production of minerals in each province or in any territory, and any other information which would aid the Commission to accomplish its end; and that financial provision be made for the same.

Your Committee further suggests that steps be taken to secure legislation to make it imperative upon mining companies to supply the Government with a yearly report of their output and the estimated value thereof, in order to render our statistics more accurate.

(Sgd.) Henri S. Béland, Chairman

Dr. Haanel's Recommendations

The following recommendations were submitted to the Committee on Minerals, at their request, by Dr. Eugène Haanel:—

First: the appointment of two competent mining engineers to make an inventory of our mineral resources so far as known, and to map their locations. To one of these officers are to be assigned the metalliferous deposits; to the other, the non-metallic deposits. Since this class of work is evidently more or less continuous, I recommend that this work be done by two officers permanently appointed on the staff of the Mines Branch.

Second: the early appointment on the staff of the Mines Branch of a thoroughly competent metallurgist, whose duty it shall be to report upon metallurgical processes practised in Canada, to render himself conversant with all new developments in metallurgical methods on this continent and abroad, to report upon the same and to recommend for special investigation such of these processes as would tend to a more economical treatment of our ores.

Third: the passing by Parliament of an act for regulating the use of explosives, for establishing a testing station for the investigation of all explosives now in use in Canada, for the purpose of eliminating and rendering illegal the use of those explosives which, on test and in practice, have proven to be dangerous; and for regulating the manufacture of explosives in Canada.

Fourth: as the Act creating a Department of Mines assigns to the Mines Branch the duty of collecting statistics for mineral production, and as, at present, the Mines Branch has no power to compel mine owners and owners of metallurgical plants to furnish this information, but is at the mercy of the good-will of mine owners and owners of metallurgical plants for their returns, it is recommended that a Bill or an amendment to the Mines Act be passed by Parliament to render returns of the mineral production by mine owners and owners of metallurgical plants compulsory.

The Chairman: The Committee has been very judicious in submitting Dr. Haanel's recommendations as they have done. They can be considered later.

The report was adopted.

COMMITTEE ON WATERS AND WATER-POWERS

THE CHAIRMAN: I shall now call for the report of the Committee on Waters and Water-powers.

In the absence of Mr. F. D. Monk, the Chairman, the report of this Committee was presented by Mr. C. A. McCool.

The report read as follows:—

Your Committee recommends:

That steps be taken to obtain and tabulate complete information on the subject of the waterways of Canada so far as available information goes, and, wherever practicable, that such information be supplemented by examination and inspection.

That this information comprise statements of the development of powers which have taken place, their scope and the market therefor, the amount used by the public and the rates charged.

That, for the use of the Committee on Public Health, information should also be collected showing how, and to what extent, the watercourses are being contaminated by drainage.

Your Committee further recommends:

That the Commission should, by resolution, declare that, in its opinion, there should be, in future, no unconditional titles given to water-powers, but that every grant or lease of powers should be subject to the following, among other, conditions:

1. Development within a specified time.
2. Public control of rates.
3. A rental with the power to revise same at later periods.

The report was adopted.

COMMITTEE ON LANDS

THE CHAIRMAN: I call on the Chairman of the Committee on Lands to present his report.

DR. ROBERTSON:—The Committee on Lands reports as follows:

Your Committee, having given consideration to the department of natural resources with which it is to deal, begs to present, as an interim report, an outline of work which it proposes to take up for the current year.

First Division

First: the collection and arrangement of available statistical information as to areas of agricultural lands, occupied and unoccupied, surveyed and unsurveyed.

Second: the collection of information as to soil areas, classified as to their characteristic contents, such as clay, loam, sandy or other formation.

Third, the collection of information for a classification of areas devoted to particular crops, particularly in regard to (a) soil formation (b) climatic conditions.

Fourth: the collection of information by investigations and the testimony of farmers and others, (a) as to whether agricultural lands are being depleted of the elements of fertility, or are being improved in that respect, and (b) as to the dangerous prevalence of weeds and other hindrances to their crop producing power.

Fifth: the collection of reasonably complete information as to the extent, character and availability of natural fertilizers, such as phosphates, mussel, muds, mucks, etc.

Sixth: a preliminary study of water supplies on farms for domestic and supplementary irrigation purposes, and a preliminary study of fuels and other natural sources of heat, power and light on farms.

Second Division

The carrying on of a campaign for the dissemination of information regarding the conservation of resources, particularly by a series of meetings in each province in co-operation with members of the Commission in the several provinces respectively.

Your Committee estimates that about thirty meetings would be required to cover the Dominion in a fairly adequate manner during the year.

Third Division

Your Committee is of opinion that a sum of money should be provided sufficient to meet the outlay necessary for carrying out the work which is herein recommended and would suggest that the Chairman of the Committee take up the matter with the Chairman of the Commission and a provisional finance committee, if such be constituted.

All of which is respectfully submitted.

(Sgd.) Jas. W. Robertson, Chairman

The report was adopted.

COMMITTEE ON PRESS AND CO-OPERATING ORGANIZATIONS

THE CHAIRMAN: We shall now have the report of the Committee on Press and Allied Organizations.

Mr. Mackay read the report as follows:—

The Committee on "Press and Allied Organizations" begs to report report as follows:

In our opinion, it will not be possible to accomplish much of a definite nature in the way of creating public opinion until such time as the other Committees have done something tangible, as we take it that our duties will largely begin where those of the other committees end. As a beginning, however, we would recommend:—

First: that the comprehensive and illuminating address of the Chairman of the Commission, Hon. Clifford Sifton, delivered at the first session of the meeting, be circulated in the widest manner possible, both in English and French, and that, to this end, the Secretary be instructed to communicate with every daily and weekly newspaper in Canada offering to supply, free of charge, the address in the form of a supplement in sufficient quantities to cover the circulations of the respective papers.

Second: that the Secretary be authorized to make arrangements for the issue of bulletins, either weekly or monthly, for the use of the press of the country, after the various publishers have signified their desire to receive the bulletins; these bulletins to consist of short, pithy paragraphs and reports dealing with the various phases of the Commission's work, and that, until such time as the other Committees have made such progress as is deemed desirable to make public, these bulletins be prepared largely from the papers read at this meeting.

Third: that in addition to the publicity which, it is hoped, will be secured through the press, efforts be made to utilize the public platform in the most effective manner possible. This, your Committee thinks, can best be done, for the time being, by the members of the Commission in their respective provinces arranging meetings in leading centres, the addresses to be made by such persons as the Commission at headquarters might from time to time be able to secure.

Fourth: that the widest publicity possible be given to the fact that it is the Commission's earnest wish to act in hearty co-operation with every organization having for its object the conserving and building up of any portion of the Dominion of Canada, and that, with this object in view, the Secretary be asked to communicate with the following bodies, and with such others as may from time to time be deemed advisable:—The Canadian Press Association, the Maritime Provinces Press Association, the Quebec Press Association, the Eastern Townships Press Association, the Western Canada Press Association, the British Columbia Press Association, the Fish and Game Protective Associations in Canada, the Canadian Forestry Association, the Canadian Clubs, the farmers' organizations of the various provinces, the Canadian Manufacturers' Association, the Trades and Labour Federation of Canada and the various Anti-tuberculosis Associations.

Fifth: that the report of this conference be issued without delay, in convenient form and in large quantities.

Sixth: We would humbly suggest a change in the name of the Committee from that of "Press and Allied Organizations" to that of "Press and Co-operating Organizations."

Lastly, we would express satisfaction that the appointment has been made to the headquarters' staff, of an experienced journalist, whose duties it will be to collect, edit and disseminate in proper form all information furthering the work which the Commission may, from time to time, have in hand.

All of which is respectfully submitted.

(Sgd.) J. F. Mackay, Chairman

Discussion on Report of Press Committee

MR. MACKAY: The Chairman's address may be secured in the form of a supplement at the rate of $2 a thousand. Supposing 200,000 copies are asked for by the newspapers, that would represent an expenditure of $400, and the Committee thought the Dominion Government has never invested $400 to better advantage than it would in offering to give this address, free of charge, to newspapers. The address would be inserted in the newspapers and circulated.

DR. RUTHERFORD: If we could get this address before the teachers and, through them, before the pupils, it would be the most effective way of giving publicity to it. We might distribute it through the inspectors and the school journals.

MR. MACKAY: The teachers' associations might be useful. It is very important to get it into the hands of the pupils.

HON. MR. HASZARD: We might send it to the Departments of Education and let them circulate it among the teachers.

Dr. RUTHERFORD: There are only 30,000 teachers in Canada.

THE CHAIRMAN: I have no objection to the report, except the first recommendation. I do not see why we should discriminate between the different papers that have been presented. For instance, I do not see why we should circulate more copies of my address than of Mr. Beck's very valuable paper on the work of the Hydro-Electric Commission. I have heard a great deal about the power policy of the Ontario Government, but I never heard it thoroughly explained before. Why should we not circulate an equal number of all the addresses in our reports?

MR. MACKAY: The Committee felt that that was the basis of the whole work of the Commission, and that it was essential we should circulate a large number of copies of it.

The report was adopted.

COMMITTEE ON PUBLIC HEALTH

THE CHAIRMAN: May we have the report of the Committee on Public Health?

SENATOR EDWARDS: Before leaving, Mr. Osler told me that it was absolutely impossible for him to make a report in the time allowed, even if he had been here.

HON. MR. FISHER: Mr. Osler told me yesterday that he suggested, as the first action, that that Committee should communicate with the health authorities of each of the provinces, and that, when he got the information at their command, he was going to call a meeting of the Committee which would discuss it and take action.

Mr. Snowball's resolution as re-drafted was then adopted. It was as follows:—

> That it is important that steps be taken at once by this Commission to protect the forests from fire, especially along the line of railways, and
> That, in particular, legislation be recommended by this Commission to bring the Dominion Government railways under the fire laws of the several provinces through which they pass, and
> That Government railways should also be made liable for damage done by fire originating from their engines, and
> That the burden of disproof should be on the railways; also
> That the legislation provide for the transportation by all railways of the chief district fire rangers and fire wardens, free of charge, when on their way to investigate or fight fires along their line of railway. Carried.

MR. SNOWBALL: I still think it is necessary to have some organization in the different provinces, with a chairman for each province, if we intend to record as much work as we would like at the next meeting of the Commission. It would be very beneficial if the provinces or groups of provinces were organized, each with a chairman, who would have authority to call together that Committee for the discussion of the broad subject of the different natural resources of the province, and we would be much better prepared than with committees from all the provinces, which probably could not meet within the year. If the chairmen of the provinces had the power, as members of the executive with yourself, to certify travelling expenses in connection with these meetings, it would be very helpful.

I would move that we discuss how to organize the provinces to the best advantage, as well as having committees on the different resources.

THE CHAIRMAN: There is a point in connection with that. We have organized a number of Committees to deal with certain subjects. Would it be well to have committees in the provinces acting independently of these committees? The Committees should find out first where we are on these different subjects. We must know what we intend to do before we start out to do it. So, while it appears that we must have organization of the kind Mr. Snowball suggests—for that is the whole object, to influence the public mind on the subject and get the governments to move—we ought first to get a definite programme laid out by our Committees, and then, when we form an organization in a province, the Chairman will be able to say what the organization has been formed to do.

GENERAL DISCUSSION

THE CHAIRMAN: What is the view of the Commission as to the next meeting? The view was expressed yesterday that the Committees should do their preliminary work and have a meeting of the Commission fairly soon, not waiting for the next annual meeting.

MR. HENDRY: What is "fairly soon"?

THE CHAIRMAN: Yesterday it was suggested within the next three months, after the Committees have had a chance to get into operation.

DR. BRYCE: June is suggested.

HON. MR. FISHER: I do not think we can make sufficient progress to report much by June. I would suggest about the first of October.

THE CHAIRMAN: People go away on their summer holidays. They return to their business and are busy for some time after the 1st of September. I think it would be better if we could have the meeting in the spring.

MR. MACKAY: And the exhibitions are held in the fall. I would move that the Commission meet in either Toronto or Quebec in June.

SENATOR EDWARDS: So far as the Committee on Forests is concerned, we will not have much to report then.

THE CHAIRMAN: You will have to work a little harder, that is all. I think we had better have it some time about June.

DR. BRYCE: The second week in June.

DR. BÉLAND: Are the Committees going to meet in the recess?

MR. HENDRY: The meeting will be of general importance. I think it should be held in Ottawa at the general offices of the Commission. This is a more central point. Then, when we get the provincial organizations, we may have meetings at Quebec or anywhere. I understand the meeting is, to a certain extent, for the purpose of bringing together our findings.

DR. ROBERTSON: I would suggest some time in the first half of July. There are on the Commission representatives of all the Universities, and these men cannot get away about the first week in June. Personally, I shall be abroad and shall not be back before July. I shall, while abroad, try to get a good deal of information of value as to methods in European countries, such as Switzerland.

DR. BRYCE: The Universities are all closed by the first of June. The convocations are over by the second week in June.

MR. MACKAY: I move that we meet in the second week in June.

DR. ROBERTSON: I move in amendment that we meet in the first half of July.

The amendment was negatived.
Mr. Mackay's motion was agreed to.

After further discussion, the place of meeting was left to be settled by the Chairman after consultation with the Prime Minister.

HON. MR. HASZARD: Dr. Robertson will visit the old country in the spring, and I think that, when he is going, probably it would be as well to give him the authority of this Commission to make enquiry on our behalf as to methods that prevail in other countries respecting the conservation of natural resources. If he was armed with this authority, it would probably place him in a better position to make enquiries than if he was simply acting on his own behalf. I therefore move:

That the Chairman of the Committee on Lands, Dr. J. W. Robertson, be authorized and directed to make enquiry and investigation in the various countries which he visits while abroad as to the methods which prevail there for the conservation of natural resources.

In moving this resolution, I think it is well to authorize Dr. Robertson to make these investigations, especially as I know that these enquiries can be made, and will be made, without any expense to the Commission.

DR. BRYCE: I have great pleasure in seconding this resolution. We discussed it in the Committee, but thought it better to have it dealt with by the Commission.

DR. FERNOW: I have arranged passage to Sweden and would be glad to have similar authorization to enquire there as to methods employed.

MR. DAVISON: I have great pleasure in moving to amend the motion by providing that Professor Fernow be granted the same authority from the Commission.

The motion, as amended, was agreed to.

THE CHAIRMAN: We now come to the question of funds. This is a very important phase of our work. My view is that, as Parliament has taken the responsibility of passing the Act which constitutes this Commission, it is presumable that it was in earnest. I presume that it did not mean that gentlemen representing all the Governments in Canada and practical men from different universities and institutions should meet here to talk and do nothing. If anything serious, if any real business, is to be done by this Commission, we must have the money to do it, and we must make proper representations to Government in regard to the amount of money we shall require.

I do not suppose any of us will be disposed to waste money, to embark on foolish or wildcat enquiries which will not bear fruit. But when we consider how this field has been neglected in the past in the sense of securing accurate information, and that we have to start at the bottom and build up, we must realize that it will cost a great deal of money. We do not wish to be identified with the operation of any Commission that does not do reliable work. Anything that we put on the public fyles as the report of this Commission must be reliable, and we must, therefore, be in a position to employ proper assistance.

HON. MR. FISHER: The staff of the Commission here in Ottawa is under Civil Service rules and the salaries of that staff are provided under the Civil Service rules. The staff provided for is: the Secretary in "A" of the first division, two clerks, technically qualified, in "B" of the first division, two clerks in "A" of the second division, and, I think, two in "B" of the third division: a total of six officials with the Secretary. We thought that, for a time, that staff would be sufficient for the office work here in Ottawa. Probably, in the future, that staff will have to be increased. A sum of $10,000 has been voted for office and miscellaneous expenses in the current fiscal year and the estimates for next year appropriate $15,000 for the same purposes. When that amount was decided on, it was arranged that we would put it in as a preliminary until we knew something of what was required, and we thought that, at any rate, during the current fiscal year, the amount provided would abundantly cover expenses. For the ensuing fiscal year, ending March 31st, 1911, there is now that item in the estimates, with the possibility of increasing it in accordance with the representations of the Commission.

DR. BÉLAND: How much is required for the officials?

MR. FISHER: Roughly speaking, about $12,500—in addition to the $10,000.

MR. HENDRY: If we are going to carry the Commission into the effective operation you propose, we will require a much greater amount than has been spoken of. In your address, you stated what you thought this Commission ought to perform for this Dominion; for it is a national Commission, it is not in any sense local. I think you will require to have at your disposal quite a large amount to be divided among the several Committees. I was considering it last night, and I believe that something like $200,000 will be required to bring this Commission into effective operation to produce the results you desire to secure. We should ask for $200,000 to be put at your disposal for use in this matter. If it is not all required, of course it will still be there. With a less amount than that, we will not be able to carry out the researches that are required in order to make this Commission of the value you wish it to be. I had thought of $250,000, but I have moderated a little to $200,000

SENATOR EDWARDS: You mean an annual expenditure?

Mr. HENDRY: Yes, for the next fiscal year.

Dr. BRYCE: How do you get at that?

Mr. HENDRY: By the work that is required to find out our resources. I am on the Mines and the Forests Committees and, if we are to do any good in the mineral line, we must have quite a lot of research to ascertain the best means of utilizing our resources. I understand this is a conservation which does not aim at conserving for future generations all the resources we have, but at providing for the use of some right away. I know that quite a little research has been made regarding the utilization of our zinc in British Columbia, but we have not arrived at a point where we can utilize it in the shape in which we have had to send it out of the Dominion to be treated. Our great forest resources will require considerable investigation if we are to bring them into the shape I understand you wish to have them in. I think that an amount less than what I have named would be inadequate for you, as Chairman, to distribute to the several Committees.

I have had a good deal to do with general business and general researches for business purposes, and I know pretty well what they cost. This is a large concern, representing, not many millions of dollars, but many billions of dollars. Of course, our recommendations are only the recommendations of the Chairman and of the Commission to the Government and to the country at their back, and I would recommend that we ask for $200,000 to be placed at the disposal of the Chairman of the Commission to use properly where needed.

The Act constituting the Commission should be amended so as to provide for the appointment of Assistant Chairmen who might assist the Chairman in various ways and take charge of meetings in the groups of provinces they would represent.

Reverting to the financial matter, what is $200,000 to this great Dominion when we know of concerns spending millions to find out what they are going to do the next year? What is this but a big concern representing billions? Next year we might want a larger amount or possibly a smaller amount.

Dr. BRYCE: I come from Winnipeg, a place where they have large schemes, but I must say that this suggestion is rather startling. The difficulty will be to know what to do with the $200,000. You must have the approval of the country. I know that the investigation suggested will take a large sum. I think we should appropriate an amount to begin some investigations in a thorough manner by choosing the right men, men who would be capable of making the investigations. I think that this might be done by adding $10,000 to the existing vote. That would strike me as a rational thing to do. In the matter of forestry and minerals there must be expert information, and in other matters we will have to make expenditures, but I certainly think, with the $20,000 now provided, another $10,000 will be as much as we ought to think of at the present time.

SENATOR EDWARDS: Personally, I am heart and soul in this work. I know that you are, Mr. Chairman, and, as one of the Commissioners, I desire to join you in carrying it out in the most effective way. I believe it is important to Canada; I think nothing is more highly important to Canada, but I do not want to shock the susceptibilities of the Canadian people on the start, and I am sure that if we ask for such an amount as this, it would not be looked on favourably. I do not think the Commission should be hampered at all; I think we should have a sufficiency; but I think we can arrive, in a year from now, more correctly at what we require. It is my opinion that, the officials being provided for, if about $35,000 were added to the $15,000, making it $50,000, it would be a reasonable sum for the first year and would be favourably regarded by Parliament. When the committees get all the information next year, we will be able to form some estimate of what the expenditure necessary for the investigations will be. I am willing to make a motion to this effect.

MR. SNOWBALL: I second the motion.

MR. HENDRY: I agree to that.

HON. MR. FISHER: It would facilitate the passing of an item of this kind through Parliament if some slight budget of the amount were prepared. My colleagues have done me the honour to entrust the work of this Commission, as far as the Government is concerned, to my hands. If a vote of that kind is proposed in Parliament, I suppose I will have to propose and defend it. While I do not think Parliament will be adverse, the size of the vote will be scrutinized. There are those who, perhaps, do not realize as we do, the importance of this work, and the Finance Minister, of course, has to guard jealously, the treasury. I would not like to ask for a vote unless there was some reasonable explanation of what was going to be done with it, and I must say I think it will take some little time to organize our work properly, so that it will be effective, and to secure men to do that work. We want to be careful, at the inception of our work, to search a little, to see that we get the best men, and, therefore, I think it will be unwise to ask Parliament for a sum which we could not reasonably explain the use of.

Dr. Fernow: It would be incumbent on each Committee to prepare a definite schedule of work with prices, just as in any other business. My view is that the Secretary should at once begin collecting information, getting out schedules, etc.

Hon. Mr. Fisher: I would be glad to make such a motion. I think one of the most important things we have to do is to commence at once on an accurate inventory. It will take a long time and the first steps can be taken at once. I think the staff will be able to do a great deal of that work, occasionally employing experts and sending out occasionally to different parts of the country.

Hon. Mr. Grimmer: I would second that motion.

Mr. Mackay: Will you incorporate in it something on public health? There is a strong feeling that this will be one of the most beneficial works of the Commission.

The Chairman: This will include public health. We should pass a resolution authorizing the officers to provide for the publication of the official record of the meetings.

A motion to this effect was adopted.

The Chairman: Then there is the question of the number of copies.

Hon. Mr. Fisher: I would be disposed to suggest that the Chairman's address be published in very large numbers for widespread circulation, and that the actual proceedings of the meeting should be published in a smaller number Perhaps 10,000 of the proceedings and 40,000 or 50,000 of the Chairman's address would be sufficient.

After some further discussion, it was ordered that 10,000 copies of the proceedings be printed in English and 2,500 in French.

The Chairman: I have been highly satisfied with the spirit in which this meeting has been carried on. So far as I can recollect, it is the first time a very comprehensive attempt has been made to do important public service of this character on purely non-partizan lines, an attempt in which men of both political parties have joined together to co-operate in the best interests of the country. For myself, I am very much gratified at the result and at the spirit in which we have been able to meet and work.

It is, indeed, a great work. We have here the first Commission of the kind ever established by a National Government, and it rests with us to show whether such a movement can successfully be brought to a conclusion. I am satisfied that if we continue along the lines on which we have begun, we will accomplish a great deal and will make a magnificent success of the Commission.

I have to thank you for your co-operation, which I have myself personally valued in the highest degree, and I trust we shall get into a satisfactory state of organization and advance the work very considerably by the next meeting of the Commission.

The Commission then adjourned.

INDEX

	PAGE
ACCIDENTS—	
in mines	10, 11
industrial (See Industry)	
Afforestation—	
in France	32
on the prairies	177
Agriculture—	
definition of	46
difficulty of directing by legislation	59
immediate object of	45
place of, in the national economy	24
Robertson, Dr. J. W., on conservation in	42
Allard, Hon. Jules—unable to be present	42
BACTERIA—	
in the soil	47
vitality of, in streams	55
Beaver in the Yukon	113
Beck, Hon. Adam, on the Hydro-Electric Power Project of Ontario	82
Beetle—	
Eastern spruce, attacks of, in New Brunswick	150
bark-boring, methods of attack of	149
Boothby, Col., on sportsmen in Maine	103
Brantford, water supply of	161
British Columbia—	
forest fires, methods of coping with	184
forest resources of	178
topography of central	155
Bryce—	
Hon. James, quoted on influence of nature on man	114
Dr. P. H., on public health	114
Bud-worm, Spruce—operations of, in Canada	146
CALGARY, water supply of	158
Cataract Power Co., water-power head of	164
Chatham, water supply of	161
Climate, as related to agriculture	52
Clover, nitrogen fixation by	48
Columbia river, as a source of water supply	156
Conservation—	
in Canada as compared with the United States	6
contrasted with reckless exploitation	6
history of the movement	5

206 COMMISSION OF CONSERVATION

	PAGE
Conservation, Commission of—	
exceptional character of..	2
committees of.	175
committees of, reports of...	176
officials of, classified..	199
provincial representation on.	5
representative membership of....	3
Coal—	
imports of, into Ontario from United States.	17
loss of life in mining..	74
longwall method of mining.	73
room-and-pillar method of mining.	73
Cobalt, waste in refining cobalt-silver ores.	68, 69
Congdon, F. T., on fur-bearing animals in Canada.	107
Coutlee, Chas. R., on the water wealth of Canada.	152
Crops—	
damage to, by insects..	56
field, area and value of in 1909.	56
the object of agriculture.	45
rotation of, advantages of.	50, 52
DENMARK, conserving soil fertility in.	57
Diptheria, deaths due to, in Canada.	121
Drainage, in Ontario.	162
EDMONTON, water supply of.	158
Education, agricultural, for mature men.	56
Edwards, Senator W. C., on concrete building construction.	172
Electrical Development Co., effect of Hydro-Electric Project on.	98
Electro-thermic process (See Smelting, Iron and Steel).	62
Entomology, relation of, to forest conservation..	143
Evans, Kelly, on fish and game in Ontario.	100
Explosives, Dr. Eugene Haanel's recommendations re..	190
FERNOW, DR. B. E.	
authorized to collect information abroad.	198
on scientific forestry in Europe.	29
on forest policies applicable to Canada.	39
on forest fires, methods of fighting.	184
on forest fires, resolution re methods of fighting.	186
summary of main points in address of.	41
on timber resources, inventory of.	183
Fertilizers—	
availability of, to be reported on.	192
use of, in England and Scotland.	58
Fish—(See under Fish and Game).	
public health, relation of supply of, to.	105
tax on non-resident anglers in Ontario.	103
white fish, depletion of supply of, in Ontario.	101

INDEX. 207

	PAGE
Fish and Game—	
economic value of	103
Kelly Evans on	100
preservation of, in Maine	102
preservation of, methods for	111
Fisheries—	
committee on	175
committee on, report of	188
Sifton, Hon. Clifford, on	11
Fish Trust, American, operations of, in Ontario	101, 105
Fires, Forest—	
aided by forest insects	144
controlling, in British Columbia, A. S. Goodeve on methods of	184
fighting, Dr. B. E. Fernow's resolution re	186
fighting, Dr. B. E. Fernow on methods of	184
on I. C. R., Hon. W. C. H. Grimmer on	181, 183
on I. C. R., W. B. Snowball on	180
on N. T. R., Hon. W. C. H. Grimmer on	180, 181
precautions against, in Ontario forest reserves	76, 77
Fires, Forest—	
precautions against railway fires in Ontario	78
responsibility of railways for, Hon. C. Sifton on	185
along railways, W. B. Snowball's resolution re	195
Sifton, Hon. Clifford, on	19, 21, 24
sportsmen, taxed, to trace origin of	104
Forests—	
area of, in the world	34
British Columbia, forest resources of	178
committee on	175
committee on, report of	176
diseases of forest trees	135
exploitation of, correct attitude towards	32
inspection of, in Germany	141
inventory of, recommended	177
methods of management of	35
municipal ownership of	36
New Brunswick, forest resources of	179
popular attitude re, necessity of change of	39
public opinion on conservation of	18
reserves in Ontario	76
reserve proposed on Eastern slope of Rockies	20
state ownership and management of	35
surveys of, necessity for	40
surveys of, in Nova Scotia	40
Sweden, Forest Conservation Boards in	38
Forestry—	
Dominion Forestry Branch	18
history of, rapid outline of	35
origination of, reasons for	33
policies applicable in Canada	39, 41

Forestry—continued. PAGE
    policies, outline of development of, in Sweden 38
    results of, in Prussia 30
    results of, in Saxony 31
    results of, in Württemberg 31
    schools of, in Canada 18
    schools of, in Germany 37
    scientific, in Europe 29
France—
    municipal ownership of forests in 36
    state supervision of forests in 36
French river, power potentialities of 164
Fungus—
    bracket 140
    damping-off 136
Funds, discussion on, for use of Commission 198, 201
Furs—
    dyeing and dressing of, in Canada 112
    production of, cycles in 110
Fur-bearing Animals
    committee on 175
    committee on, report of 188
    reserves for, advocated 111, 112
Fur-Trade—(See Furs, and Fur-bearing Animals.)
    losses in, causes of 109
    marten skins, increasing value of 110
    statistics re 108

GAME—
    committee on 175
    committee on, report of 188
    fur-bearing animals in Canada 107
    fur-bearing animals, destruction of 109
Gas, Natural—
    waste of, in Ontario, fine for 82
    production of, in Ontario 81
    tax on, in Ontario 82
Germany—
    forests, municipal ownership of, in 36
    forestry schools in 37
    wheat yield, in 1909 57
Gibson, Arthur, investigation of attacks of spruce bud-worm, by 146
Gold, in the Yukon 10
Goodeve, A. S., on forest fires in British Columbia 184
Government management, efficiency of 90
Grand Falls Power Co., power development of 165
Great Britain, wheat yield in 57, 58
Grey, Earl, address by 27
Grimmer, Hon. W. C. H.—
    on forest fires along I. C. R. 181, 183
    on forest fires along N.T.R. 180

INDEX

	PAGE
HAANEL, Dr. EUGENE.	
on economies in mineral production.	60
recommendations of, to Committee on Minerals.	190
Haileybury, water supply of.	162
Hamilton, contracts for power with Hydro-Electric Power Commission.	93
Health, Public—	
Bryce, Dr. P. H., on.	114
committee on.	175
committee on, report of.	195
pollution of waters.	12, 154
preventive measures in.	130
Sifton, Hon. Clifford, on.	12
tuberculosis, discussed in House of Commons.	12
Hewitt, Dr. C. Gordon, on forest insects.	142
Hopkins—	
quoted on damage to forests by insects.	144
quoted on damage by bark-boring beetles.	149
Housing problem.	134
Howard, L. O., experiments in control of destructive insects.	149
Hungary, wheat yields in.	57
Hydro-Electric Power Commission—	
Beck, Hon. Adam, on.	82
municipalities, contracts with.	95
municipalities, cost of power supplied to.	95
municipalities, amount of power supplied to.	95
Ontario Power Co., contract with.	94
powers of	86—91
prices, reduction of, in Hamilton.	93
prices, reduction of, in Ottawa.	92
savings effected by.	96
Hydro-Electric Project—	
Beck, Hon. Adam, on.	82
cost of.	97
Hydro-Electric Power Commission appointed.	85
legislation of 1908 and 1909, re.	87
municipalities, commission appointed by.	84
Ontario Government acting as agent in.	88
Ontario Government commission.	85
INDUSTRY, deaths due to.	129
Infant depots.	119
Insects—	
attacks of, on ornamental trees.	144
beetles, bark-boring.	149
beetles, Eastern spruce, in New Brunswick.	150
damage done to Canadian crops by.	56
forest, classification of.	144
Hewitt, Dr. C. Gordon, on destructive forest.	142
larch sawfly.	145
loss occasioned by forest.	144

Insects—continued.   PAGE
  moth, brown-tail.. 147
  spruce bud-worm.. 146
Intercolonial Railway, forest fires along......................... 180, 181, 183
Iron—(See Smelting.)
  importation of, into Canada.. 61
  ore, magnometric method of locating..................................... 65
  ore, commercial, minimum standard of.................................. 61
  ore, limited supply of... 61
Irrigation—
  in Southern Alberta... 159
  in the North West.. 15
  on the Pacific coast.. 154
  on prairie rivers.. 159

KAFFIRS, deaths of, by accidents in South African mines................ 74
Kaministikwia river, water-power on....................................... 163
Klinck, Prof., evolves new variety of Indian corn.......................... 54
Kootenay river, as a source of power...................................... 157

LACHINE RAPIDS, power from... 164
Lands—
  Canada, landed estate of.. 44, 45
  committee on.. 175
  committee on, report of.. 191
  necessity of, for the people.. 44
  Ontario, area of Crown lands in.. 75
  Ontario, kinds of, for settlement...................................... 75, 76
  Robertson, Dr. J. W., on conservation of agricultural resources...... 42
Larch Canker.. 138
Life—(See Mortality.)
  Loss of, in coal and metalliferous mines................................ 74
Lindsey, James A., quoted on struggle for existence................... 114
London, water supply of... 161
Long Sault dam... 164
Lumbering, evils of present methods of..................................... 19

MACKENZIE basin, water supply of....................................... 157
Magnometric measurements... 65
Maine, preservation of fish and game in............................. 102, 103
Manufacturers' Associations, Canadian, interested in Niagara power.... 84
Manufacturing, importance of cheap power for............................ 99
Marten—
  value of skins of... 113
  increasing value of skins of... 110
Medicine Hat, water supply of... 158
Milk supply—
  municipalized... 120, 130, 131
  regulations re, in Wellington, N.Z..................................... 131

INDEX 211

	PAGE
Minerals—	
committee on.	175
committee on, report of.	189
extent of mineral resources.	9
Haanel, Dr. E., on economies in production of.	60
Sifton, Hon. Clifford, on.	8
value of annual production of, in Canada.	9
waste of.	10
Mines, Department of.	9
Mortality, statistics re.	117
Mortality, infant—	
Bryce, Dr. P. H., on.	117
prevention of.	130
Moth, Brown-Tail—	
life history of.	148
operations of, in Canada.	147
Municipalities—	
contract of, with Hydro-Electric Power Commission.	95
taking power in Ontario from Hydro-Electric Power Commission.	95
cost of power to, when obtained from Hydro-Electric Power Commission	95
NAISH, Dr. A. E., quoted on milk depots.	119
Natural Resources, Hon. F. Cochrane, on conservation of, in Ontario.	75
Navigation, inland—	
in British Columbia.	155
Great lakes system of.	163
in lake Winnipeg basin.	159
Nelson river, water-power potentialities of.	160
Nesbitt, Wallace, quoted on attraction of capital by fish and game.	105
New Brunswick—	
forest resources of.	179
water-power in.	165
New Liskeard, water supply of.	162
Newman, Dr. George—	
quoted on infant diseases.	117
quoted on infant death rate in England.	118
New Westminster, water supply of.	153
Niagara river, power developments on.	164
Nickel, wasteful methods of treating ore.	67
Nipigon river, water-powers on.	163
Nitrogen—	
as a plant food.	48
supply of, in the soil.	49
supply of, Sir Wm. Crookes quoted on.	48
Nova Scotia, water-powers of.	165
North American conference, declaration of principles.	5, 8
OKANAGAN VALLEY, water supply of.	156

Ontario—

	PAGE
conservation of natural resources in.	75
water-powers, regulations re granting of rights to.	79, 80
Ontario Power Co., contract with Hydro-Electric Power Commission.	94
Organization, discussion on.	170

Organizations, co-operating—

committee on.	175
committee on, report of. . .	193

Ottawa—

Hydro-Electric Power Commission secures power for.	92
water supply of.	162
Ottawa basin, description of upper part of. . . .	166
Ottawa river, average volume of flow in. . . .	167

PACIFIC COAST—

rain fall on. .	153
water supply of.	153
Patten, H. C., quoted on public health. . . .	117

Peat—

commercial importance of.	69, 70
experimental fuel-testing station at Ottawa. . .	71
extent of Canadian bogs. .	70
peat mull, uses of.	72
Petroleum, in Ontario.	81
Phosphorus, supply of, in the soil. . . .	49
Plant growth, elements of, in the soil. . .	49
Plant life, essentials of.	48
Pointe du Bois, power station at.	161
Poison, use of, in killing fur-bearing animals. . .	109

Pollution of Streams—(See Public Health.)

C. R. Coutlee on.	154
Polyporous volvatus.	140

Population—

relations of trade returns to. .	116
value of, as a national asset.	115
Port Arthur, secures power through Hydro-Electric Power Commission. . . .	93
Potassium, supply of, in the soil. .	49
Prairie lakes, characteristics of. .	158
Prairie rivers, characteristics of.	158

Press—

committee on.	175
committee on, report of. . .	193
Prussia, forestry appropriations in. . .	35, 36

Public Health. (See Health.)

Publicity—

proceedings ordered printed.	202
recommendations for securing.	193

Pulpwood—

export duty on, in Sweden.	39
export of, prohibited from Ontario Crown lands. . . .	79
supplies of, along N.T.R.	78

INDEX 213

	PAGE
QUEBEC, power supply of city of...................................	165
RABBIT, relation of, to supply of fur-bearing animals....	111
Railways, fires caused by...22,	23
Ross, Hon. G. W., regulations by government of, re Niagara power.........	86
Ross, R. A., consulting engineer of Hydro-Electric Power Commission.....	97
Reforestation—	
on eastern slope of Rockies.	20
importance of...	20
in Northern Ontario..	21
Prussia's annual expenditure for.....	35
Regina, water supply of...	158
Resources, natural, inventory of.	7
Ripley, W. Z., quoted on environment..........	114
Robertson, Dr. James W.—	
authorized to collect information abroad	198
on conservation of agricultural resources...	42
contribution of, to scientific agriculture....	25
Russia, wheat yield in, 1909....	57
Rust, white pine........	137
SANITATION—(See Health.)	
in schools..	121
Saunders, Dr. William—	
contribution of, to scientific agriculture..	25
contribution of, to seed growing.............................	54
Sawfly, larch—	
life history of...	145
operations of, in Canada......	145
Schools—	
health of children in... 121,	132
medical inspection of, in England...	118
medical inspection of, in New York..	122
Seedlings, importation of white pine, into Canada.	137
Seeds—	
good seed, increased yield from.................................	54
seed grain used in Canada, 1909..........................	53
Shawinigan falls, power at.....	165
Sifton, Hon. Clifford—	
inaugural address...	1
on agriculture. ..,...	25
on funds for Commission..	198
on influx of capital into Canada...........................	26
on organization of Commission..	170
party politics, dissociation from.......	5
responsibility of railways for setting forest fires.....................	186
Silver—	
smelting and refining ores from Cobalt...	10
waste in refining cobalt-silver ores...................................68,	69

	PAGE
Smelting—	
cobalt-silver ores.	10, 68, 69
iron ores, difficulty of smelting with blast furnace in Canada.	61
iron ores, electro-thermic process of.	62
iron ores, electro-thermic process in Sweden.	64
iron ores, results of experiments with electro-thermic process.	63
zinc	66, 67
Snowball, W.B., resolution re forest fires along railways.	195
Soil—	
accumulation of, rate of.	47
fertility, economic advantages from conserving.	53
fertility, depletion of, in Canada.	56, 57
organisms in.	47
Spanish river, power on.	163
Steel, electro-thermic process of making	63
St. Lawrence basin.	161
Storage works, on the Upper Ottawa.	167
Swamps, effect of, on regulation of stream flow	162
Sweden—	
forest policy, development of, in.	38
forest resources of.	37
Switzerland, water-power law in.	17
TAFT, PRESIDENT, on conservation in his message to Congress	42
Taxation—	
non-resident anglers' tax in Ontario.	103
uneconomic, of forest lands in United States	6
Ties, scarcity of railway.	23
Timber—	
export duty on, in Sweden.	39
export of unmanufactured Crown Land timber prohibited in Ontario.	79
lands, government policy on lease of.	19
licenses, Dr. B. E. Fernow on.	40
pine, reserves of, in Ontario.	76
supply of, world's.	34
Trade, Board of, in Toronto, investigates Niagara power.	83
Transcontinental Railway, National—	
forest fires along.	180
forest fires along, precautions against.	78
forest fires along, prevention of.	24
Transmission, electrical—	
high voltage, in Ontario.	91
system of, Hydro-Electric Power Commission.	94
Trees, diseases of, classified.	135
Tuberculosis—	
as an after effect of other diseases.	120
conditions conducive to.	127
deaths from, in Canada in 1900.	127
loss, economic, due to.	128
Perley, G. H., on, in House of Commons.	12

INDEX 215

Tuberculosis—continued. PAGE
    prevention of.......... 133
    treatment of, "fresh air," in Germany. 134
Typhoid—
    decrease of, in England and Wales. 125
    decrease of, in German cities. 125
    on the farm. 55
    in military camps. 125
    prevention of. 132
    preventive measure, effectiveness of. 126
    prevalence of. 123
    at Sault Ste. Marie. 124
    in United States cities. 125, 126

UNITED STATES—
    furs, imports of, from. 108
    wheat yield, 1909. 57

VANCOUVER, water supply of. 153
Vested interests, effect of Hydro-Electric Project on. 97

WATER—
    C. R. Coutlee on water wealth of Canada. 152
    as an essential of plant growth. 52
    increase of available quantity of. 14
    sources of supply of. 12
    streams in Ontario forest reserves. 79
    uses of. 13, 152
Water-power—
    in central British Columbia. 156
    committee on. 175
    committee on, report of. 191
    development and use of, laws and regulations for. 15
    estimated horse-power of, in Canada. 16
    equivalent of, in tons of coal. 17
    on French river. 164
    Grand Falls Power Co., development of. 165
    on Kaministikwia river. 163
    on Kootenay river. 157
    from Lachine rapids. 164
    on Nelson river. 161
    in New Brunswick. 165
    on Niagara river. 164
    on Nipigon river. 163
    in Ontario, conditions re disposal of. 79, 80
    in Ontario, conservation of. 82
    in Ontario, Hydro-Electric Power Commission, policy re. 15
    in Ontario, leased under Act of 1898. 80
    on the upper Ottawa. 166
    on the Pacific coast. 155

Water-power—continued.

	PAGE
at Shawinigan falls.	165
on Spanish river.	163
on St. Lawrence river system.	163, 164
Swiss legislation re.	17
titles to, conditional, recommended.	191
uses of.	14
in lake Winnipeg basin.	160
on Winnipeg river.	161

Water supply—

of farm houses.	54
pollution of.	132
pollution of, Senate's action re.	132

White, James, appointment of, as secretary.	1
White fish, depletion of supply of, in Ontario.	101
Whitson, J. F., quoted on forest fires.	19, 21, 22
Wind-power, for light and heat.	55
Winnipeg, basin of lake.	157
Winnipeg river, water-power on.	161
Wolves, destruction of fur-bearing animals by.	110

YUKON—

export of furs from.	108
fur-bearing animals in, extermination of.	111

ZAVITZ, Prof. C. A., contribution of, to seed growing.	54

Zinc—

experiments in refining ore	66
Sifton, Hon. Clifford, on.	10
smelting of, European processes for.	67

CPSIA information can be obtained
at www.ICGtesting.com
Printed in the USA
BVHW041057220219
540923BV00016B/119/P

9 780365 478676